LIFE SCIENCE LIBRARY

DRUGS

TIME
LIFE
BOOKS
®

LIFE WORLD LIBRARY

LIFE NATURE LIBRARY

TIME READING PROGRAM

THE LIFE HISTORY OF THE UNITED STATES

LIFE SCIENCE LIBRARY

INTERNATIONAL BOOK SOCIETY

GREAT AGES OF MAN

TIME-LIFE LIBRARY OF ART

TIME-LIFE LIBRARY OF AMERICA

LIFE SCIENCE LIBRARY

DRUGS

by Walter Modell, Alfred Lansing
and the Editors of LIFE

TIME INCORPORATED, NEW YORK

ABOUT THIS BOOK

As THIS BOOK POINTS OUT, a drug is any chemical that can change the functioning or structure of the body: thus, the smoke that pollutes the city air, no less than the aspirin tablets in the medicine cabinet, must be considered a drug. How drugs have been used—and misused—is the subject matter of this volume, which traces the origins of modern drugs and examines some of the most important and common ones: alcohol, antibiotics, tranquilizers and contraceptives.

Each text chapter of the book is accompanied by a picture essay. For example, Chapter 1, "Poisons That Save Lives," examines the prescientific origins of drugs, while Essay 1, "The Pharmacist's Ancient Art," reviews the history of drugs up to the beginning of modern pharmacology.

THE AUTHORS

WALTER MODELL is Professor of Pharmacology at the Cornell University Medical College in New York City, a consultant to the Surgeon General of the Army, and a member of the Executive Committee of the *U.S. Pharmacopoeia*. Dr. Modell is also editor of several publications in his field, including *Pharmacology for Physicians* and *Clinical Pharmacology and Therapeutics*. He has done original research on drugs and has written numerous articles, is author of the book *Relief of Symptoms*, and is editor of *Drugs of Choice*.

ALFRED LANSING, a free-lance writer, is the author of many magazine articles and the best-selling book *Endurance*, an account of a British expedition to the Antarctic from 1914 to 1916. Mr. Lansing has served as a staff writer for *Collier's* magazine and as an editor of TIME-LIFE BOOKS.

THE CONSULTING EDITORS

RENÉ DUBOS, a member and professor of The Rockefeller University, is a distinguished microbiologist and experimental pathologist who was awarded the Arches of Science Award in 1966. His books include *Mirage of Health* and *Man Adapting*. He is also coauthor of *Health and Disease* in this series.

HENRY MARGENAU is Eugene Higgins Professor of Physics and Natural Philosophy at Yale, and an authority in spectroscopy and nuclear physics. He wrote *Open Vistas*, *The Nature of Physical Reality*, and is coauthor of *The Scientist* in this series.

C. P. SNOW has won an international audience for his novels, including *The New Men*, *The Affair* and *Corridors of Power*, which explore the effects of science on today's society.

ON THE COVER

Lined up in ordered rows, newly dipped gelatin capsules at the Eli Lilly and Company plant in Indianapolis stand ready for drying and loading with drugs. Capsules like these are used to package about 600 different kinds of drugs sold in the United States. The back cover drawing shows a special capsule, called a Spansule, emptying its drug pellets, designed to dissolve at different time intervals in the body.

Published simultaneously in Canada. Library of Congress catalogue card number 67-25859.
School and library distribution by Silver Burdett Company.

CONTENTS

TIME-LIFE BOOKS

EDITOR
Maitland A. Edey
EXECUTIVE EDITOR
Jerry Korn
TEXT DIRECTOR Martin Mann
ART DIRECTOR Sheldon Cotler
CHIEF OF RESEARCH
Beatrice T. Dobie
PICTURE EDITOR
Robert G. Mason
Assistant Text Directors:
Harold C. Field, Ogden Tanner
Assistant Art Director: Arnold C. Holeywell
Assistant Chief of Research: Martha Turner

PUBLISHER
Rhett Austell
General Manager: Joseph C. Hazen Jr.
Circulation Director: Joan D. Manley
Marketing Director: Carter Smith
Business Manager: John D. McSweeney
Publishing Board: Nicholas Benton, Louis Bronzo, James Wendell Forbes

LIFE MAGAZINE

EDITOR: Edward K. Thompson
MANAGING EDITOR: George P. Hunt
PUBLISHER: Jerome S. Hardy

LIFE SCIENCE LIBRARY

SERIES EDITOR: Martin Mann
Editorial Staff for *Drugs:*
Associate Editor: Robert G. Mason
Text Editors: William K. Goolrick, William Frankel
Picture Editor: Nancy Genet
Designer: Charles Mikolaycak
Assistant Designer: Raymond Ripper
Staff Writers: Leon Green, Victor Waldrop
Chief Researcher: Marjorie Pickens
Researchers: Sarah Bennett, Leah Dunaief, Linda Ferrer, Pamela Johnson, Alice Kantor, Linda Kridel, Gail Lowman, Cynthia J. MacKay, Irene Yurdin
EDITORIAL PRODUCTION
Color Director: Robert L. Young
Assistant: James J. Cox
Copy Staff: Marian Gordon Goldman, Madge Raymond, Dolores A. Littles
Picture Bureau: Margaret K. Goldsmith, Barbara Simon
Traffic: Douglas B. Graham
Art Assistant: Gloria Cernosia

This book, from its conception to final editing, was under the professional direction of Walter Modell, with the editorial guidance of Alfred Lansing. The text chapters were written by Robert Claiborne, the picture essays by Nancy Genet and the editorial staff. The following individuals and departments of Time Inc. were helpful in producing the book: LIFE staff photographers Yale Joel, Mark Kauffman and Michael Rougier; the Chief of the LIFE Picture Library, Doris O'Neil; the Chief of the TIME-LIFE News Service, Richard M. Clurman; and the Chief of the Bureau of Editorial Reference, Peter Draz.

INTRODUCTION

LIFE IS CHEMICAL—all living cells and the organs and creatures they form function as organized systems of chemical reactions. That fundamental fact explains why drugs are so important to human well-being. For drugs are the chemicals best able to enter into the living reactions of cells and alter their structure or function, hopefully but not always for the better. Indeed, it may be said that the effort to find and use beneficial drugs to treat the ills of body and mind has been the major effort of civilized medicine in its millennia-long struggle against suffering. The victories, stalemates and defeats of that effort are excitingly told in this book.

By now we have accumulated a vast pharmacopoeia ranging from deadly poisons to lifesaving, bacteria-destroying antibiotics. We have mind-influencing drugs such as anesthetics, pain-relievers, tranquilizers and psychic energizers. We have alcohol, caffeine and nicotine and other depressants and stimulants. Drugs to regulate mood and emotion can alleviate mental illness, while others that may improve learning and memory are under investigation. We have isolated or synthesized natural body products—hormones such as insulin, thyroxin, sex hormones and cortisol, to substitute for the output of deficient glands. Some hormonal substances synthesized by chemists are more effective than are the natural hormones themselves—modified hormones can block normal reproductive processes and thus serve in birth control pills. But we also have the much praised and damned LSD, one of many substances that modify a person's view of himself and reality. And there are many diseases that still torment mankind for which drugs are urgently needed.

The effort to find and use beneficial drugs goes on at an accelerated pace and in a new, more effective way. Discoveries in the past have usually come from trial and error, but 20th Century advances in science, especially those of recent years, are teaching us how chemicals enter into the complex reactions of cells and tissues. Thanks to these advances, pharmacologists are learning to produce drugs that act more powerfully and directly against many ailments, and that even raise the hope of ultimate victory over such killers as cancer and disorders of the heart and blood vessels. With this new knowledge, here explained in clear detail and informative case histories, the deadliest enemies of mankind may yet be conquered.

—HUDSON HOAGLAND

Executive Director

Worcester Foundation

for Experimental Biology

1

Poisons That Save Lives

Today's drugs come in varied packages. An open capsule *(far left)* spills powder; next to it is a Spansule loaded with "time pills." The ampule *(center)* holds liquid for injection. Stacked at right are *(top to bottom)* gelatin, uncoated and coated pills.

In the hospital emergency room, a physician bends over an unconscious two-year-old. The child's breathing is rapid and shallow, his pulse is pounding. His terrified parents, huddled nearby, can say only that the boy swallowed "some pills."

The doctor has the patient's stomach washed out and orders a quick blood test. The test confirms what he had already suspected: the child is suffering from acute salicylism, the result of gulping a fistful of aspirin tablets. He has been brought near to death by a drug that is one of the most useful known to science—and also the leading cause of accidental poisoning in children.

Deep in the Amazon jungle, a Jivaro hunter quietly loads his blowpipe with a dart whose needlelike tip is covered with a brownish gum. Leveling the 15-foot tube at a monkey perched on a tree 30 yards off, he sends the tiny missile on its way with a silent puff of air. The monkey jumps at the prick of the dart, chatters a few moments, sways and falls from its perch. In less than five minutes, it has stopped breathing.

The brownish gum that killed the monkey is curare—one of the most toxic natural substances known. In purified form it is also a valuable adjunct to surgery: injected in minute doses, it relaxes the muscles of the abdomen (even as it first relaxed and then paralyzed the monkey's muscles) so that the surgeon can operate on his patient without fear that an involuntary muscular spasm will complicate his task.

These two anecdotes sum up what is probably the most fundamental fact about drugs: all drugs are poisons, and all poisons are drugs. It is no accident that the words "poison" and "potion" come from the same root, or that the Greek word *pharmakon,* which we find rooted in our own words "pharmacy" and "pharmacology," originally meant both a healing draught and a deadly one.

In the broadest sense, a drug—or a poison—is any chemical that can effect an alteration in the function or structure of living tissue. (A bullet, striking the body at high velocity, can unquestionably alter its functioning—but does so mechanically rather than chemically, and therefore could not be classed as a drug.)

As commonly used, of course, the word "drugs" implies *medicinal* chemicals—those substances that, in carefully regulated doses, produce desirable changes in the human body, counteracting disease or relieving distress. These beneficial poisons have nearly wiped out some diseases and can at least alleviate the impact of most of the rest. They can speed a flagging heart or slow a racing one, raise the blood pressure or lower it, stimulate the kidneys to excrete more or less, and perform scores of other medically useful tasks.

They can alter the functioning of the nervous system: anesthetics can blot out the pain of the surgeon's knife; tranquilizers can allay the anxieties of the neurotic or psychotic. But their action on the nervous system is not always for the better. Alcohol can induce euphoria —or comatose stupor; the opiates can relieve pain—or "hook" addicts. Hallucinogens such as LSD may perhaps expand the consciousness on occasion, and they may also warp the mind to the point of insanity.

The ambiguous qualities of these central nervous system drugs point up a basic truth about all drugs: improperly used, or sometimes even properly used, they become poisons without qualification, producing unwanted reactions ranging from temporary nausea to death. Even the most beneficial drugs notoriously possess adverse effects. Some experts estimate that perhaps one American hospital patient in 20 lands in the hospital as a result of reactions to drugs. The best one can say of any drug is that its beneficial effects outweigh its harmful ones—for most patients, most of the time.

The search for drugs that will do more jobs more effectively and more safely has occupied men for millennia. The quest has taken them to strange places: to the South American jungles, where curare originated; to the brews of medicine men and "wise women" skilled in the use of herbs, which have yielded at least a score of useful drugs; and, increasingly, into the submicroscopic labyrinth of molecules, whose complexities are slowly yielding clearer answers to the questions of why drugs do what they do and how they can be made to do it better.

THE OLDEST PRESCRIPTIONS were inscribed in angular cuneiform writing on a clay tablet by a Sumerian physician of the Third Millennium B.C. The portion of the tablet seen here in close-up contains two prescriptions. The column on the left prescribes the seed of "carpenter plant," gum resin of markhazi and thyme, all pulverized and dissolved in beer. The column on the right calls for powdered root of "moon plant" and white pear tree dissolved in beer. The diseases for which these drugs were prescribed are not known.

Soap and water as drugs

However, for the pharmacologist, the scientist who specializes in the study of drugs, and indeed, for people of all sorts, the "drug problem" is far broader than the search for new and better medicines, broader even than the widespread medical and social dilemmas that stem from the abuse of some drugs. Substances that can affect us chemically are all about us, constantly entering our bodies though we may never let a pill pass our lips. Thus, the soaps, rinses, deodorants and depilatories in the family bathroom are drugs; so are the detergents, cleaners and metal polishes in the kitchen. The do-it-yourself homeowner works with paints and their solvents. The farmer and home gardener have chemical fertilizers, pesticides and weed-killers. With every breath we draw, we inhale carbon monoxide, hydrocarbons and oxides of nitrogen from automobile exhausts, sulfur dioxide and soot from smoking chimneys—drugs every one of them. If we smoke, we inhale several hundred more. Indeed there is not one substance in our environment that cannot, under certain circumstances, act as a drug. Even the purest distilled water, consumed in large enough quantities, can leach enough salt out of the body to produce a condition akin to heat exhaustion. Children who have swilled down a gallon of water have died of water poisoning.

In today's world, nonmedicinal drugs are far more numerous, far less avoidable and for the most part considerably less well understood than the medicinal drugs. Yet a better understanding of environmental drugs is no less essential to civilized man than is knowledge of medicines. We are just beginning to comprehend some of the ways in which our environment, which most emphatically includes the drugs in it, can make us healthy or unhealthy, vigorous or debilitated. Without a deeper comprehension of drugs, civilization stands an excellent chance of poisoning itself with its vast array of chemical and industrial by-products.

If drugs in the broad sense are conspicuously products of civilization, in the narrow medical sense, they almost surely antedate civilization. "The desire to take medicine," quipped the noted Canadian physician Sir William Osler, "is perhaps the greatest feature which distinguishes man from the animals." The evidence suggests that there is a good deal of truth in Osler's witticism. Nearly all of the still-primitive peoples use at least one or two drugs. The Australian aborigines, for example, usually classed as the least civilized culture on earth, chew the pituri plant for its narcotic effect. They use the same drug to poison fish.

It is a reasonable guess that our prehistoric ancestors employed similar potions 10,000 or even 50,000 years ago. Indeed, some degree of pharmacological sophistication was a condition of man's survival, for his palate, when he is hungry enough, is notoriously unchoosy. Even the most apelike primitives must have distinguished, by instinct, intelligence or unhappy experience, between nutritious berries and poisonous ones, between roots that would maintain life in time of famine and those that would end it in agony.

Whatever we may guess about precivilized man, we know quite definitely that the first civilized men were medicine-takers. The Sumerians, who built the earliest civilization along the valley of the Euphrates and Tigris rivers 4,300 years ago, compounded medicines from salt and saltpeter, cassia, myrtle, asafetida and thyme; from the seeds, roots or bark of the willow, fir, pear, fig and date trees. Scratching on tablets of damp clay, their doctors set down prescriptions such as this: "The seed of the carpenter plant; gum resin of markhazi; thyme. Pulverize. Dissolve in beer. Let the man drink." Unfortunately, the Sumerian physicians failed to give specific quantities in their recipes or to identify the complaints for which they were intended. Today, we can only guess at their efficacy.

Judging from the much more comprehensive and precise medical documents of the ancient Egyptians, the therapeutic batting average of their early prescriptions could not have been high. Many, indeed, contained substances that we can identify as drugs, but in all except a few instances the effects of the drug, or its quantity, or its method of application were quite inappropriate to the complaint.

AN ANCIENT DRUG made of goat's blood and white earth from the Mediterranean island of Lemnos was used throughout Europe for 16 centuries. Shown at about twice its actual size, the medically useless, square pellet called *terra sigillata* (sealed earth) was prescribed by Roman physicians as early as 100 A.D. In its heyday, it was renowned as an antidote against poison and a remedy for dysentery, hemorrhages and ulcers, but it fell into disfavor in the 16th Century when it was widely but futilely used against the bubonic plague.

A cure from the liver of an ox

When the Egyptian physician prescribed an extract of pomegranate root to combat roundworms in the intestines, the result was probably excellent, since the root does contain a potent vermifuge. More remarkable was the prescription of "liver of ox, roasted and crushed," to cure night blindness. We now know that this disorder is due to vitamin A deficiency, and since liver is an excellent source of the vitamin, the Egyptian prescription doubtless worked more often than not. But when the doctor purported to cure blindness by mixing pig's eyes, antimony, red ocher and honey and then pouring the concoction into the sufferer's ear, he was operating far out of his medical depth—despite the optimistic hieroglyphic message that describes the remedy as "really excellent." And the Egyptian ointment for baldness, a condition whose cure still eludes medical science, was equally useless: "Fat of lion, fat of hippopotamus, fat of crocodile, fat of cat, fat of serpent, fat of ibex. . . ."

These recipes are taken from a papyrus written about 1550 B.C. Strangely enough, equally picturesque and equally ineffectual remedies continued to crowd the pages of medical texts for nearly 3,500 years more—almost down to the 20th Century. With hindsight, it is easy to chuckle over the gullibility of physicians and patients of past ages. Yet considering the difficulties faced by drug-makers during most of human history, the wonder is not that most of their remedies were useless but that any were at all useful.

In the first place, the physician did not really know what he was treating—or what he was treating it with. Until the advent of modern physiology, nobody could know what a disease did to the body; without modern analytical chemistry, the Egyptian or Greek or even 18th Century physician could know only in the most general way the contents, let alone the strength, of his prescriptions.

A CRUDE EYE REMEDY, prescribed in 13th Century Europe, applied a drug made of "the juice of wild lettuce and its leaves macerated with Attic honey." The worthless prescription was based on the theory that since eagles eat wild lettuce and have sharp eyesight, a salve made of lettuce must be good for weak eyes. The drawing shown here is from a book of medicinal plants that also prescribed pig dung and herb ointment for scrofula, and gladiola with goat's or ass's milk for internal pains.

The touchy business of testing drugs

However, the physician's lack of scientific knowledge, though a very real handicap, was not the significant factor in his inability to develop useful drugs. The physician, after all, was no more scientifically ignorant than any other craftsman. The swordsmiths of Damascus and Toledo knew as little of metallurgy as their medical contemporaries did of pharmacology—yet they hammered out blades that were very nearly as good as the best we can produce today. The chief reason why drug-making was, and long remained, perhaps the most backward of the crafts lies deeper, in the profound difficulty of assaying the effects of any drug. This difficulty still forces today's pharmacologists, with all their knowledge, into elaborate and sophisticated procedures to determine the value of drugs, new and existing. And even these meticulous test methods on occasion yield erroneous or ambiguous answers.

In modern terminology, what misled the Egyptian physicians, and their successors for some dozens of centuries, were two phenomena: spontaneous recovery and the "placebo effect." Both benefit human well-being by alleviating illness, but both complicate medicine because they occur illogically and erratically.

The first term, spontaneous recovery, refers to the fact that the majority of diseases are self-limiting. That is, the patient, treated or not, will sooner or later get well. In such disorders—which are estimated to account for at least 75 per cent of human illness—it is impossible, without modern scientific methods, to say whether the patient recovered because of the treatment or in spite of it.

Even more confusing to drug-makers is the placebo effect, the seemingly miraculous cures worked by prescriptions that, according to any scientific criterion, are utterly worthless. The word placebo comes from the Latin verb meaning "to please" and is classically defined as any medicine adapted to benefit the patient by pleasing him. It has been demonstrated on countless occasions that a placebo, a "medicine" containing harmless and inactive ingredients, can relieve anxiety and tension, and alleviate pain—even the acute discomfort from major surgery. Moreover, it can cause or cure nausea or diarrhea, reduce stomach acidity, even "cure" the common cold.

Senseless prescriptions that work

Significantly, the curative value of the placebo effect has been found to be most widespread among people who are both uneducated and deeply religious. Considering that for most of human history the great majority of people fell into this category, it is apparent that even the most nonsensical prescription often did cure the patient, if he was curable at all.

When these difficulties in assaying the true worth of drugs are added to the abysmal state of science, it is easier to understand why only a small minority of ancient prescriptions, out of the hundreds that have come down to us, were pharmacologically effective, and produced by their own action some significant change in the patient's body. Almost all of the effective preparations were designed to produce changes that were immediately and conspicuously noticeable to physician and patient alike. And only a very few of this already small group were both effective and appropriate, in the sense that the changes they produced were truly beneficial.

Most of this last select group were drugs to relieve pain and discomfort. The Egyptians used the juice from poppy seeds—a crude form of opium—to soothe crying babies (paregoric, an opium preparation, is still used for colicky infants, and morphine, the active ingredient of opium, remains the most widely used reliever of acute pain). The Greeks added decoctions of mandrake, one of whose active ingredients, the alkaloid scopolamine, was employed until quite recently to ease the pangs of childbirth. The Greeks also discovered that an infusion of the autumn crocus could end the agony of gout (purified, it is still used for this purpose), and that extracts of willow bark could reduce fever (a job that a remote descendant, aspirin, still does as effectively as any drug we know). The Arabs contributed various forms of mercury as a cure for scabies (popularly known as "The Itch"); these remained in use until fairly recently, when they were replaced by safer preparations.

Among the ancient remedies that were conspicuous in their activity, but often less than beneficial, were the purges and emetics. The Egyptians, for example, used castor-oil seeds to "expel the disease in the belly"; this is perhaps the first record of the theory, still held by some people, that the first thing to do in case of illness is to "clean out the system." Modern physicians know that purges and emetics are seldom beneficial and at times even harmful. In most cases, therefore, these harsh potions—along with the dozens of purely magical recipes—must have served as simply placebos, though very active ones.

It was the conspicuously active drugs that won favored places in the papyruses, parchments and crudely printed books that record the millennial fallacies of prescientific pharmacology. For a placebo to exert its full effect (and, presumably, for the physician to collect his full fee) the patient needed to be impressed with the fact that something was being done for or to him. Purges and emetics obviously had this quality in full measure. So did the innumerable horrid-tasting potions that have made the phrase "take one's medicine" a byword for accepting an unpalatable but necessary situation. So, too, did dozens of odoriferous prescriptions containing human or animal excrement or such substances as asafetida, whose name means "stinking gum."

When drugs were gems

These psychologically if not pharmacologically beneficial preparations did well enough for the ordinary citizen. The upper classes, however, wanted something more for their money. For them, "impressive" tended to mean "costly"—as indeed it often still does. Thus one Bulleyn, an English physician who in the reign of Henry VIII enjoyed the equivalent of a modern "society practice," described a remedy containing "two drachms of white perles, two little peeces of saphyre . . . emerauldes . . . thin peeces of gold and silver." Kings and noblemen, said the doctor, "have used this for their comfort."

The inveterate desire of kings, noblemen and ordinary folk for potions that would heal, soothe or stimulate made drugs no inconsiderable factor in commerce and, at times, in history. The spices—cloves, cassia and "lucent syrops tinct with cinnamon"—for which Vasco da Gama rounded Africa and Columbus fared forth across the Atlantic were valued as much for their supposed medical virtues as for their culinary properties. Not much over a century ago, England fought two wars with China to keep the opium trade going. And it was a dispute over tea (which owes its stimulating properties to the drug caffeine) that helped launch the American Revolution.

THE HORN OF THE UNICORN, a mythical beast, was believed in medieval and Renaissance times to possess magic healing powers. Fake "unicorn's horns"—elephant or rhinoceros tusks, in reality—commanded high prices. Jellies prepared from them were said to restore failing strength; scrapings presumably prevented fevers. Believed to be antidotes against poisons in food or wine, hollowed-out horns were used as drinking cups by kings. The fame of unicorn horns as a cure-all finally faltered when they failed to cure victims of the Great Plague of 1665.

As articles of commerce, drugs were no less subject to fads and fashions than were other commercial products. A new drug was often impressive—and therefore psychologically effective—*because* it was new. But familiarity sometimes bred pharmacological contempt. In another of his witty observations, made at the beginning of this century, Osler said that "one should treat as many patients as possible with a new drug, while it still has the power to heal."

Amid fashions and fantasies, the list of truly useful drugs expanded —but at a very slow pace. As late as 1860, the American physician and author, Oliver Wendell Holmes, could still declare that except for "opium . . . wine . . . and the vapors which produce the miracle of anesthesia—I firmly believe that if the whole *Materia Medica,* as now used, could be sunk to the bottom of the sea, it would be all the better for mankind— and all the worse for the fishes."

Dr. Holmes, in his eloquent disgust, was a trifle unjust to the pharmacology of his day, for he must have known of other drugs that had proved their value. But not very unjust; most prescriptions still depended for their efficacy on the misplaced faith of doctor and patient, and if faith failed, so did the drug. Yet even as Holmes penned this indictment, a revolution was underway in pharmacology and related sciences. Ether and nitrous oxide, the anesthetic vapors that he mentioned appreciatively, were themselves products of that revolution—specifically, of the developing science of chemistry, which was already purifying old drugs and synthesizing new ones. Simultaneously, the new sciences of experimental pharmacology and physiology were developing ever more exact ways of appraising the effects of drugs in living organisms.

The drug revolution can be said to have started in 1806, when a German apothecary, Friedrich Wilhelm Adam Sertürner, isolated from opium some bitter, colorless crystals. These he described, correctly, as "the specific narcotic element of opium." This isolation of morphine, soon followed by the isolation of other pharmacologically active compounds such as strychnine and quinine, made possible the partial lifting of the veil that until then had obscured the physician's view of drugs. At last the doctor could know precisely what he was giving his patient. No longer was he forced to rely on some brew of herbs and roots, heterogeneous in composition and uncertain in strength; henceforth he could administer measured doses of some specific substance.

Even more important than the rise of pharmaceutical chemistry was the development of sound methods for evaluating drugs. Though many men contributed to this advance, its leaders were two Frenchmen, François Magendie and Claude Bernard. They, along with researchers in other lands, worked out the basic techniques, still used today, for determining what drugs *do* in the body of an animal or a man.

Poisons that save lives

It was Bernard, sometimes called the "father of experimental physiology," who summed up the ambiguous relationship between poisons and drugs. At the same time, with true French clarity and terseness, he summed up the task of all the pharmacologists who followed him.

"Poisons," said Bernard succinctly, "can be employed as agents of life's destruction or as means for the relief of disease." But in addition, he continued, "the poison becomes an instrument that dissociates and analyzes the most delicate phenomena of the living machine."

Today's pharmacologist, though he dispenses far more of such poisons than Bernard ever dreamed of, employs them precisely according to this definition. Seeking new means "for relief of disease," he also searches for safeguards against chemical "agents of life's destruction." But even more important, he sees his drugs as ever more precise instruments, which by their selective effects on individual parts of the body, reveal how those parts work and analyze "the most delicate phenomena" of living organisms. For he understands what Bernard understood: we can preserve life only to the extent that we comprehend it.

TRAVELER AND TRADER, Marco Polo brought back two durable drugs, camphor and rhubarb, when he returned to Venice from China after 25 years at the court of Emperor Kublai Khan. The 13th Century merchant and explorer is pictured above on the title page of a medieval German edition of his famed travelogue, which included glowing descriptions of great forests of camphor trees in southwestern China. Both camphor and rhubarb are still in use as drugs today, the former as a counterirritant to burns and itches, the latter as a laxative.

The Pharmacist's Ancient Art

Of the millions of people who reach every day for the aspirin bottle or the bicarbonate of soda, probably not one in ten thousand realizes that he is using a remedy that is scores of centuries old. Long before the era of modern science, ancient physicians had built an extensive pharmacopoeia, consisting mostly of fantastic concoctions of no therapeutic value but including some substances that medicine still relies on. The Egyptians of Pharaoh's time knew that castor oil was a laxative; the Babylonians were the first to use deadly belladonna to relieve the spasms of coughing; the ancient Chinese discovered that liver and iron cured anemia.

The great Greek physicians, like Hippocrates, collected and prescribed the most efficient drugs of older civilizations and in turn passed the knowledge along to Rome, which gave the world standardized prescription drugs and the first drugstore. In the Middle Ages Arabian alchemists applied their skills to the making of drugs, and many of their discoveries—distilled alcohol, vegetable extracts—survived to stock the shelves of 17th Century pharmacies like the one opposite, alongside such older and often bizarre ingredients as crushed pearls, powdered wolf's teeth and ground mummies.

A 17TH CENTURY DRUGSTORE

This busy Paris pharmacy, shown in a 1624 illustration, prepared all of its medicines from a floor-to-ceiling stock of drugs stored in decorative boxes, urns and canisters. The pharmacist stands at the left with his prescription book, while an apprentice uses a mortar and pestle to compound a remedy for one of the fashionably attired customers at the counter.

Drugs of the Ancient World

The earliest record of man's use of drugs is a 4,000-year-old clay tablet, on which an unknown Sumerian listed a dozen remedies for unspecified sicknesses. About 500 years later, an Egyptian physician recorded about 800 remedies containing more than 700 drugs. One of his prescriptions, administered to children for excessive crying, contained poppy seeds—the source of the opium contained in paregoric—and the excrement of flies. The priestly physicians of Egypt administered drugs in at least 14 different forms, from pills to poultices, and special ointment kitchens *(below)* mixed drugs with animal fat to produce medicinal salves.

The logical Greeks, among the first to attempt a practical evaluation of medical treatments, discarded many of the drugs they had inherited. Hippocrates limited himself to only 260 types including squill, an effective but now outmoded heart stimulant. The Greeks also scoured the Mediterranean world for drugs like highly touted silphium from North Africa *(right)*.

Rome brought its genius for organization to the gathering, preparation and sale of Greek drugs. Detailed prescriptions, calling for precise quantities of specific ingredients, were scrupulously compounded.

Far beyond Rome's world, other great civilizations had also evolved extensive pharmacopoeias. Chinese Emperor Shen Nung, who ruled about 48 centuries ago, put together the *Pen T'sao,* in which he rated 365 herbs as superior, mediocre or inferior. One of the best was a shrub now known as *Ephedra sinica,* used for lung ailments. It is the source of ephedrine, effective against asthma and other allergic conditions.

Less is known of the drugs used by pre-Columbian civilizations in America, but at least one—the pain-killing coca leaf—is still chewed by Peruvian Indians as their Inca ancestors did 14 centuries ago *(opposite, below)*.

An Egyptian tomb painting of an ointment kitchen shows, from the left, men crushing drugs with mortar and pestle, shaping the ointment into

MEDICINE AS PRECIOUS AS GOLD
A Sixth Century B.C. Greek bowl illustrates the weighing and loading of precious silphium on board a ship under the watchful eye of King Arkesilas of Cyrene. Silphium was a carrotlike plant used as a cathartic and said to be worth its weight in gold.

balls and melting drugs in a pot of boiling animal fat.

ELEGANT DRUG CONTAINERS
These handsome vessels were used as drug containers by two great civilizations. The gold Inca chalice at the left held coca leaves—the source of the drug cocaine—chewed by revelation-seeking priests around 500 A.D.; a coca chewer forms its handle. The Chinese porcelain apothecary jar at the right, from the Ming Dynasty of the 14th to 17th Centuries, may have been copied from an earlier Arabian jar called an albarello. Jars made of nonporous porcelain were highly prized in Europe for storage of liquids and syrups until well into the 19th Century.

Dioscorides, depicted in Moslem garb in this Arab illustration, explains the properties of mandrake, a plant often used as a pain-killer.

The Heritage of Dioscorides

The knowledge of drugs accumulated by the Greeks and Romans reached Arabia during the Middle Ages largely through the works of Dioscorides *(opposite, right).* He was a Greek who served with the Roman legions during the First Century and traveled the Roman Empire from Spain to Asia Minor. Wherever he went, Dioscorides investigated the properties of local plants that might be useful as drugs. This information was eventually published in his five-volume work, *De Materia Medica,* which became the basic catalogue of drugs and their effects for the next 15 centuries.

With the fall of Rome, the heritage of Dioscorides traveled eastward, first to Byzantium and then to the Near East, where Arabic translations helped make Moslem physicians supreme in the Middle Ages. Baghdad became the world's leading medical and drug center, and the *Arabian Nights,* describing the ample stock of one of the city's drugshops, listed "precious flasks . . . balms . . . salves . . . powders . . . syrups held in crystal . . . pomades made up of the sap of three hundred rare kinds of herbs."

A cramped open-front drugstore, typical of 13th Century Baghdad, displays its wares in glazed earthenware pots and leather pouches.

The Golden Age of Arabian Drugs

As Arab alchemists brought their technical skills to bear on the old remedies of Greece and Rome, the art of drug making began to evolve into the science of pharmacology. During the golden age of Arabian drugs, the Eighth to the 13th Centuries, these skilled men produced a new constellation of extracted, distilled and fermented drugs that provided concentrated, purified medicines. One of these potions, prescribed "for catarrhs, coughs, swelling of the belly, and loosening of the stomach," is shown being made below. The ingredients—myrrh, iris, white pepper and anise—are pounded to powder, tied in a rag and left to soak and fer-

ment for three days in a jug of wine. The wine is then strained out *(center)* and "drunk after exercise."

While the Arabian experiments provided effective new formulas, they also produced many nostrums as impractical as the worst of the Egyptian remedies. For example, Avicenna, the great Arab physician who successfully used mercury ointment for skin diseases, prescribed thin coatings of gold or silver on his pills—an elegant but hardly therapeutic addition. Nevertheless, medicine owes much to the Arab pharmacopoeia of more than 2,000 drugs, which became available to Western physicians as Europe emerged from the Middle Ages.

DRUG DISPENSERS OF EUROPE
In his drugshop *(above)*, a 13th Century Venetian pharmacist dispenses vinegar syrup to be drunk on the spot. Two centuries later, a German pharmacist *(below, standing)* and his assistant take inventory of the shop's drugs, ranked in their cryptically labeled containers.

An illustration from one of Guy de Chauliac's works, published in 1478, shows this famed

The First Pharmacies

The introduction of Arab drugs into Christian Europe late in the Middle Ages brought into being a new specialist—the pharmacist—to prepare and dispense them. As early as the 13th Century, Venice was studded with tiny, open-fronted shops, like the one at the upper left, where a man suffering from a bad cough or dysentery could obtain a soothing draught of medicine prepared to the exact formula devised by the Arabs.

During the 14th and 15th Centuries, the drugshops evolved into the larger enclosed pharmacies that became the centers of medical practice in European cities. Doctors met their patients at the local pharmacy. There, also, the ailing could seek remedies from a pharmacist—who often prescribed the drugs he dispensed.

Not all physicians were willing to accept the independent pharmacist as a reliable supplier of drugs. The

urgeon *(center)* in his Paris clinic, directing his personal herb gardener and pharmacist to prepare the ingredients required for one of his drugs.

brilliant 14th Century French surgeon, Guy de Chauliac, urged physicians to compound their own medicines, and to carry some with them when they visited the sick. De Chauliac included a private herb garden and pharmacy in his Paris clinic *(above)*.

The prescription book appeared on the pharmacist's counter by the end of the 15th Century *(lower left)* and formalized a relationship between prescriber and dispenser that still exists. Then, as now, physicians used Latin shorthand to specify drugs that might range from *terra sigillata*—"sacred earth" brought from the isle of Lemnos for use against diarrhea —to such weird concoctions as *spiritus antepilepticus sanguinis humani*. A liquid distilled from human blood mixed with angelica water and a solution of peony blossoms, it was frequently prescribed as a remedy for asthma, apoplexy, palsy and epilepsy.

Symbols of a Powerful Faith

"Heal the sick, cleanse the lepers, raise the dead, cast out devils."
Matthew 10:8

Christ's instructions to his disciples *(above)*, established the Christian church as the healer of body and soul, and made it an important influence in medicine from medieval to modern times. As early as the Sixth Century,

the monasteries had become the repositories of medical knowledge in Europe. Using bits of information gleaned from salvaged Greek and Roman texts, the monks produced excellent drugs from such homegrown herbs as peppermint, fennel and mustard. By the 14th Century, every sizable monastery had not only its own hospital and physician, but often a well-equipped pharmacy as well. The monk-pharmacists were the first to distill liqueurs like the famous Benedictine for digestive and respiratory ailments.

The strong link between religion and medicine, still evidenced by religion-affiliated hospitals, medical missionary groups and nursing orders of nuns, was forged during the Middle Ages. Some of the best physicians of that period were bishops who could prescribe both physical and spiritual remedies. For believers, both were potent medicines; reflecting this conviction, drugs of the spirit are prominent in ancient portrayals of Christ as a pharmacist *(below)*, a decoration found in many European pharmacies up to the 18th Century.

THE HEAVENLY PHARMACY
Beneath a banner that reads "Come here and buy without money and for nothing," Christ is shown dispensing drugs for the body and spirit in this allegorical painting done by a German artist in 1731. The square drug containers on the counter are labeled faith, hope, charity, patience, contentment, help and mercy.

A PRESCRIPTION FOR MANKIND
An ornate French pharmacy of the 16th Century is the setting of this illustration, which depicts Christ as a pharmacist prescribing a spiritual "restaurant" (restorative) for Adam and Eve, who represent mankind. On the shelves, clove stalk and maize mingle with such spiritual remedies as confidence and patience.

A drug guild's shield adorns this old tile.

New Drugs from Old

By the 17th Century, the first stirrings of scientific progress in drugs could be felt in European pharmacies like the one at right. They still purveyed many of the roots used since ancient times as medicines, but distilled extracts of plants and minerals were turning numerous older remedies into unwanted "drugs on the market."

Well-equipped 17th Century pharmacies contained not only the traditional mortars and pestles, but also equipment like alembics and condensers for distillation. Pharmacies were the first laboratories of scientific chemistry, producing such discoveries as phosphorus and fluorine.

Under the rigorous supervision of powerful guilds like the Worshipful Society of Apothecaries of London, whose emblem appears on the pill tile above, 17th Century pharmacists became specialists in the making of both galenical drugs—pure extracts of vegetables, like carrot oil —and chemical drugs like smelling salts, made by combining ammonium carbonate with ammonia water.

Today only the ghosts of many old drugs remain, their essential ingredients chemically isolated into the alkaloids, glucosides and amines of modern medicine's superior drugs.

IN A DUTCH DRUGSTORE

A richly detailed view of a mid-17th Century Dutch pharmacy, often attributed to Emmanuel de Witte, shows a well-dressed pharmacist at the left, holding an unidentified medicinal herb. Among the drugs that can be identified on his spic-and-span shelves are camphor, sassafras and saltpeter. A visiting physician writes a prescription while the pharmacist's wife holds a lemon, a traditional sign of welcome.

A WOODEN PHARMACIST

This life-sized wooden figure of an apprentice pharmacist once served as a house sign outside a Swiss pharmacy. Although such figures are now museum curiosities, the mortar and pestle used to grind and mix various ingredients have remained a universal symbol of pharmacy.

A Heritage of Ancient Drugs

Even in this age of man-made miracle drugs, medicine is still using effective drugs derived from ancient herbs like the ones shown on these pages, each linked with its present-day role.

Some of these drugs once had sinister reputations. The Roman Emperor Claudius was poisoned with belladonna, Hamlet's father with henbane and Romeo with aconite. But mild dosages of belladonna and henbane are now valued for their muscle-relaxing effects, while aconite has been used as an ointment to relieve the acute pain of ailments like neuralgia and rheumatism.

Another ancient poison was meadow saffron, known to the Romans as *Colchicum autumnale* (autumn crocus). From it comes colchicine, useful in treating gout and arthritis.

In medieval times, physicians knew that squill, an onionlike plant found near the Mediterranean seashore, was a good heart tonic. They did not know they had an even better heart stimulant, digitalis, employed chiefly as an external remedy for skin conditions until the 18th Century, when it was first used to treat heart disease.

One of the best of the old drugs is cinchona which, like ipecac, was introduced into Europe from South America in the 17th Century. The powdered bark of a Peruvian tree, cinchona was exported in large quantities once colonists realized its remarkable ability to halt the recurrent high fevers of malaria. Not until the 19th Century did scientists isolate from cinchona one of its active ingredients, quinine, prescribed for malaria today.

CINCHONA (ANALGESIC)
IPECAC (EMETIC)
SQUILL (STIMULANT)
ACONITE (ANALGESIC)
MEADOW SAFFRON
(GOUT REMEDY)
WHITE POPPY (SEDATIVE)

2

Alcohol: The Oldest Drug

A basketful of purple grapes from Burgundy, France, stands ready for processing into wine. Its production of 1.6 billion gallons of wine annually makes France a major source of alcohol, the world's oldest and still most popular drug.

THE MOST WIDELY USED DRUG in the world is not aspirin, nor penicillin, nor any other substance commonly prescribed by physicians. It is a material of only minor medical importance, yet it is consumed daily by tens of millions of people, sometimes in dangerous quantities, and on occasion by hundreds of millions more. Indeed a large majority of the world's people have probably partaken of it, or will partake of it, at some time during their lives.

This drug is a colorless, volatile liquid known to the chemist as ethanol, or ethyl alcohol, but to almost everybody else it is simply alcohol. Because of its widespread use—and abuse—it is the object of intensive study by many medical scientists. And the extensive nature of this research makes it possible to draw a full-length portrait of the drug that can serve as a case study of how any drug is investigated scientifically. For the questions a pharmacologist asks about alcohol and the kind of answers he gets have close parallels in all drug research.

On several counts alcohol deserves first place in any discussion of drugs. Not only is it one of the most common of all drugs, but it is better understood than most. It is almost certainly the oldest drug, and perhaps the most important.

Alcohol has been produced and consumed by man since before the dawn of civilization. Every civilized or uncivilized people on earth today that lives by farming produces some form of alcoholic beverage. These potables are fermented from grain (beer, whiskey), potatoes (vodka), fruit juices (wine, cider), honey (mead) and half a dozen more exotic substances. Even food-gathering tribes ferment alcoholic beverages, and some anthropologists have suggested that the very invention of agriculture may have been stimulated as much by a desire for alcohol as by the need for a more copious food supply.

Certainly in the earliest civilizations, alcohol was accorded a place little, if at all, inferior to that of the basic food, bread. The very first written documents that have been found, a collection of clay tablets dug from a mound in Mesopotamia and dating from about 2100 B.C., include alcohol in a wage list: what seems to be a series of proper names is followed by the notation: "Bread and beer for one day." In the tomb inscriptions of ancient Egyptian notables, one of the commonest boasts is "I gave bread to the hungry, beer to the thirsty. . . ."

Ancient civilizations and their barbarian neighbors alike enjoyed alcohol—often to excess. As early as the First Century A.D., the Roman naturalist Pliny the Elder sourly observed that "in no part of the world is drunkenness ever at a loss." Subsequent explorers, though they enormously expanded the known world of Pliny's day, seldom failed to find alcohol at the end of their quests. In the 16th Century, Bernal Diaz del Castillo, a companion of Cortés in the Spanish conquest of Mexico, described that land as "full of Magueys [a large, fleshy-leaved plant], from which they make their wine." Mexicans still consume quantities of maguey "wine," called pulque, as well as its distilled essences, such as tequilla. Some 250 years after Cortés, Captain James Cook sailed into

MEDIEVAL DRUG PREPARATION, although it relied on crude methods, attempted to produce uniform dosages. These illustrations from a 14th Century manuscript of the works of Avicenna, the famous Arab physician, show how pharmacists compounded medications with mortar and pestles *(top)* and rolled pills by hand *(center)* to provide doses of roughly equal size for the patient *(bottom)*. Methods little different from Avicenna's were common practice until the 20th Century.

the South Seas and found the Polynesians in their idyllic islands imbibing kava, fermented from a variety of pepper. A generation later, the great English explorer Mungo Park, pushing his caravan into the Sahara, was entertained by African tribesmen with "a liquor which tasted . . . much like the strong beer of my native country (and very good beer, too). . . ." There is no country in the world today—including those where alcohol is officially forbidden or frowned on—in which the drug is not consumed. Americans imbibed some 212,245,000 gallons of alcohol in 1965—2.27 gallons (equivalent to 182 quarts of beer or 36 pints of 100-proof whiskey) for every man and woman over 16.

The reasons behind the worldwide importance of alcohol are to be found in its actions in the human body. For alcohol, more than for most other drugs, these actions can be explained in some detail. There are reasonably certain answers to the basic questions that the pharmacologist asks about all drugs. What organ or organs does it affect, and how? Does it speed up the heart or retard it, stimulate the brain or depress it, accelerate or retard the waste-eliminating action of the kidneys? What permanent changes does it cause? How does it get into—and out of—body tissues? And most important of all, how is each of these actions related to the amount of the drug consumed: in the pharmacologist's own phrase, what is the dose?

How alcohol really works

In the case of alcohol, general answers to these questions are simple to find. Its direct actions in the body seem to be limited strictly to one organ: the brain, which controls the body's other activities. On this organ, it acts as a depressant, not as the stimulant it is commonly believed to be. Unlike true stimulants, such as caffeine or amphetamine, alcohol retards rather than accelerates the brain's control mechanisms. Its depressant action, depending on the dose, can cause mild or serious mental disorganization, loss of muscular control (most conspicuous in the inebriate's slurred speech and staggering gait), sleep, coma and even death.

For a more precise picture of what alcohol does in the body, it is necessary to examine the question of dose. A doctor, in prescribing a drug, obviously needs to know how much of it will produce the desired effect on the patient, how much more will make him seriously ill, how much more will kill him. But the answers to these questions are seldom unequivocal. The effects of a given amount of a given drug will depend on the size, physiology and state of health of the person receiving it, and on other things as well.

The simplest measure of dosage is furnished by the bloodstream because alcohol, like most drugs, is carried to its target in the body by the blood. Moreover, the effects of varying amounts can usually be related to the concentration of alcohol in the blood.

The effects of alcohol become noticeable, at least in the drinker's behavior, at a concentration in the blood of around .05 per cent—five parts of alcohol to ten thousand parts of blood. At .10 per cent, intoxication is noticeable in the form of loud or slightly slurred speech and uncertain equilibrium; at .15 per cent, the drinker is legally defined as "under the influence of alcohol," meaning that his ability to drive a car safely is considered to be significantly impaired; at .20 per cent, he will be staggering; at .30 per cent, he may be unable to stand. By .40 per cent, if not sooner, he will probably be unconscious—and will therefore hardly be in a position to raise the level further. However, a few determined drinkers have managed this—often with fatal results. Some years ago, a Chicago commuter boasted to some barroom companions that he could swallow 17 martinis in less than an hour. He did—but the 17th proved to be his last drink, for he dropped dead after swallowing it. An alcohol blood level of .50 to .60 per cent is almost invariably fatal.

These figures are, of course, averages. People vary in their response to drugs as they do in height, intelligence and temperament. And quite apart from individual idiosyncrasies, a number of other factors influence the complex connections between alcohol levels and dose. The effects of a given concentration of alcohol in the bloodstream depend on the route it takes to get there, the speed at which it travels, the other substances it meets along the way and even the size of the body it is moving through.

The route followed by alcohol is, of course, indirect. It is swallowed and reaches the bloodstream by way of the gastrointestinal tract, its first stop being the stomach. There, part of it passes into the blood vessels of the stomach wall. How much is absorbed in this way, and how fast, depends mainly on how dilute the alcohol is. A glass of beer (4 per cent or more alcohol) or a dilute highball (10 to 20 per cent) are absorbed much more slowly than a straight shot of whiskey (43 per cent) and therefore produce far less of an immediate effect.

The greater part of the alcohol is not absorbed in the stomach at all, but must wait until it passes into the small intestine. There its absorption, in the words of one writer, is "rapid, constant and complete." Thus a major factor in how rapidly ingestion is followed by intoxication is how rapidly the alcohol passes from the stomach to the intestine.

Well-pickled herring in Russia

Food slows this passage—particularly proteins and fats, which being less easily digested remain in the stomach longest, together with any alcohol mixed in with them. The Russians, known for their consumption of potent potations (some varieties of vodka contain as much as 72 per cent alcohol), often cushion the effect by interspersing their explosive drinks with mouthfuls of herring, sausage or caviar—all prime sources of fats and protein.

Oddly enough, Russians may receive additional protection from the very robustness of their national drink. At concentrations above 40 per cent, alcohol is actually absorbed more slowly in the stomach. Moreover, high-proof liquors irritate the pyloric valve that acts as a gate between stomach and small intestine; on contact with really fiery drinks, the sensitive valve closes, keeping the drug out of the small intestine and thereby still further slowing the intoxicant's absorption by the body.

Carbon dioxide, on the other hand, speeds up the passage of alcohol into the intestine. It is dissolved CO_2 that gives champagne its extra kick and makes whiskey mixed with carbonated soda more immediately potent than a whiskey and water highball.

The final complication in assaying the dose of alcohol comes from the fact that once it gets into the blood it immediately begins to be removed from the body. When straight whiskey is swallowed on an empty stomach, nearly all the alcohol is absorbed in a matter of minutes, almost before the body has time to begin eliminating it. The same amount of alcohol diluted in beer might be consumed and absorbed over an hour or more—during which time a sizable proportion of it would be eliminated.

Since the dose of alcohol depends on the drinker, the drink and the circumstances, the effects on an individual of a given amount of drinking cannot be predicted with accuracy. But much more is known about how those effects are produced. Alcohol's action is highly selective. Even in stupefying concentrations, it seems to exert no direct effect on any organ except the brain. And even there, its effects are selective. Small concentrations of alcohol depress the reticular activating system, the part of the brain that alerts the cerebral cortex—the thinking and learning portion of the brain that integrates its activities. Freed from control, the cortex begins to function in a less organized manner. Activities requiring alertness, such as driving, or concentration, such as adding a column of figures, are carried out less efficiently. At the same time, ideas and images may flow more freely, if less coherently.

Whiskey's phony glow

Also affected at this point are two other portions of the brain; those controlling the blood vessels and the kidneys. In the circulatory system, alcohol causes the capillaries that are located just under the skin to dilate so that they can carry more blood. The skin, flushed with warm blood, feels warmer. So does the drinker—but this, like many effects of alcohol, is an illusion. In fact, body temperature does not rise but falls, because much internal heat is carried by blood to the skin and dissipated there. Despite the folklore of the St. Bernard dog who brought comfort with his keg of brandy to travelers marooned in snowdrifts, alcohol has never kept anyone warm in cold weather. Indeed, in really cold weather it can lead to dangerous chilling. In hot climates, by contrast, the loss of body heat can be a boon. The Empire-building Englishmen in the tropics who went out in the midday sun preserved their British *sang-froid* with the aid of innumerable brandy-pegs, gin-and-tonics and Singapore slings. As a result of habitual heavy drinking, the dilation of the tiny capillaries can become permanent, producing the drunkard's traditional flushed face and cherry nose. The retired Indian Army colonel, a cliché of British literature, did not owe his fiery complexion to sunburn.

Alcohol's effect is as marked on the kidneys as on the blood vessels. It depresses a center in the brain that normally slows the kidneys' excretion of water. The result is reflected in the famous remark of the comic porter in Shakespeare's *Macbeth,* who described drinking as a provoker of "nosepainting, sleep and urine."

In slightly higher concentrations, alcohol extends its domain in the brain to the cortex itself. In the words of a standard text, "the finer grades of discrimination, memory, concentration and insight are dulled and then lost. Confidence abounds, the personality becomes expansive and vivacious, and speech may become eloquent and occasionally brilliant. Mood swings are uncontrolled, and emotional outbursts frequent."

The staggering effect of heavy drinking

Still higher concentrations of alcohol depress more resistant parts of the brain. When the drug reaches the cerebellum, which controls muscular coordination, the tippler's speech becomes garbled and his gait uncertain. The next victims are the brain centers that control consciousness—at which point the drinker blacks out. The deepest and most primitive portions of the brain, which keep the heart and lungs operating, are fortunately almost unaffected by any reasonable concentration of alcohol. Only the most determined and suicidal drinkers have managed to ingest enough of the drug to court death from heart or respiratory failure.

While alcohol is fogging the brain into intoxication, it is simultaneously being removed from the body. At one time, it was believed that elimination occurred entirely through the lungs, skin and kidneys, which disposed of the drug unchanged. This theory was exploded more than a century ago in a historic series of experiments by the great German scientist Justus von Liebig, one of the founding fathers of physiological chemistry. He showed that the drug combined with oxygen in the body, and was ultimately transformed into carbon dioxide and water. Moreover, he pointed out, since this change, which is called oxidation, is always accompanied by the production of energy, alcohol is a food as well as a drug. In fact, we now know that a martini has about the same caloric value as a baked potato.

Subsequent experiments have shown that von Liebig was not completely correct. A small portion of the alcohol does leave unchanged in urine, sweat and exhaled air, but all the rest is, indeed, oxidized. The organ that begins this job—on alcohol and some other drugs—is the liver.

The first step in the transformation of alcohol in the liver is the drug's conversion into the compound acetaldehyde. This is even more toxic than alcohol. But luckily, acetaldehyde is itself transformed almost immediately into a harmless compound, acetic acid (the same substance that makes vinegar sour). At this point the liver's job ends, for acetic acid can be utilized by almost any cell of the body. But the liver remains the bottleneck, since it is only there that the crucial first steps can take place. Any excess of alcohol—the overload that the liver cannot transform—continues to circulate with the blood, eventually causing intoxication.

The body can under no circumstances eliminate more alcohol than the liver can handle—about one fourth ounce an hour. If a person limited his alcohol intake to this amount—about half a shot of whiskey or half pint of beer per hour—he could drink indefinitely without getting drunk—if he enjoyed that kind of activity. But an intake even slightly exceeding the liver's capacity will, sooner or later, build up to intoxication.

The liver's sluggish chemistry cannot be substantially accelerated by any of the traditional treatments for insobriety—vigorous exercise, cold showers or sweat-inducing Turkish baths. The only effective remedy for intoxication is time. But some symptoms of intoxication—such as sleepiness—can be alleviated by counteracting alcohol's depressant effects with a stimulant, thus fighting one poison with another. Most common of the stimulants is caffeine, in the form of strong coffee; the amphetamines ("pep pills") are also used.

Once alcohol has disappeared from the body, its aftereffects are few. The "morning after the night before" has a powerfully unpleasant reputation—and a deserved one. Yet most discomforts of even the most monumental hangover are only partly caused by the drug alcohol, though they are entirely caused by drinking.

The most common symptom—fatigue—has precisely the same cause as any other kind of fatigue: overactivity. Alcohol, though it does not banish fatigue, blocks off the mind's awareness of it, so that the drinker is likely to continue carousing well past the point at which he would otherwise succumb to exhaustion and sleep. On sobering up, he feels tired because he *is* tired. The pounding hangover headache, which Norwegians describe graphically in a phrase that literally means "I've got carpenters," is partly the result of fatigue (it can be brought on by overwork as well as overindulgence) but also of changes in brain fluids brought on by alcohol.

The nausea that frequently accompanies a hangover is apparently due partly to alcohol but also to its "congeners"—chemicals of various sorts that become incorporated into alcoholic beverages during their manufacture. Liquors high in congeners, such as bourbon whiskey, are widely —and probably correctly—considered to have a greater "hangover potential" than congener-poor gin and vodka.

The day after's unslakable thirst

What is probably the most universal hangover symptom of all, however, is entirely caused by alcohol. This is the parched tongue and raging thirst that the French eloquently call "wooden mouth." Alcohol not only speeds up excretion of water, which of course induces thirst, but also temporarily shifts some of the water remaining in the body from the interior of the cells to the so-called extracellular fluids. This partial dehydration of the cells affects the "thirst centers" in the brain, causing the hangover sufferer to feel more thirst than is warranted by his body's need for water.

Unlike many drugs, alcohol does not seem to produce cumulative changes in the body—apart, of course, from a certain degree of tolerance —so long as it is consumed in moderate amounts. Despite the ominous preachments of prohibitionists, there is no proof that a lifetime of

COMPOSITION OF ALCOHOLIC BEVERAGES

BEVERAGE	PER CENT ALCOHOL	PER CENT CONGENERS
GIN, 90 PROOF	45	.0039
BOURBON, 86 PROOF	43	.246
RYE WHISKEY, 86 PROOF	43	.111
SCOTCH, 86 PROOF	43	.0950
BRANDY (COGNAC)	42	.212
RUM	40	.0482
VODKA, 80 PROOF	40	.0026

RECIPE FOR A HANGOVER, shown in the table above, includes both the alcohol in a drink and congeners—toxic substances formed during fermentation. These two share responsibility for the nausea and splitting headaches that characterize hangovers. The special importance of congeners can be seen when the effects of common drinks are compared. Gin contains more alcohol than any of the other beverages listed, yet it does not cause the worst hangovers because its congener content is remarkably low. Bourbon and brandy contain slightly less alcohol but can produce fiercer hangovers because their congener content is considerably higher.

moderate indulgence interferes with normal health. The habitual use of large amounts of the drug is something else again. Not only is it harmful to the personality, but the evidence of bodily damage is unequivocal. Cirrhosis, which destroys the working cells of the liver, is common among longtime heavy drinkers and is most often caused by alcohol.

Even in moderate doses, alcohol can lead to serious and occasionally lethal effects when it is taken in combination with certain other drugs. These include some sedatives, such as the barbiturates, and many tranquilizers. Such drugs, like alcohol, are depressants, and have an additive effect when combined with it. Normally this is not very serious; a person who has been taking barbiturates or a depressant tranquilizer and begins to drink will simply get drunk more quickly and more thoroughly than he expects. But if an evening of heavy drinking is followed by the drunken gulping of a large number of barbiturate sleeping pills, the two drugs together may produce a fatal dose.

When liquor is poison

Oddly enough, the interaction of alcohol with another chemical has been used to treat the most serious problem associated with the drug. Some 20 years ago, two Danish physicians were studying the compound disulfiram as a possible cure for intestinal worms. As part of their testing program, they dosed themselves with small quantities of the compound. Attending a cocktail party soon after, they suddenly found themselves flushed, dizzy and violently nauseated, with splitting headaches. On recovery, they suspected and soon confirmed that disulfiram was to blame. This substance, it turns out, inhibits the liver's transformation of alcohol. It blocks the second step in the process, in which acetaldehyde is transformed into acetic acid, thereby quickly producing a toxic pile-up of acetaldehyde in the body.

Anyone who has taken disulfiram (known commercially as Antabuse) cannot drink even a single glass without becoming violently ill. Unfortunately, as a treatment for alcoholism, disulfiram is seldom successful; the alcoholic usually finds he can give up disulfiram more easily than alcohol.

The limited usefulness of disulfiram indicates the frustrations the pharmacologist faces in trying to deal with the widespread disease of alcoholism. It cannot be explained, or even defined, in pharmacological terms alone. There is no known pharmacological reason why some people destroy their lives by drinking; neither dosage nor physical effects offer an infallible guide. A man who drinks heavily five nights out of seven may on occasion get drunk, but he is not necessarily an alcoholic. Some alcoholics, by contrast, may stay sober for days or even weeks at a time. But once they start drinking, they cannot stop short of abysmal intoxication. They are addicts, "hooked" on the drug alcohol. And addiction to alcohol, like addiction to any other drug, is essentially a psychological compulsion—and therefore the problems it raises are far more psychological, medical and social than pharmacological.

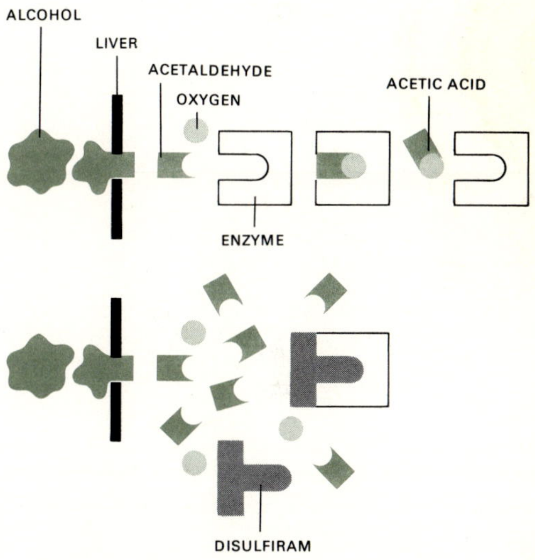

THE ACTION OF DISULFIRAM, a drug intended to discourage alcoholism, disrupts liver functioning so that an imbiber gets sick after drinking. The upper diagram shows how the liver normally handles alcohol. Entering the liver from left, alcohol is first converted into acetaldehyde, a poisonous substance, but this chemical and oxygen are quickly fitted together by an enzyme, forming harmless acetic acid. When disulfiram is taken *(lower diagram),* alcohol is converted into acetaldehyde, but disulfiram joins with the enzyme and prevents acetaldehyde from linking with oxygen to form acetic acid. As a result, toxic acetaldehyde collects, and the drinker becomes nauseated.

The Mind Influencers

The mind is affected by a variety of drugs that induce sleep, calm madness, block sensation, stimulate imagination. Most of them act on the nervous system at a point called the synapse, where the tip of a nerve fiber, called an axon, touches another nerve. One nerve cell may be in contact with—and may receive signals from—as many as 25,000 axons *(inset, opposite)*. The operation of this signal system, like all fundamental life processes, is partly electrical and partly chemical. As researchers identify the chemical reactions and map their locations, the way in which the chemicals known as drugs modify nerve reactions becomes easier to understand.

Some signals excite the cell to action, others inhibit it; drugs can either intensify or suppress both kinds of signals. There are up to 20 billion nerve cells in the human body, each transmitting signals to the others at rates as high as 600 impulses per second. At the same time, the cells are coordinating the signals, enabling the brain to think about the sensations it is receiving and then to put its thoughts into action. The long-sought explanation for drugs' subtle power to influence the brain approaches as scientists learn more about the structure and function of the cells of the nervous system.

THE NERVE CELLS: DRUG TARGET

Deep in thought, this girl is using the key element of her brain, the nerve cell *(inset, white)*. Touching the cell are seven bulb-tipped axons *(green and gray)* bringing signals *(incoming arrows)* from other nerve cells. The green fibers carry signals that prepare the cell to fire its own signal down its own axon *(outgoing arrow)*. The gray axons may inhibit this firing.

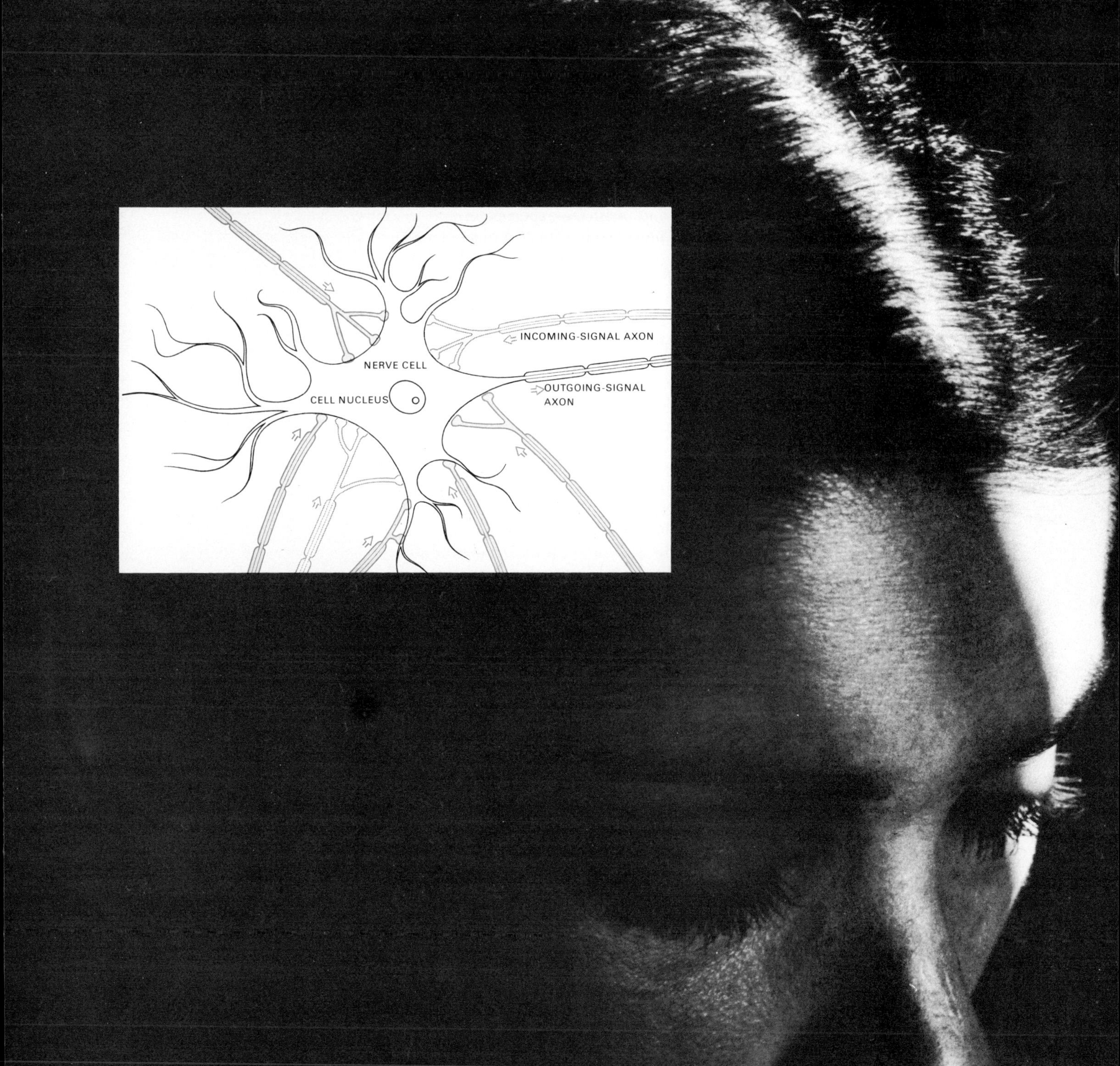
INCOMING-SIGNAL AXON
NERVE CELL
CELL NUCLEUS
OUTGOING-SIGNAL AXON

LSD: Visions and Ghastly Danger

One of the most talked-about drugs of recent years, LSD, has fascinated scientists not only because of its tremendous potency—1/300,000 ounce can produce a trance in which a man may dance with his own shadow *(opposite)*—but because its action offers clues to nerve-cell chemistry. The LSD molecule—technically lysergic acid diethylamide—contains an important section that closely resembles a major part of the molecule of a chemical called serotonin. Serotonin may be one of the brain chemicals that transfer signals from an axon tip across the synapse to another nerve cell. The similarity between LSD and serotonin may explain LSD's power.

According to one theory, an LSD molecule can fool a nerve cell into accepting it as a signal-carrying serotonin molecule. But LSD cannot forward impulses the way serotonin does, so signals are altered. Thus, the drug may both increase the number of signals, amplifying sensations, and also distort the signals so that the sensations received are exaggerated beyond ordinary experience.

The visual effects of a dose of LSD are extraordinary. Colors brighten and glow, and familiar objects may seem wondrously beautiful. But the drug can also make a user writhe on the floor, terrorized by grisly visions, or imagine himself so indestructible that he walks into a moving car.

Some of the psychic disturbances induced by LSD resemble those of schizophrenia, a severe mental illness. These effects do not always wear off, and use of the drug has led to insanity. Because of the risk of such lasting harm, the Commissioner of the U.S. Food and Drug Administration, Dr. James L. Goddard, has described LSD as "one of the most dangerous compounds I know of."

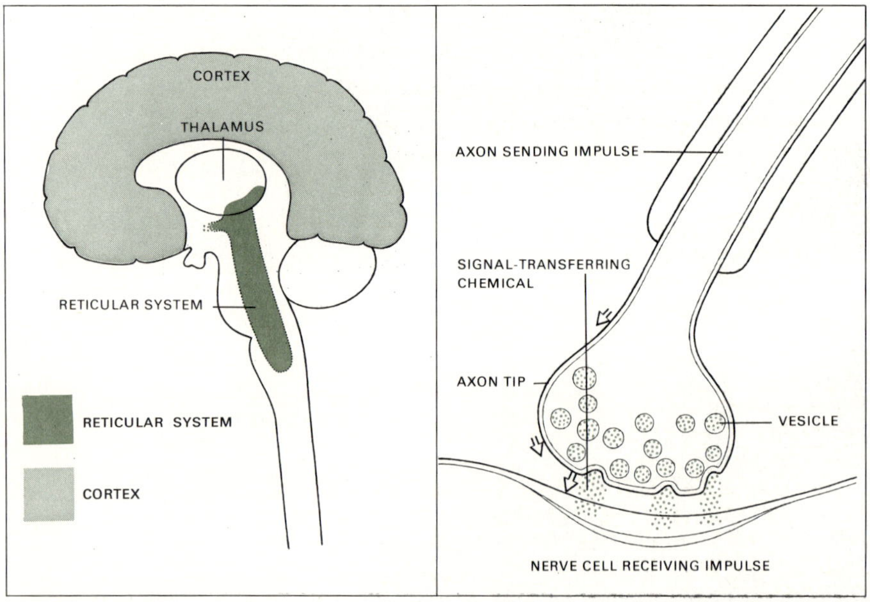

A CONFUSION OF SIGNALS

LSD, it is believed, affects some of the brain areas shown above at left. The reticular system *(dark green)*, which sorts sensory signals going to the cortex *(light green)*, may be overstimulated by the drug, thus distorting its response to the signals. The strange visual effects of LSD, one study indicates, arise in the thalamus, which relays vision signals to the cortex. In all three areas, LSD appears to interfere with the normal transference of signals from axons to nerve cells *(above, right)*. Normally, impulses *(arrows)* move down an axon to its bulbous tip, there to release from tiny vesicles a chemical that transfers the signals to the cell. LSD's interference in this neural process usually causes disquieting alterations of its user's perception.

A Los Angeles "acid head" dances with his

shadow after taking LSD, acid made from a rye mold. LSD's stimulation lasts about 10 hours, but may be followed by confusion or insanity.

Before tranquilizers, violent psychotics had to be tied to their beds *(left);* even less disturbed men and women patients could not be allowed

Tranquilizers for Sick Minds

As recently as the early 1950s sights and sounds in even the best mental hospital could be harrowing—the violent patients kept under restraint by straps or bed sheets; seriously disturbed psychotics yelling in mental torment; others huddled in frozen silence. By the mid-1950s, the wards were transformed because of the introduction of two drugs that helped ease disturbed minds. Neither drug—reserpine, made from rauwolfia, a root found in India, nor chlorpromazine, first synthesized in France—cures sick minds. Each, however, can calm violence, relieve anxiety, and end withdrawal, enabling patients to benefit from psychotherapy and often to go back to home and job.

Both reserpine and chlorpromazine, like LSD, have chemical structures that resemble the nerve-signal carrier serotonin, but their effects are completely different from those of LSD. LSD seems to overactivate the brain; the tranquilizers, on the other hand, seem to calm brain activity. The tranquilizers appear to affect brain areas that include the limbic system, which is involved with the emotions and instincts for survival—fear, feeding, mating—and the hypothalamus, the "fight or flight" center.

The relief of anxiety is so important in our society that tranquilizers—reserpine, chlorpromazine and a less powerful drug, meprobamate, which is used by healthy people to reduce tension—are now among the most commonly prescribed drugs in the United States. Together, they account for one in seven prescriptions.

to mingle. Today, patients can work together *(above)* in a hospital garden, their wildness calmed and their tensions eased by the new drugs.

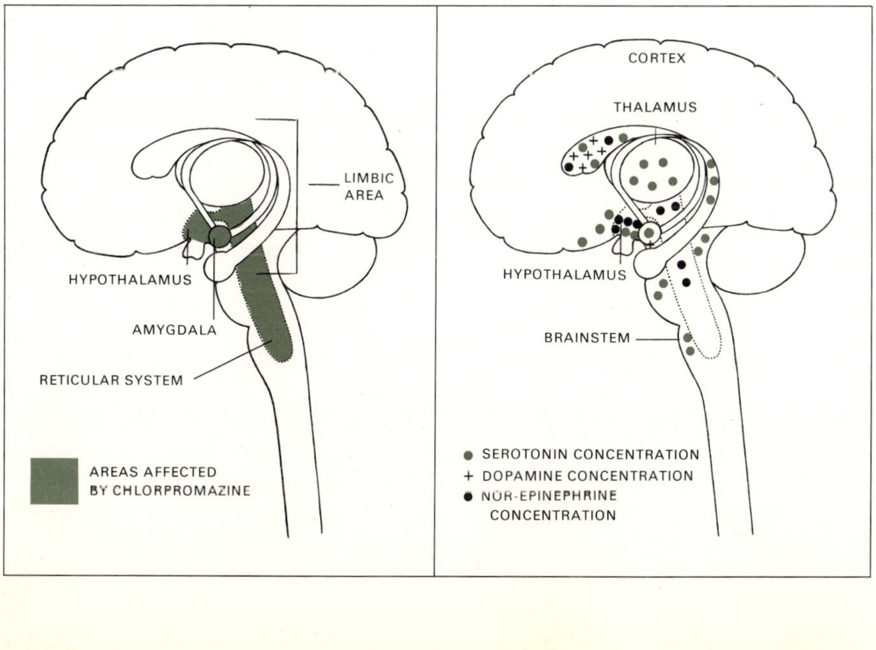

CALMING THE BRAIN'S SIGNALS
Tranquilizers affect the brain's sites of basic drives and emotions, diagramed at left. Chlorpromazine may act on areas shown in green at far left: the signal-transmission center of the reticular system; the hypothalamus, which responds to danger; and the amygdala, which regulates emotions like rage and aggression. While the exact sites of reserpine's influence are unknown, it seems to reduce the brain's supplies of certain chemicals that may transfer signals—serotonin, nor-epinephrine and dopamine. These are concentrated, as indicated on the drawing at near left, in the hypothalamus, the reticular system and the brainstem, as well as in the signal-integrating areas in the thalamus and in the emotion sites of the limbic area.

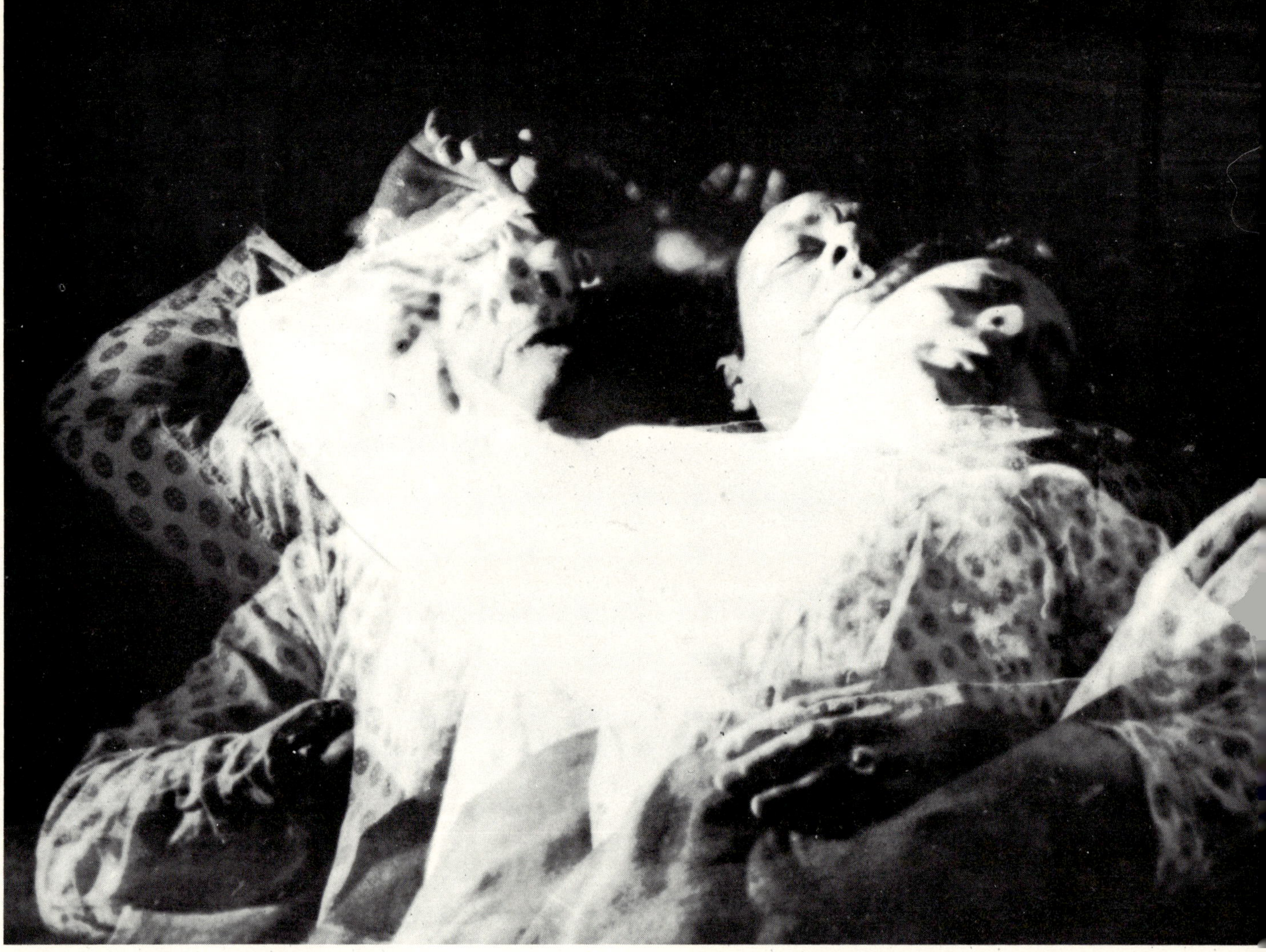

The barbiturates are commonly used to bring on restful sleep, as demonstrated in the multiple exposure above. It shows a person who—until

Soporifics to Bring on Sleep

Half the people in the United States have insomnia; they take about 200 tons of barbiturates every year to help them sleep. How these drugs work is only dimly understood because the phenomenon of sleep itself still awaits a complete explanation.

Falling asleep seems to depend on two opposing actions: an increase in certain brain signals coupled with a decrease in others. The increase has been detected by measuring the electrical waves generated by the brain. Since some of them become more pronounced during sleep, it is assumed they represent signals that actively order the brain to sleep. They may do so by decreasing brain signals that cause wakefulness.

One source of "stay-awake" signals seems be the reticular system, which coordinates sensory impulses before passing them along to stimulate the brain's thinking area, the cortex. A decrease in this stimulation is also a factor in sleep. If the signal flow from the reticular system stops altogether, unconsciousness follows—experimental animals lapsed into a coma when their reticular systems were severed. Even if the signals are not cut off, but are merely monotonous—like those induced by the drone of a boring lecturer—they may fail to stimulate the cortex, and a drowsy brain will drift into sleep.

The flow of signals between reticular system and cortex is at least one target of modern barbiturates. These drugs first depress the reticular system, which is particularly sensitive to them. The result, presumably, is that fewer stimulating signals are sent on, and the cortex is lulled. But the drugs may also affect the cortex directly.

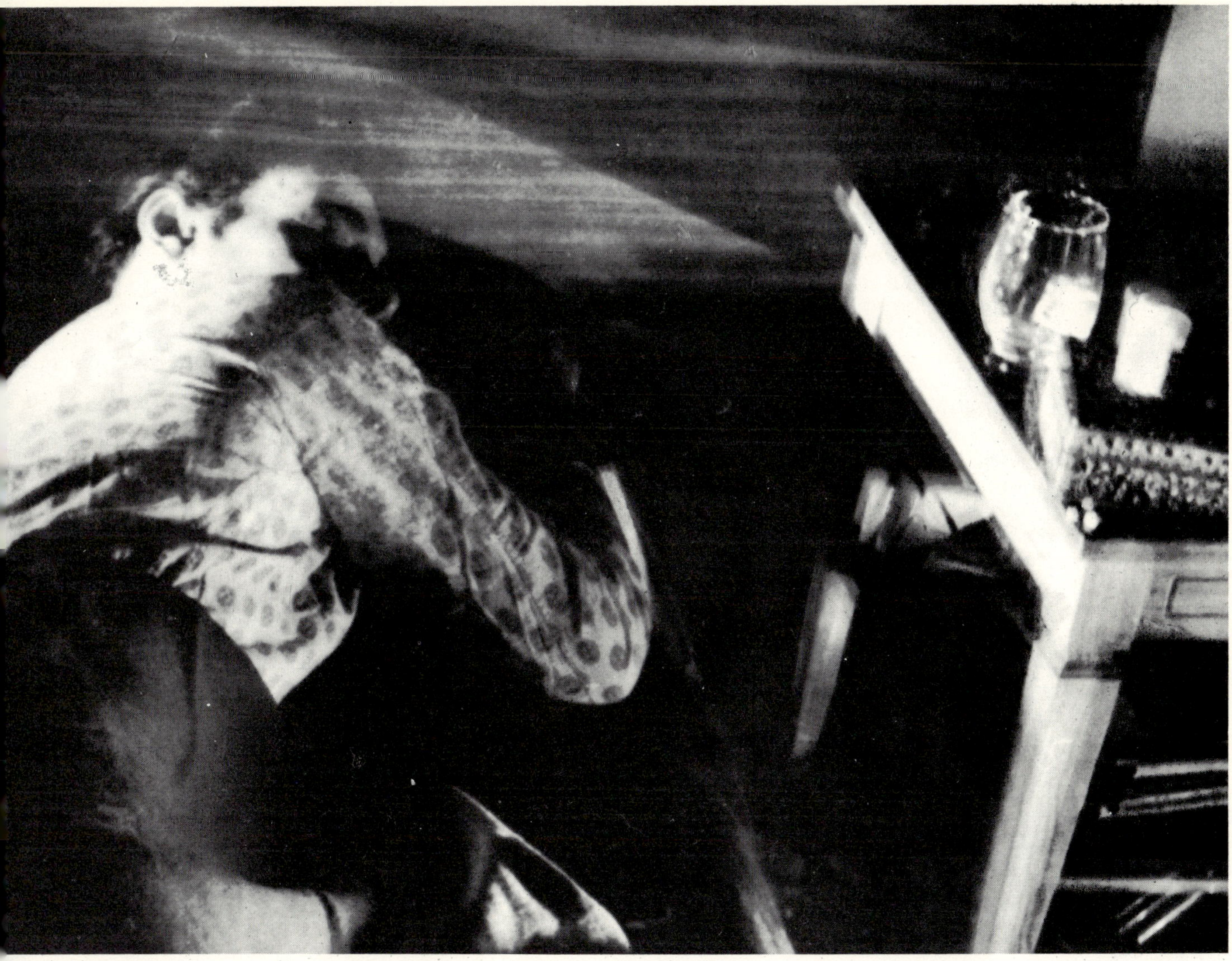

the drug works—tosses and turns in bed, his brain kept active by severe tensions and worries that overstimulated him during a stressful day.

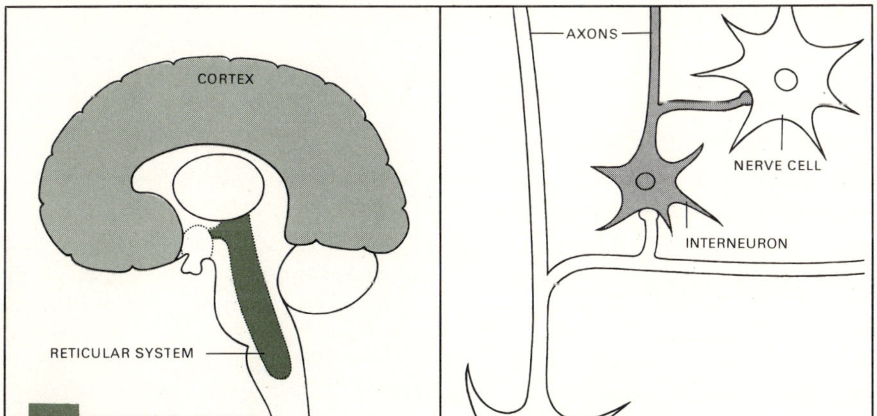

LULLING AN ACTIVE BRAIN

Barbiturates may act on the cortex *(far left, light green)* by depressing thoughts and memory and lulling those areas that help to analyze sights and sounds. This action induces calmness; deep sleep comes when the same barbiturates quiet other areas *(dark green)* that make up the body's arousal mechanism, the reticular system. The sedatives act in particular upon the reticular interconnections called interneurons *(left, gray)*. The interneurons join nerve cells in the spinal column and lower areas of the reticular system with nerve cells higher up in the reticular system.

Psychic and Physical Blocks to Pain

Pain is such a complex phenomenon that the anesthetics and analgesics used to relieve it must influence brain functions as diverse as thought, memory and action. A soldier's agony *(opposite)* is alleviated by an injection of morphine—in part because the drug blocks the brain's ability to recognize some levels of pain.

The physical part of pain consists of signals initiated by sensitive nerve endings in the skin. As these signals travel toward the brain, they may leap from one pathway to another, particularly in the reticular system. Here interconnecting relay cells—the interneurons, which are sensitive to drugs—modify and sift the signals. Only after this processing do signals from the pain-sensitive nerve endings reach the brain areas that perceive pain. The drugs that dull pain affect both the pathways that signal pain and those parts of the brain that perceive it.

But physical sensation alone is not always enough to make a person feel pain. To be felt, pain must also stimulate conscious thinking in areas outside the sensory regions. This kind of thinking apparently takes place in the prefrontal lobes of the brain, which seem to be the zones of anxiety, remembrance of past pain, and fear of the connotations of present pain. Pain-killers also lessen signal reception by the prefrontal lobes.

That the circumstances of past and present affect awareness of pain has been demonstrated by many experiments. Even the circumstances at the time of injury can outweigh all physical influences: when a battle ends, many of the survivors are so relieved by their escape from death that they barely notice their wounds.

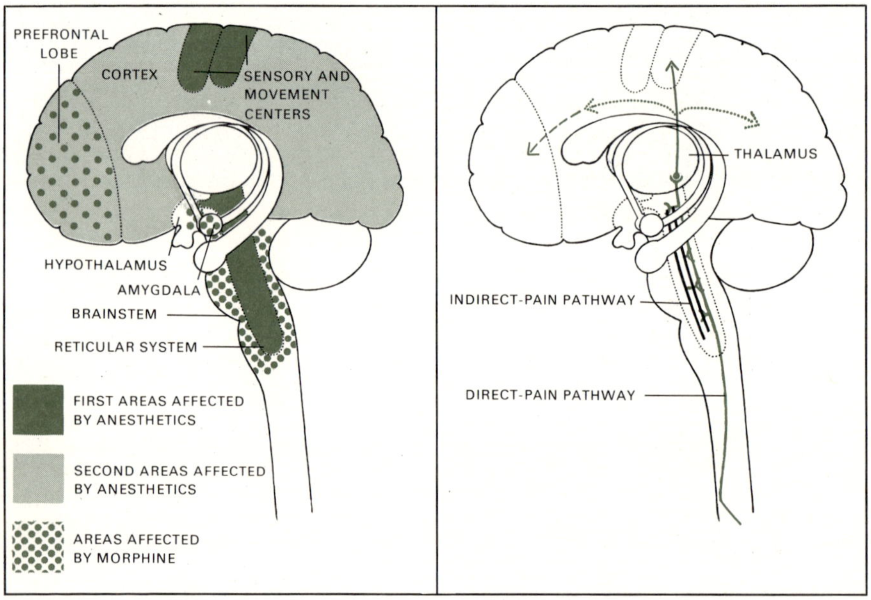

PAIN-KILLERS' PROGRESS
Various pain-killers influence brain areas in different sequences as diagramed at left above. General anesthetics first depress the reticular system's arousal mechanism, then they affect centers for movement and sensation in the cortex and then the entire cortex. Morphine acts first on the reticular system, then on the hypothalamus arousal center, prefrontal anxiety areas and the amygdala's emotional centers. The sensations in these areas are generated by signals that originate in nerve endings in the skin and travel the path *(above, right)* indicated in green. Ascending the spinal column into the reticular system, the path branches and interconnects with two indirect-pain paths *(black)*. Signals move back and forth between these paths, modifying the quality of the pain before it gets to the sensory center of the cortex *(solid arrow)*, the cortex *(dotted arrows)*, and areas of consciousness and anxiety *(dashed arrows)*.

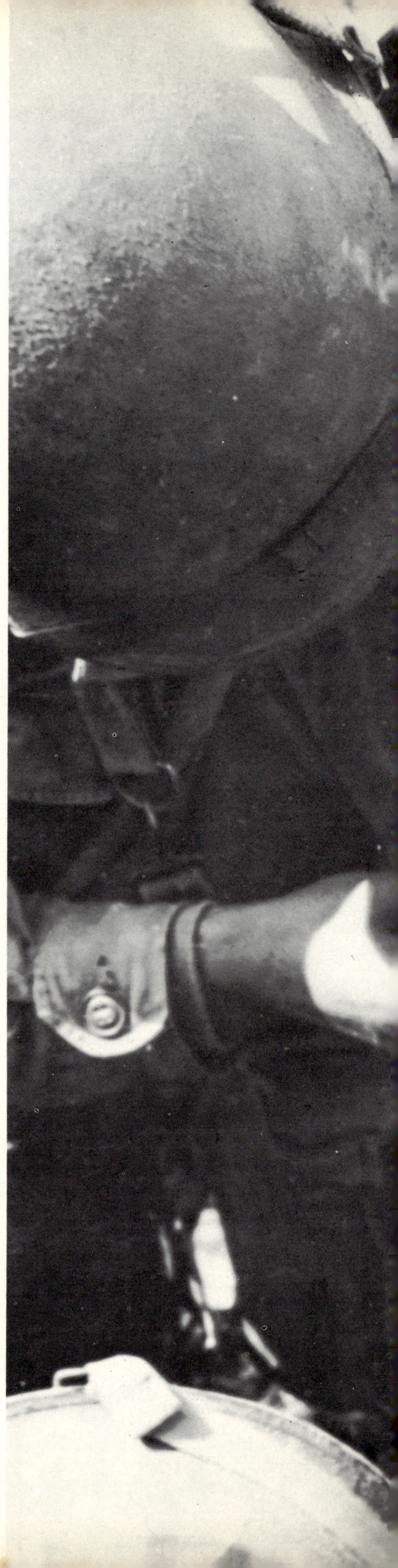

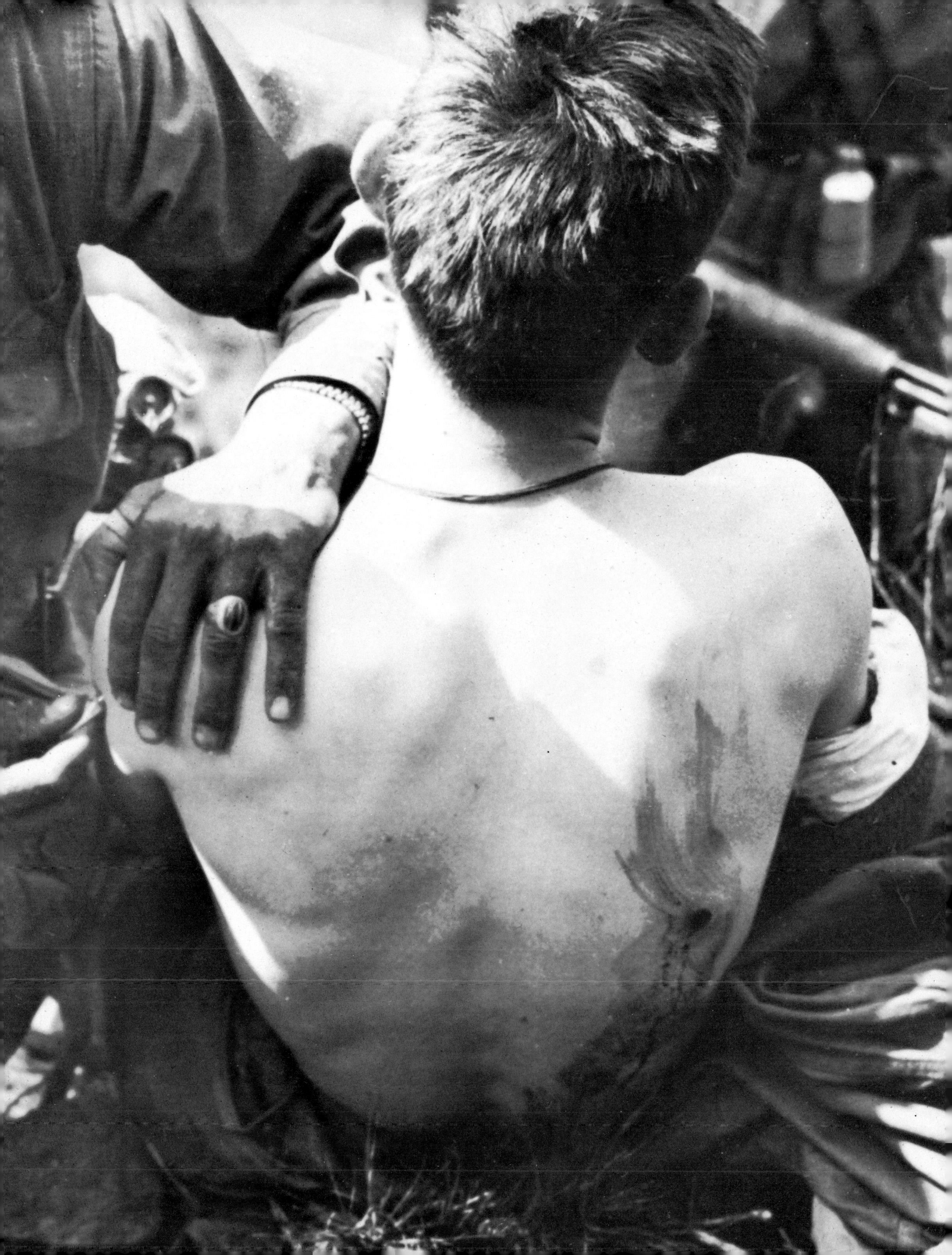

3

Escape from Reality

One of the "mind" drugs that have revolutionized the care of mental patients is Compazine, the liquid in the ampules being held here. Thanks to Compazine's tranquilizing effect, thousands have resumed nearly normal lives.

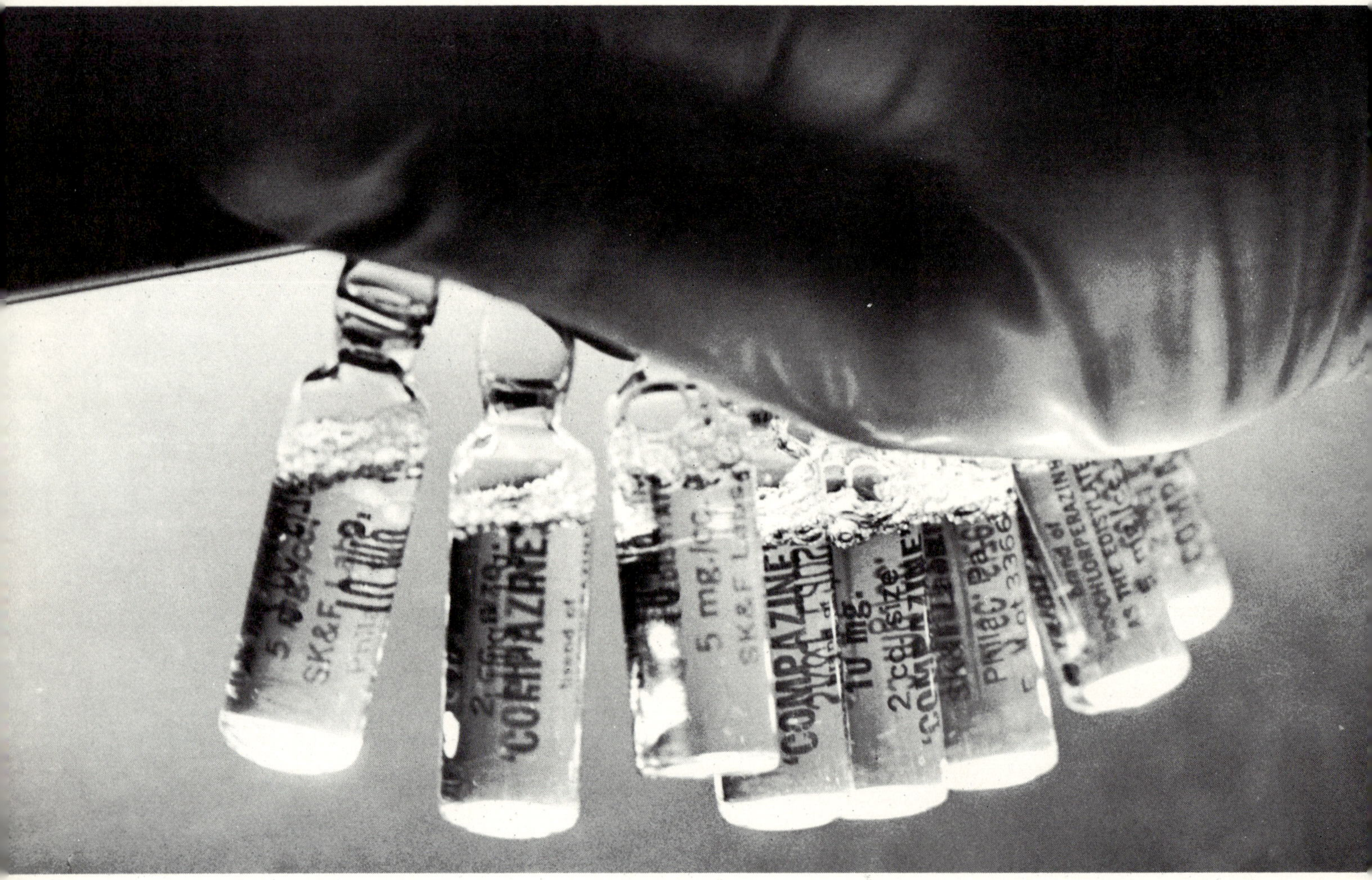

THE DRUGS THAT FASCINATE man most—the ones that inspire him to poetry or drive him to murder—are those that affect the brain and the spinal cord on which it rests. These organs make up the central nervous system (CNS), the control center not merely of the body itself but also of sensation, of emotion, of thought, of everything that we call the mind. The drugs that act on this center are as diverse in their actions as is the mind itself. They can cheer, depress, excite, stupefy; calm the frenzies of a schizophrenic; soothe the agonies of a cancer sufferer; blunt thought and feeling or twist them into visions ecstatic or horrible. They include some of the most commonplace drugs (alcohol, caffeine, nicotine), some of the most useful (ether, procaine), some of the most controversial (LSD, hashish), some of the most dangerous (cocaine, heroin).

The CNS drugs have throughout history been the most dynamic of all drugs in their impact on society at large, and the most troublesome as well. All of them have the power, in greater or lesser degree, to alter man's perception of himself and of the world around him. Their ability to ease the abrasive contact between man and reality has made them coveted and widely used commodities. With ancient traders came a tide of wine to waft Mediterranean civilization into the barbarian lands of northern and western Europe; much later, a torrent of cheap whiskey helped to open up the American frontier—and to separate the Indians from their lands. The trade in tobacco created the first great American fortunes; the commerce in tea sent white-winged clipper ships racing around the Horn. And today's illicit traffic in narcotics is probably the most lucrative of underworld enterprises.

Man's worldwide use and abuse of CNS drugs to manipulate his mind has repeatedly embroiled the drugs with religion and superstition. Religious cults have hailed them as gifts of the gods—even as pathways to mystical enlightenment. Other cults have denounced them, no less ringingly, as instruments of the devil. Unfortunately, these passions and counterpassions have contributed nothing to a rational understanding of the drugs and indeed have often hampered scientific study of them. This is a pity, because only clear and dispassionate understanding of their medical—and extramedical—significance is likely to give rise to intelligent use and wipe out abuse.

From the medical standpoint, these drugs first appear on the stage of history as pain-relievers. Some, like opium, could actually reduce pain and discomfort. Others, like alcohol and hashish, merely made man indifferent to pain. None could "make the patient better," but all could make him *feel* better.

Predictably, the illusion of a cure was often taken for the reality. Before the Third Century B.C., Chinese physicians were prescribing a hemp derivative somewhat similar to marijuana for gout, rheumatism, malaria, beriberi and absentmindedness. Some centuries later, the Greek physician Dioscorides recommended extracts of mandrake root, already well known as an effective pain-reliever and soporific, as a cure for tumors and snakebite.

Alcohol was not particularly esteemed as a cure-all until the invention of distilled spirits, in which the drug is far more concentrated and therefore far more potent. "Spirits of wine" (later called brandy) seems to have been introduced to medicine around 1300 A.D. by the French physician Arnauld de Villeneuve. Entranced—perhaps intoxicated—by his discovery, he described it as "really a water of immortality." The German Hieronymous Brunschwig, writing a few centuries later, was equally sweeping and considerably more specific. He recommended brandy for (among other things) baldness, indigestion, jaundice, dropsy, gout, bladder stones, malaria and rabies.

Tea leaf and coffee bean, tobaccoweed and coca plant in their day also won similar glowing testimonials. But unfortunately for the health of mankind, no ancestral wonder drug has lived up to its advertisements. Today only two of them play an important role in the pharmacopoeia. Opium, refined into its active principle, morphine, remains a powerful and reliable pain-killer; highly diluted, it is the main ingredient of paregoric, an equally reliable remedy for diarrhea. The coca leaf furnishes the procaine that makes dentistry bearable. Tea and coffee find very limited medical uses, and tobacco none at all.

To the physician, there are (apart from the pain-relievers) only two really important groups of CNS drugs, and these are relatively new ones, discovered in the 19th and 20th Centuries. They are the anesthetics and the so-called psychotropic agents, which include both the tranquilizers and the drugs that relieve depression. The first group revolutionized surgery; the second began a new epoch in the treatment of mental illness.

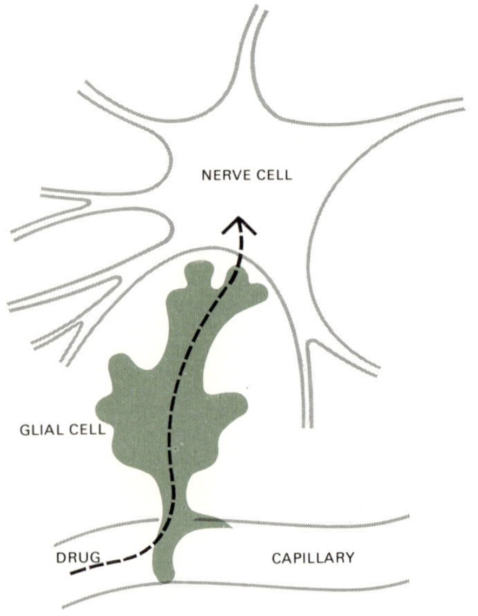

THE GATEWAY TO THE BRAIN, through which drugs affecting the central nervous system must pass is a layer of so-called glial cells between the capillaries and the brain's vital nerve cells or neurons. As the drug-bearing blood approaches the brain in a capillary the drug must seep through the capillary wall and the glial cell in order to reach the nerve cell. Through a mechanism not fully understood the membranes of the glial cells act as a screen permitting some drugs to go through easily admitting limited amounts of others and completely barring the rest.

Without anesthetics to control pain and muscular reactions, surgery could not have developed into a modern lifesaving science. An agonized, writhing patient was not only an offense to humane feelings but he could also gravely hamper the surgeon's activities—and do himself serious injury.

A knock on the head for anesthesia

Some early methods of anesthesia were brutally direct. The Assyrians, a notably bloody-minded people, choked boys into insensibility before performing the operation of circumcision; at other times and places, the patient was simply knocked on the head. Such "anesthesia" often turned out to be permanent.

More cautious physicians used CNS drugs like alcohol, opium and mandrake. But these, though they could dull pain somewhat, could not —at least, not safely—abolish it. In modern terms, they were not sufficiently "selective," meaning that a dose large enough to render the patient insensible would produce too many dangerous side effects. Opium, for example, was, and is, a safe analgesic (pain-reliever) because the analgesic dose is relatively small. As an anesthetic, however, it is no better than a simple knock on the head. A dose of opium that would make a patient completely unconscious would also depress his breathing so much that he would be almost certain to die of the drug, if not the operation. With only unselective drugs of this sort, the surgeon of necessity concentrated not on reducing pain but on shortening its duration; master surgeons of the early 19th Century boasted that they could saw off a leg in less than 60 seconds.

The surgeon's speed offered the only safe relief from the brutality of an operation for 4,000 years. The 19th Century discovery of anesthetics seems to have occurred for the same "reason" as many other scientific achievements: its time had come. As one commentator has put it, "When it is time to invent locomotives men will invent locomotives." In the 1840s, it was evidently time to develop anesthesia. Between 1842 and 1847, it was employed on four occasions by four different men—using three different drugs.

Exhilarating ether jags

First of the four discoverers was Dr. Crawford W. Long of Jefferson, Georgia. His drug was ether. Like alcohol and many other CNS drugs, ether can induce a euphoric feeling of buoyancy as well as unconsciousness, and Long had made its acquaintance through the "ether jags" that were a fad when he was a medical student. Even after he had begun his practice he frequently intoxicated himself and his friends with the drug, a sport which, he later remarked, "became quite fashionable in the country"—partly, one suspects, because it was deemed more high toned than simple boozing.

During these ether parties, Long was evidently not too exhilarated to use his eyes, for he noticed that many of his intoxicated friends became quite insensible to pain. In March 1842, he put his observations to work. He gave a young man ether to breathe and then painlessly removed a tumor from the youth's neck. Long continued to use the drug effectively in his own medical practice, but because he was merely a young country doctor, he was too diffident to report his results to any medical journal.

The second and equally inconclusive discovery of anesthesia was made by a Hartford, Connecticut, dentist, Horace Wells. In 1844, he attended "A Grand Exhibition of the effects produced by inhaling Nitrous Oxide, Exhilarating or Laughing Gas." As its name indicates, this drug too was known to produce euphoria and intoxication, though the "exhibition" was planned and advertised as "in every respect a genteel affair." Fortunately for science, it was not. A volunteer who inhaled the gas became sufficiently belligerent to jump from the stage, trip over a chair and gash his leg. Recovering his wits, he realized with surprise that he had felt no pain despite his injuries. Wells, seated nearby, noticed this, quickly realized the medical possibilities, and soon began using laughing gas on his patients.

But when he sought to demonstrate his discovery to the medical profession at Boston's famous Massachusetts General Hospital, the experiment was a humiliating failure. (Nitrous oxide was, and still is, difficult to administer safely in the dosages that are needed for the deep anesthesia used in surgery.)

Third time lucky. In the fall of 1846, another dentist, William T. G. Morton of Charlton, Massachusetts—who knew of Wells's work—performed his famous public demonstration of ether anesthesia, again at Massachusetts General, and wrung from a skeptical attending surgeon the historic testimonial: "Gentlemen, this is no humbug." A year later, the Edinburgh surgeon James Young Simpson began the successful use of another anesthetic, chloroform.

Unhurried surgery

No longer was the surgeon forced to race against time. With the aid of anesthesia (and, of course, many other medical advances) he could attempt ever more complex and lengthy procedures. Today, he can labor for hours on a relaxed, untroubled patient, rebuilding a face smashed in an auto accident, cutting away a tumor from the delicate tissue of the brain, repairing a living heart, even removing an organ from one individual and grafting it into another.

Ether, nitrous oxide and chloroform succeeded as effective anesthetics where older drugs had failed because they were more selective in their actions. They can abolish pain, and at higher doses can blot out consciousness entirely. At still higher doses, they abolish most of the body's reflexes, in particular those that cause many muscles to contract convulsively when cut by the surgeon's scalpel. (This is an especially important consideration in abdominal surgery, since the reflex is so highly developed in the abdominal muscles that their violent contraction can thrust part of the patient's viscera out of his body.) Yet even while the patient is unconscious and insensitive to pain, his heart and lung action can continue.

SATIRIZING THE USE OF ETHER, this 1847 French cartoon published shortly after the drug's discovery shows a small boy anesthetizing himself to avoid the sting of a whipping. Many authorities of the time welcomed ether as a universal panacea that might cure even epilepsy and mental disorders. Although these ideas were quickly discarded, ether continues to be valuable in its original role as a general anesthetic for surgery.

Revolutionary as these selective CNS drugs were, they ultimately proved to be not selective enough. Like all drugs, they had undesirable side effects: ether irritates the breathing passages; chloroform damages the liver, and so on. They have now been supplemented by newer drugs, which, while they do cause side effects of their own, enable the physician to select a combination best suited to the task at hand. Ether, for example, is now usually administered to induce deep anesthesia only after another drug, such as a barbiturate, has been given to counteract ether's irritating effects and also to make the patient sleepy. For a complicated procedure like heart surgery, the anesthesiologist may employ over a dozen drugs, each chosen to perform one part of the task of bringing the patient safely and painlessly through the operation.

If in the 1840s it was time to discover anesthetics, in the 1950s it was equally the time to discover the psychotropics, the "mind drugs" that have so revolutionized the treatment of the mentally disturbed. That decade saw three great developments: the first psychiatric use of the so-called strong tranquilizers, chlorpromazine and reserpine; the introduction of the first "mild" tranquilizer, meprobamate; and the appearance of the first modern antidepressants, iproniazid and imipramine.

Both the strong tranquilizers and the antidepressants are far more selective than the anesthetics. (The mild tranquilizers are puzzling in their action and are seldom prescribed for serious illness.) The first group can calm a violent psychotic without rendering him unconscious or, in most cases, even sleepy. The second can elevate the mood of a depressed patient without the unpleasant side effects, such as accelerated heartbeat or insomnia, of some other stimulants. Indeed, the best of both groups seem to distinguish even between normal and psychotic individuals, since they exert more pronounced and actually different effects on those suffering from severe mental disorders.

Precisely how psychotropic drugs manage to be so selective in their actions is still one of nature's secrets, but their impact on mental disease has been great. Prior to the discovery of strong tranquilizers and antidepressants, mental hospitals were places of horror. Frenzied patients had to be restrained with straps and straitjackets for their own and others' protection. Depressed ones sat immobile for hours, trapped in the unspeakable horrors of their own thoughts. The erratic and unpredictable behavior of many patients kept physicians and attendants busy simply supervising them, leaving little time for attempts to treat them. Nor, for that matter, was there much hope of helping them: most psychotics were too far out of touch with reality to be reached by anything less drastic than the unpleasant and occasionally dangerous shock treatments. And the situation was getting worse. The rising number of mental patients, increasing faster than the population as a whole, crowded new hospitals faster than they could be built.

The psychotropic drugs radically changed this grim picture. As physicians learned how to use them, thousands of patients began to emerge from the hospitals; thousands more who previously would have required confinement could be treated as "outpatients," remaining at home with their families and visiting a clinic at intervals for their pills. Between 1955 and 1965, the number of hospitalized mental patients in the United States dropped by 15 per cent—despite an increase in the general population of some 17 per cent. And even for those still remaining in the hospitals, life became, if not happy, at least less agonizing.

The mind drugs, which have notably alleviated psychic pain, and the anesthetics, which have done so much to banish physical pain, are the bright side of the CNS drugs. The dark side, of course, is the problem of drug addiction.

A life-wrecking compulsion

Defining addiction is a tricky business—and it is made no easier by the confusion that arises from the use by physicians of such terms as "physical addiction," "psychological addiction" and the like. For all general purposes, addiction can be defined as the compulsive use of a drug to an extent that seriously impairs the user's capacity to lead a normal life. The addict, that is, takes his drug not merely because he wants to but because he has to. And the compulsion to consume (and, of course, to obtain) the drug—a compulsion that may arise from the chemical nature of the drug or from the social and psychological situations in which it is consumed—so dominates the addict's life as to leave him little time or energy for constructive pursuits.

People can become addicted in this sense to almost any drug, provided they find its effects pleasant. At least one man is known to have become addicted to sodium bicarbonate—apparently because he liked the sensation of belching. The great majority of addicts, however, have less outlandish tastes, getting their "kicks" from among half a dozen problem drugs.

From alcohol to LSD

By far the worst offender, at least in Western countries, is alcohol, whose addicts, called alcoholics, number an estimated five million in the United States alone. In second place, probably, are the various derivatives of Indian hemp. In such forms as hashish, ganja, majoun, bhang and perhaps 200 others, hemp is consumed by scores of millions in the Muslim world and in India, where alcohol is frowned on or forbidden. Not all of these people can be considered addicts, however, nor can all the undetermined number of Americans who smoke marijuana (the Mexican name for hashish). Less popular than the hemp drugs but more vicious in their effects are opium, consumed fairly widely in the Orient, and its derivatives, morphine and heroin, whose addicts in the United States are estimated to number more than 60,000. Serious problems are also posed by the barbiturates and the amphetamines ("pep pills"). Finally, a growing threat, whose extent is still unclear, is the use of such drugs as LSD, technically classified as hallucinogens or hallucination-producers.

The very real hazards raised by these problem drugs are often obscured by purely imaginary hazards that are mistakenly attributed to them—misconceptions that can hamper effective action against drug addiction. In the first place, only a few of these drugs directly give rise to violent or criminal acts. Even alcohol, though it can remove inhibitions against violence, does not stimulate brutal acts. The "dope fiend" of popular folklore was in fact a cocaine addict; large and repeated doses of this stimulant can indeed bring on paranoia and violent behavior. Cocaine addiction is rare nowadays—perhaps because, as one addict put it, "If you aren't nuts before you use it, you sure are afterward." But the all-too-popular pep pills, which do not contain cocaine, seem to have similar effects in triggering violence.

Nevertheless, the principal connection between drugs and crime comes not from the physiological effects of the drugs but from the need for large sums of money to buy them—money that often must be obtained by criminal means. And there seems to be no connection at all between drugs of any kind and one type of crime—sexual offenses—for which they are widely blamed.

None of the drugs, without exception, can turn an individual into a "sex maniac"; if anything, they do the opposite. The opium derivatives reduce or abolish the sex drive; the hemp drugs have a similar though less-pronounced effect. ("A hashish-eater would not lift a finger for the most beautiful maiden in Verona," wrote the French author and hashish addict Théophile Gautier.)

Imaginary dangers aside, the genuine hazards of drug addiction are severe ones. The degree to which they harm an individual depends on three factors. The first is pharmacological, and involves the complicated ways that a drug may take part in bodily reactions and, indeed, may become necessary to them. The second, probably far more important but still very poorly understood, concerns the psychology of the individual drug taker. The third is sociological, and involves the cultural patterns that surround the drug in a particular society or ethnic group.

The physical and chemical processes of the human body can, in some degree, tolerate or adapt to almost any drug. For some drugs, this tolerance reaches astonishing proportions. The sodium bicarbonate addict previously mentioned was consuming half a pound of the stuff a day when he was hospitalized—a quantity that would make the ordinary person very ill. Sometimes tolerance involves merely the stepping up of the processes by which the drug is removed from the body. Habitual use of barbiturates can do this, with the result that much of a given dose of the drug is eliminated before it can get to the brain.

The perils of tissue tolerance

But many drugs (including the barbiturates) can engender another, and more dangerous, type of tolerance, called "tissue" or "cellular" tolerance. This results from the remarkable capacity of the human body to alter itself in response to disturbing stimuli. Just as a heavily exercised muscle will, over the long pull, develop more and thicker fibers to carry the increased load, so organs whose functions are repeatedly altered by drugs may respond by readjusting their functions to restore the status quo. Repeated doses of an alkali such as sodium bicarbonate increase the effect of the body's acids; repeated doses of the opiates will lead the nervous system to function more energetically to counteract the drug-induced depression.

At this point, the individual has become physically dependent on the drug. Adjustment to the drug's presence is gradual, and once adjustment is achieved, readjustment to its absence is no less so. If the drug is suddenly withdrawn, the body responds to the absence of the drug on which it has become dependent by "withdrawal symptoms," which are always unpleasant and occasionally harmful. Thus the bicarbonate addict, deprived of his daily doses, developed a condition known as metabolic acidosis; it would probably have killed him if he had not been treated. Likewise, a heroin addict, when the hyperactive control centers of his body are no longer lulled by the drug, will develop such symptoms as sleeplessness, vomiting, sweating and cramps.

The degree to which tissue tolerance and physical dependence can be established depends on the drug and—like so many drug effects—on the dose. Alcohol can induce moderate tolerance, but only if the dose exceeds a certain minimum. The tired businessman can enjoy the effects of his evening martini for 20 years, with no need to increase his alcoholic consumption and no aftereffects. But the problem drinker who swallows a fifth of whiskey every day for a week will become less and less obviously intoxicated by his daily bottle—and will develop delirium tremens ("the D.T.s") if he suddenly stops drinking.

The high cost of tolerance

The all-time championship for tolerance and dependence is held by the sinister opiates. To a person unaccustomed to morphine, for instance, an injection of .004 ounce is normally fatal. Yet in controlled experiments addicts have taken up to 50 times this amount in one day and survived. The result of the body's ability to adapt to opiates is that a morphine or heroin addict must gradually increase his dose if he is to obtain his accustomed "kick." And, given the black-market prices for these drugs, he must almost certainly take to crime to support his habit. Many addicts, indeed, will enter a hospital and go through the unpleasant process of withdrawal simply to lose their tolerance, thereby reducing their habit to a financially supportable level—for a while.

Physical dependence, and the resulting desire to avoid withdrawal symptoms, unquestionably play their part in addiction to some drugs—chiefly the opiates. But it is worth emphasizing that physical dependence is not the same thing as addiction. Most smokers, for example, are physically dependent on nicotine, in the sense that they feel jumpy and uncomfortable without it. But they are not addicted to it, since it does not disrupt their lives. Habitual cigarette smoking over many years can produce severe and even fatal physical damage—but it does not lose people their jobs, break up their marriages or land them in jail. By contrast with nicotine, hemp drugs, the amphetamines and cocaine seldom if ever produce physical dependency—but they unquestionably produce addicts.

PUFFING TOBACCO, a Mayan priest, depicted on a Fifth Century bas-relief from a temple in Mexico, uses one of the world's most popular drugs. First cultivated in the Western Hemisphere, tobacco has provoked many taboos through its long history. In modern times it has been prohibited by some religious sects and has been condemned as a menace to health. Yet it is now enjoyed by smokers in nearly every part of the world—including 70 million people in the United States alone—for its pleasant, tension-relaxing effect.

Thus the addict may or may not be physically dependent on his drug, although he is unquestionably psychologically dependent on it. The drug's effects satisfy some deep need in his personality—but there is little agreement on just what this need is. Obviously he feels he must escape from something. What he is escaping from, and why he chooses alcohol or heroin as his ticket to Nirvana—instead of watching television or becoming a hobo—are subjects on which there are almost as many theories as there are schools of psychiatry.

On the third aspect of the drug problem, the sociological, there is considerably more agreement. With some drugs, at least, the problem seems to be much less with the drug than with the circumstances under which it is consumed.

Alcohol is a good example. A number of sociologists have conducted extensive studies to discover why alcoholism is very rare among certain U.S. ethnic groups—notably Jews and Italian-Americans. Nearly all Jews and Italian-Americans consume alcoholic beverages, but they are generally moderate drinkers and they rarely become addicted to alcohol. Studying the ways in which these people did their drinking, the researchers found that for both groups the use of alcohol was tightly integrated into the life of the family and its social circle. By and large, members of these two groups did not drink in order to get drunk, but as part of a social occasion, or of the family meal (Italian-Americans) or of periodic religious observances (Jews). The moderate use of alcohol was built into their culture so that they learned from childhood to use alcohol without becoming addicted to it.

Like alcohol, the hemp drugs seem to be "culture dependent"—i.e., harmful in some societies but not in others. In parts of North Africa, hashish is often consumed immoderately and habitually—and is considered responsible for producing a great deal of chronic mental disease. In many other places, however, hemp derivatives are consumed almost as widely, as moderately and with as few ill effects as is alcohol among Jews and Italian-Americans. This latter fact has caused some American young people to ask, in effect, "Why is marijuana worse than alcohol?" The definitive answer, credited to the musician Mezz Mezzrow, is "It can put you in jail." Its use is not accepted in our society. In the United States, marijuana is mixed up with the whole illegal drug subculture, which is permeated with criminality and psychological illness. As a result, not a few of its users are induced to try more dangerous drugs such as the opiates—which in the contemporary drug "scene" are all too readily available.

When a drug becomes a cult

Even more directly culture-dependent are the powerful hallucination drugs, the best known of which is lysergic acid diethylamide, or LSD. Depending on the environment and mental outlook with which he takes the drug, the user may experience visions of sheer ecstasy or sheer horror. Used under medical supervision, LSD has shown some promise in the treatment of mental illness—especially, and ironically, addiction to alcohol and heroin. Used promiscuously, however, it can lead to mental illness lasting long after its effects have worn off—and perhaps cause permanent damage.

Unfortunately, the still problematical value of LSD has been obscured by the cultist atmosphere that has grown up about it. Its partisans tout it as a solution of all psychological—and even social—ills. But their claims differ little from those made long ago for alcohol, for hashish and for half a dozen other CNS drugs. The "acid head" may see himself as the vanguard of a new era, but in fact he is marching at the end of a long line of seekers for instant salvation. The chances are overwhelming that, like his predecessors, he will find the illusion of health rather than the reality.

PUFFING HASHISH, best known in the United States in the form of marijuana, a Persian lady of the 14th Century enjoys an ancient drug that is still the subject of much controversy. Made from the dried flowers of hemp, hashish produces intoxication and hallucinations that may persist for hours. It is sometimes smoked, sometimes taken in the form of pills or pellets, or mixed with sugar and eaten like candy. While its use has long been accepted in Asia Minor and the Orient, the drug is illegal in the United States.

The Doctor Who Vanquishes Pain

In an age of medical specialties, the anesthesiologist is a specialist in the use of drugs to prevent suffering. The pain of surgery is his first concern, as it has been for more than 100 years—and since about 12 million operations annually are performed under some form of anesthesia in the United States, he does not lack for work.

But the modern anesthesiologist is a far cry from the "ether-pourer" of the 19th Century, whose sole job was to render surgical patients unconscious and keep them that way until the operation was over. Today the anesthesiologist brings swift relief to accident victims, treats ailments of the respiratory tract, eases the agony of incurable diseases. And he draws on an extensive range of instruments and drugs: machines that temporarily substitute for body organs, gases that can induce a dreamy doze or deep unconsciousness, tranquilizers that banish fear, injections that block pain.

So precise is the control afforded by these new tools and techniques that the anesthesiologist can, in effect, suspend life for hours at a time, making possible some of the most dramatic achievements of modern surgery, such as the repair of a damaged heart or the replacement of a diseased kidney.

SOOTHING A TROUBLED HEART
Holding a life in his hands, an anesthesiologist squeezes a breathing bag to force more oxygen into the lungs of a patient whose heart has faltered during an operation. To counteract the erratic heartbeat, he has just administered a dose of procaine amide; now his eyes are glued to an electrocardiograph, not visible here, which records the heart action.

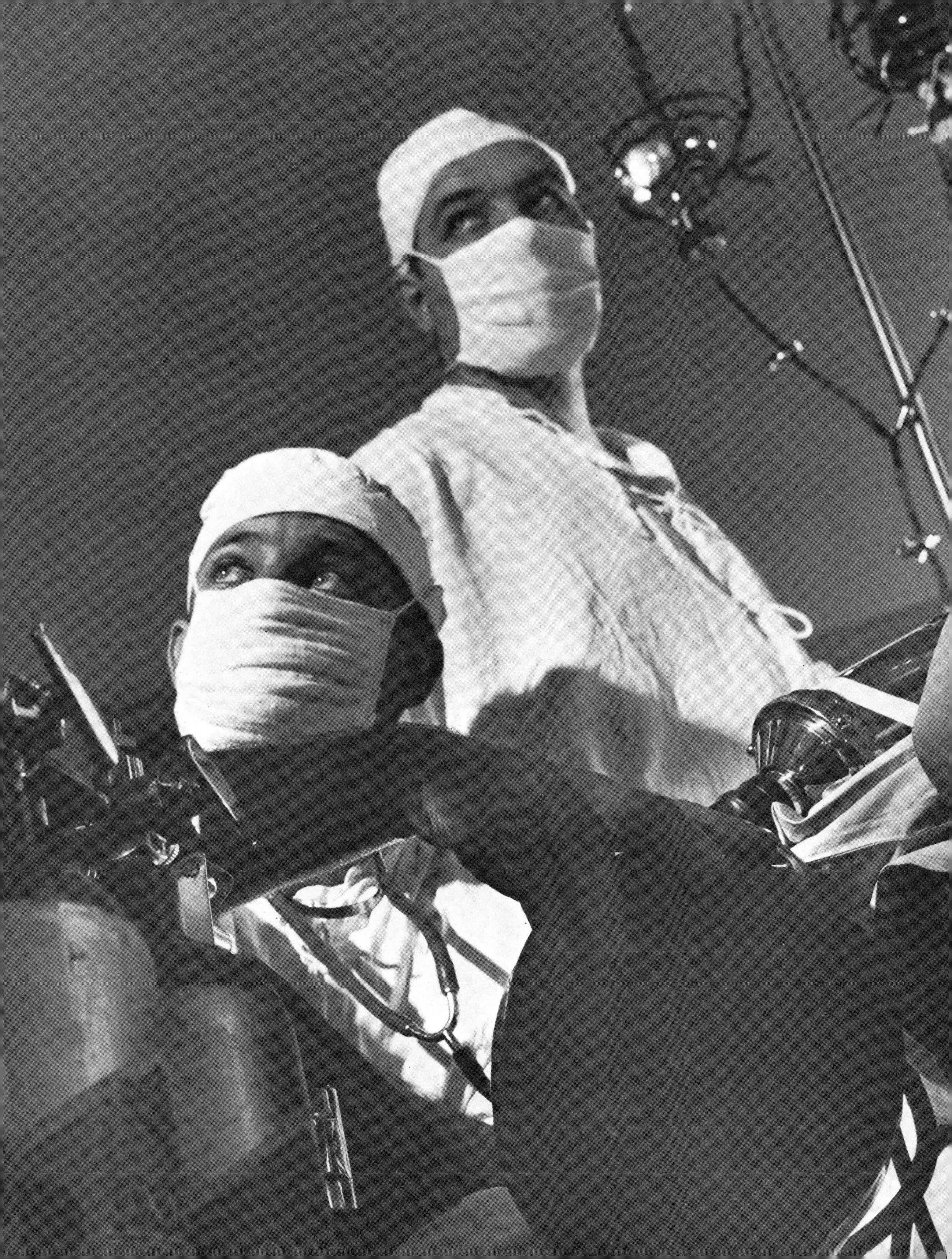

A Slow Journey into Deep Sleep

In 1842, a Georgia physician named Crawford Long made medical history when he held an ether-soaked towel over a patient's face until he was unconscious. Then Dr. Long removed a small neck tumor; the patient experienced no pain. It was the first successful use of surgical anesthesia.

Today ether—obtained by distilling ethylene with sulfuric acid—remains one of the most effective drugs for inducing the deep, relaxed sleep required for major surgery. But ether has an unpleasant, often nauseating odor, it irritates the respiratory system and it is dangerous to use because of its explosive nature. In one method of overcoming these drawbacks anesthesiologists use only very small amounts of ether, often mixed with another anesthetic, as the finishing touch in a step-by-step procedure of inducing sleep. This technique, tailored to the individual, employs a series of drugs designed to achieve successively deeper anesthesia.

In a typical procedure, a pleasant relaxation is induced by injections of scopolamine and morphine. Calm and relaxed, the patient is now ready for an intravenous injection of sodium pentothal that will bring on the first stage of anesthesia, a light doze, followed by the second stage, loss of consciousness and dulling of the brain's pain response. The third stage, complete unconsciousness, generally requires some drug as strong as ether. The anesthesiologist inserts a plastic tube into the trachea, or windpipe, so that a mixture of ether, nitrous oxide and oxygen can be fed directly into the lungs without irritating the breathing passage. Only when he is certain that the patient's central nervous system is completely insensitive to pain will the anesthesiologist give the quick nod that indicates the operation may begin.

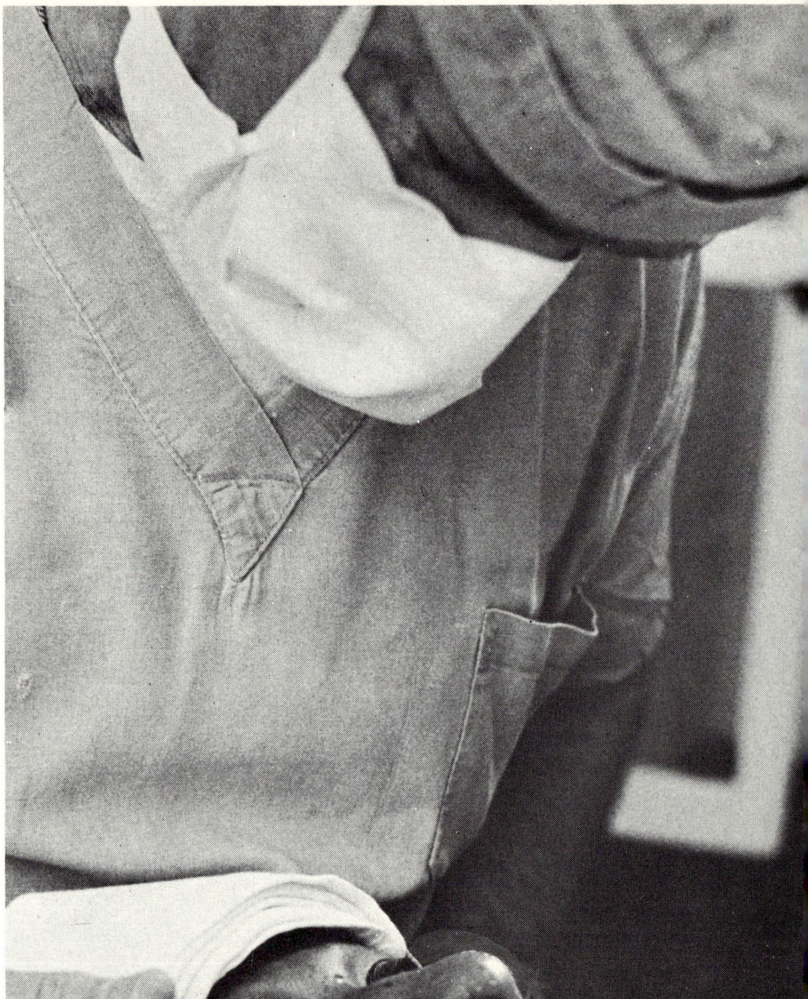

RELAXED . . .
After injections of scopolamine and morphine, a woman about to undergo an operation for removal of a benign tumor at Chicago's Cook County Hospital chats with an anesthesiologist. She is now mentally and physically ready for a sleep-inducing drug and the first stage of anesthesia.

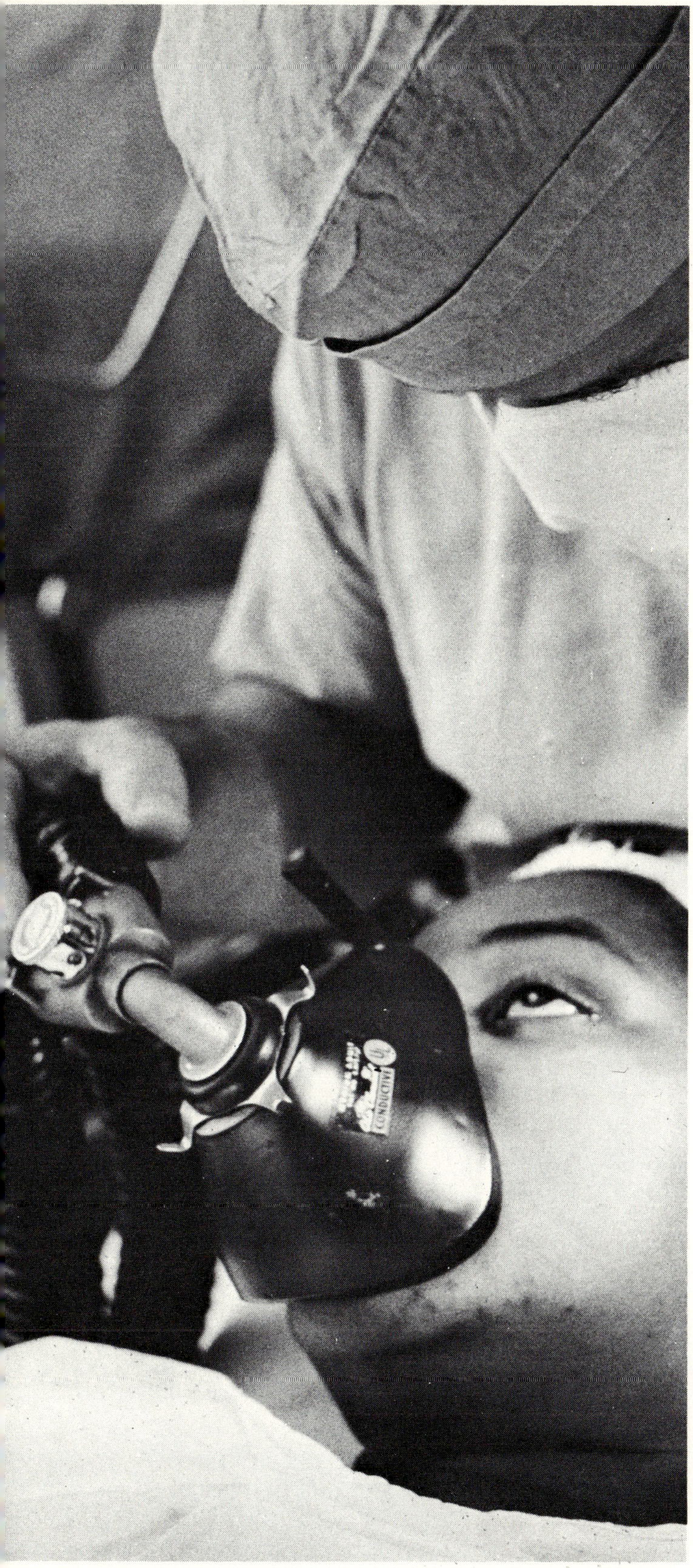

. . . DROWSY . . .
While a face mask supplies pure oxygen to ease her breathing, the patient drifts gently into the light sleep of the first stage of anesthesia induced by an injection of sodium pentothal. The face mask will then be replaced by a tube that supplies a mixture of anesthetics and oxygen.

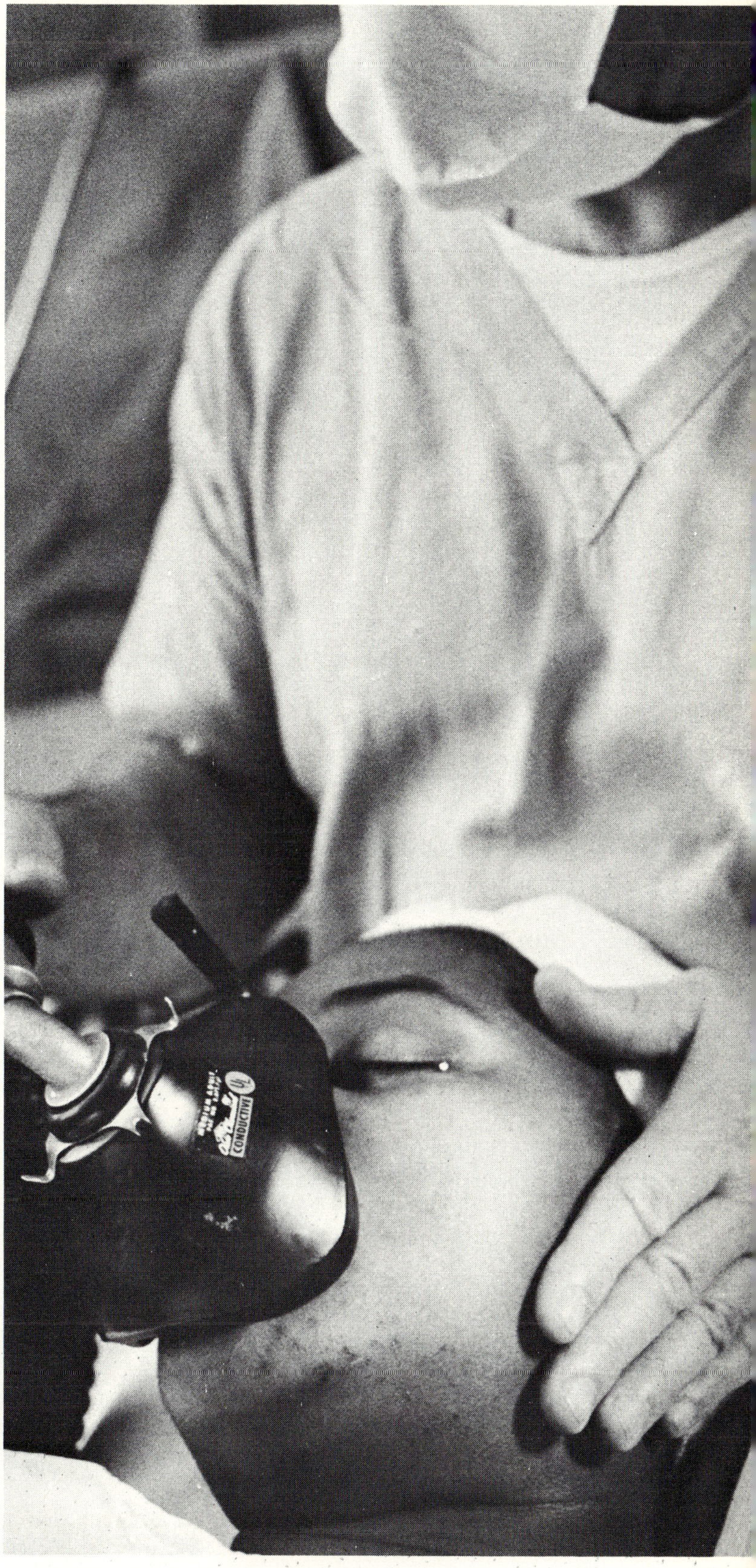

. . . ASLEEP
Unconscious, the patient has entered the second, or dream, stage of anesthesia. One by one, the sensory centers are shutting down—vision first, hearing last. Finally the brain areas controlling voluntary reactions are stilled, though many reflexes, like that of swallowing, remain active.

Lifeguard of a Helpless Body

Once surgery has begun, the anesthesiologist becomes the watchdog of the operating room, the man responsible for keeping the unconscious patient alive.

Keeping an eye on the work of the surgeon, the anesthesiologist concentrates on changes in the patient's blood pressure, pulse and breathing. He checks to be sure that the anesthetic gas mixture contains 28 to 30 per cent oxygen, for even a brief dropoff may cause asphyxiation. He examines the patient's eyes *(opposite)* for subtle changes that mean the anesthetic is wearing off or that it is sinking the patient into a dangerously deep sleep. If muscle-stilling drugs like curare or succinylcholine have been injected—a common procedure when surgery requires the blocking of reflex action in the abdomen—their effect must be monitored *(below)* to gauge how much general anesthetic need be administered.

After surgery is completed the anesthesiologist faces one of his most difficult tasks: he must restore his anesthetized patient to complete consciousness as smoothly and painlessly as possible. The best drug for this purpose is oxygen. Flooding into the lungs, oxygen forces the anesthetic gases out of the patient's body and also eases the work of the heart and respiratory system as the patient awakens.

"If we've done our job well," says Dr. Vincent Collins, head of anesthesiology at Cook County Hospital, "the first thing the patient wants to know is whether he's been operated on."

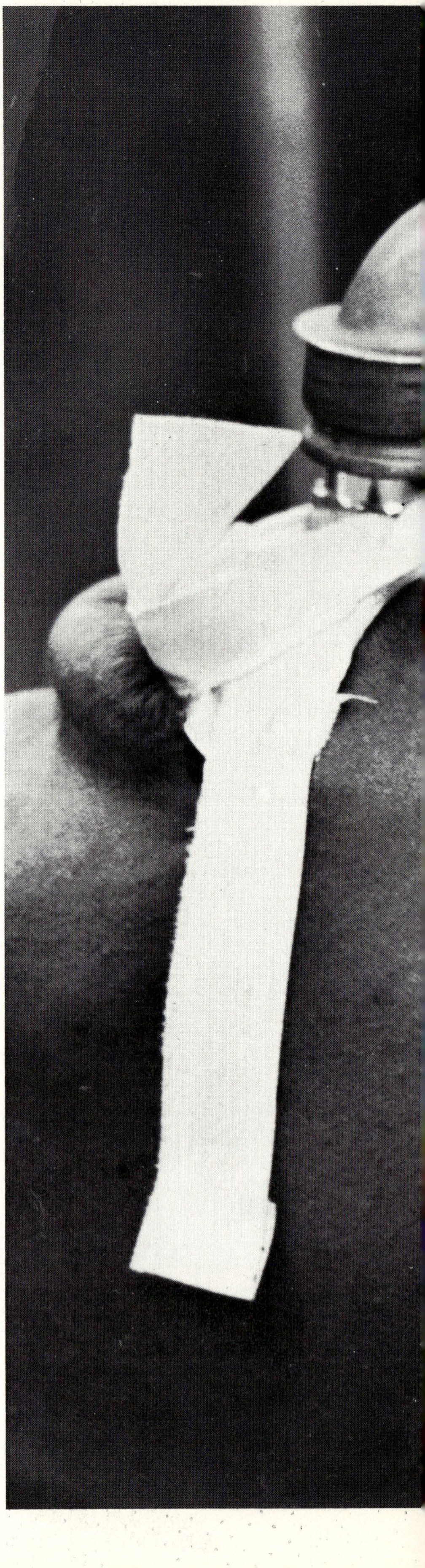

A SHOCK TEST FOR CURARE
Testing the muscle-paralyzing effect of curare, a drug derived from South American poison, an anesthesiologist sends a mild electric shock through a patient's arm. The extent to which fingers twitch indicates how well the drug has blocked the nerves' control of muscle reflexes.

A TEAR THAT MEANS ALL'S WELL
A patient in the third, or surgical, stage of anesthesia breathes a mixture of oxygen, ether and nitrous oxide through a tape-secured tube extending into the trachea. The tear at the corner of the staring but sightless eye is one of the many indications of the level of the anesthesia.

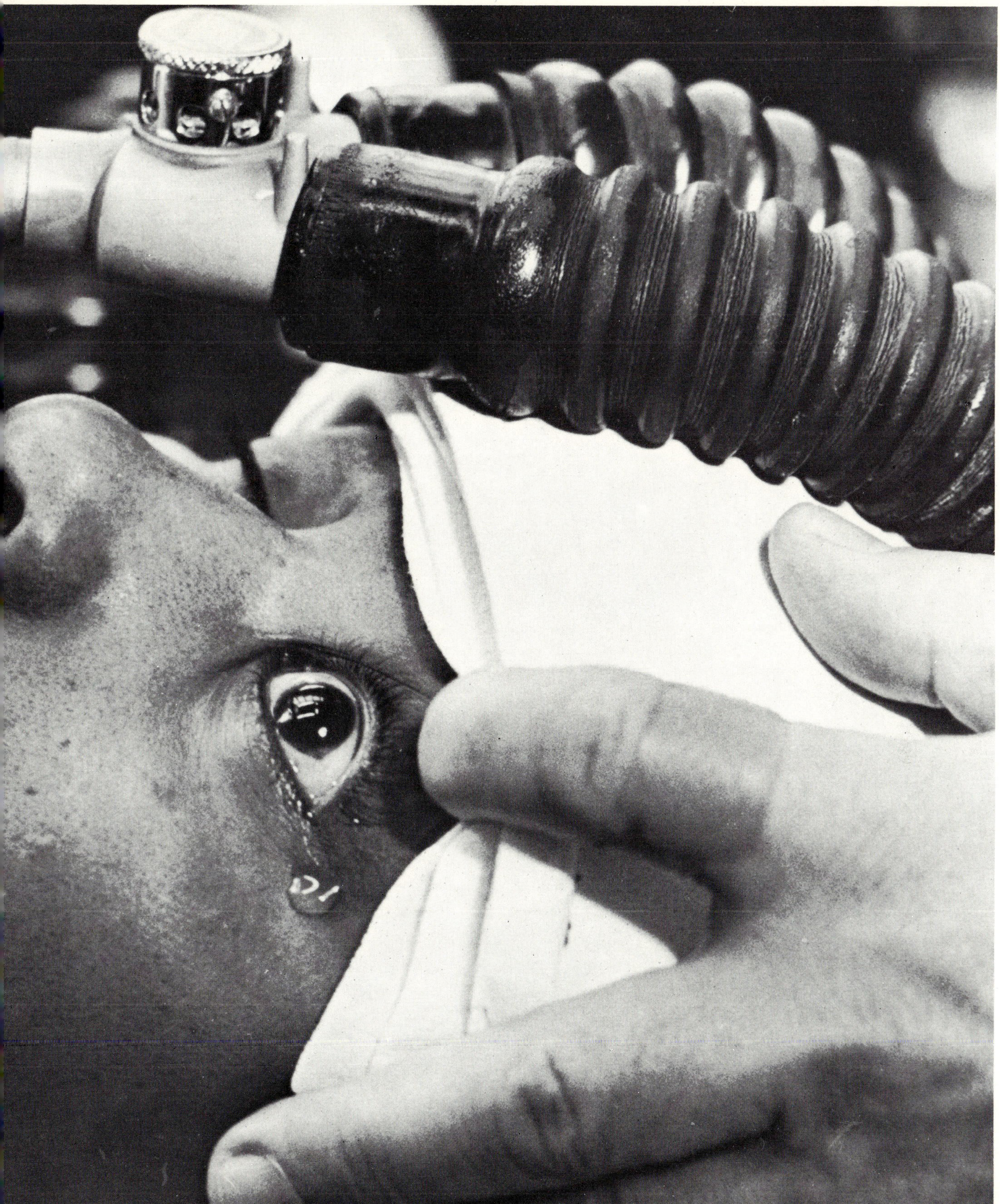

The Tools of the Anesthesiologist

In order to get his drugs to the parts of the body where they will do the most good, the anesthesiologist relies on an intimate knowledge of physiology and an assortment of ingenious tools and techniques, some of which are shown in use below.

One basic piece of equipment is the curved, flexible endotracheal tube *(left)*, designed to deliver the anesthetic mixture to the lungs. To place the tube properly in the trachea, the anesthesiologist must first slide an instrument called a laryngoscope into the patient's throat, then insert the tube alongside the laryngoscope. A miscalculation can cause a painful postoperative sore throat or even damage the vocal cords.

To anesthetize nerves in the spinal cord—a procedure often used to "freeze" a portion of the lower body for abdominal surgery—the anesthesiologist follows a precise three-step procedure. First he presses an "introducer," resembling a large, hollow-

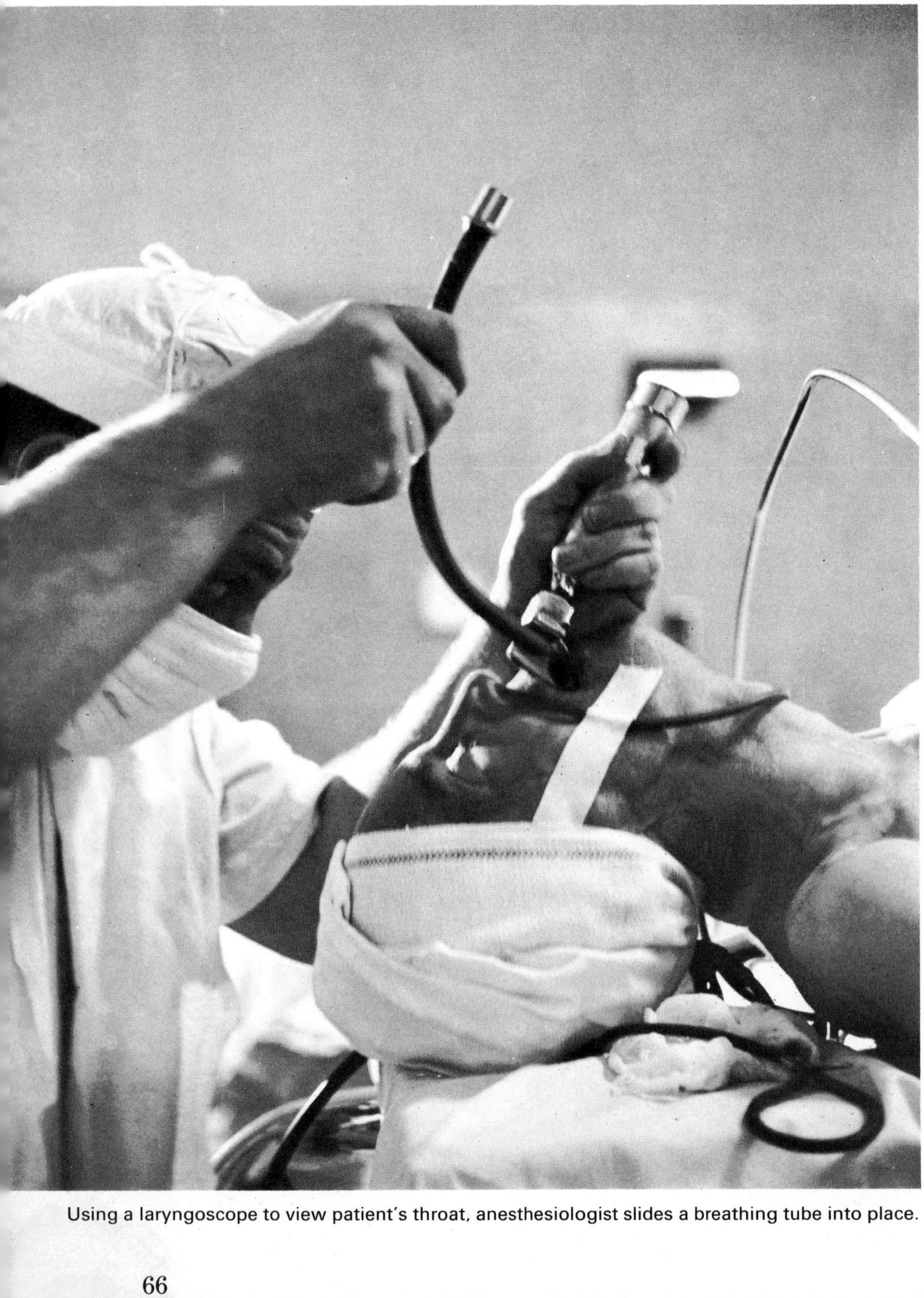

Using a laryngoscope to view patient's throat, anesthesiologist slides a breathing tube into place.

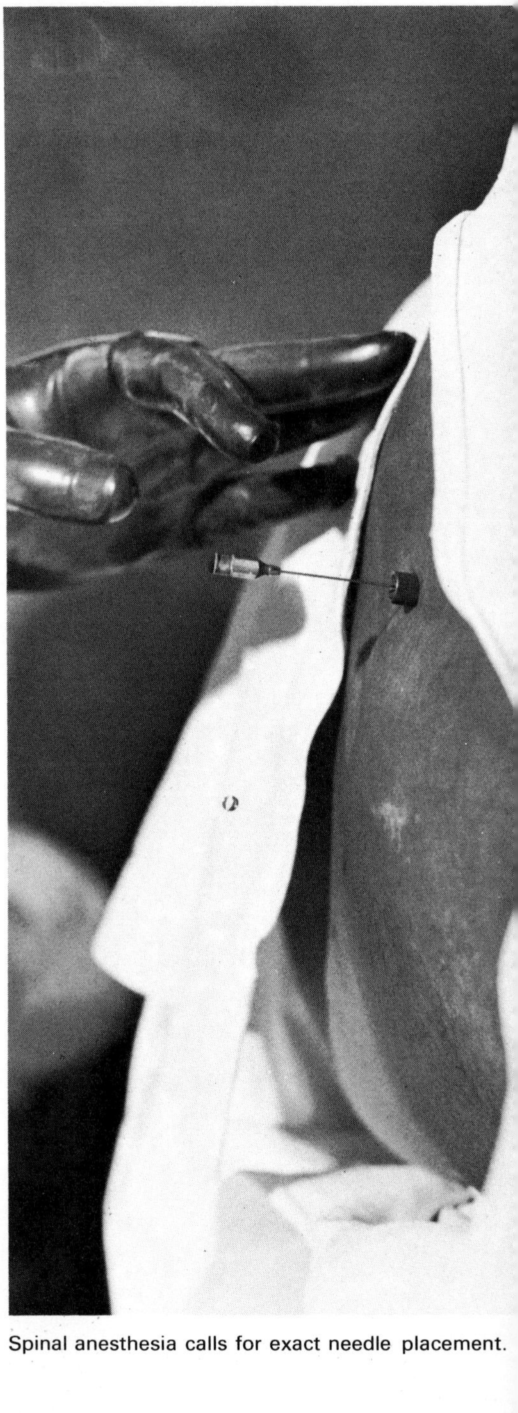

Spinal anesthesia calls for exact needle placement.

stemmed thumbtack, between two vertebrae in the lower back, piercing the ligaments. Then he inserts a hollow needle through the introducer to puncture the tough membrane surrounding the fluid-filled cavity containing the spinal nerves. With this spinal tap completed *(center)*, a syringe containing a local anesthetic, such as procaine or tetracaine, is attached to the needle and injected into the spinal fluid.

Other tools help the anesthesiologist overcome such problems as those caused by mucus secretions that often collect in the lungs during anesthesia. He may remove secretions by washing and vacuum-cleaning the lungs with a flexible tube passed in through a bronchoscope *(right)*, which can reach beyond the trachea and into either of the two main "air pipes" leading into the lungs. The anesthesiologist sprays in liquefying agents to dissolve these secretions and then draws them out by suction.

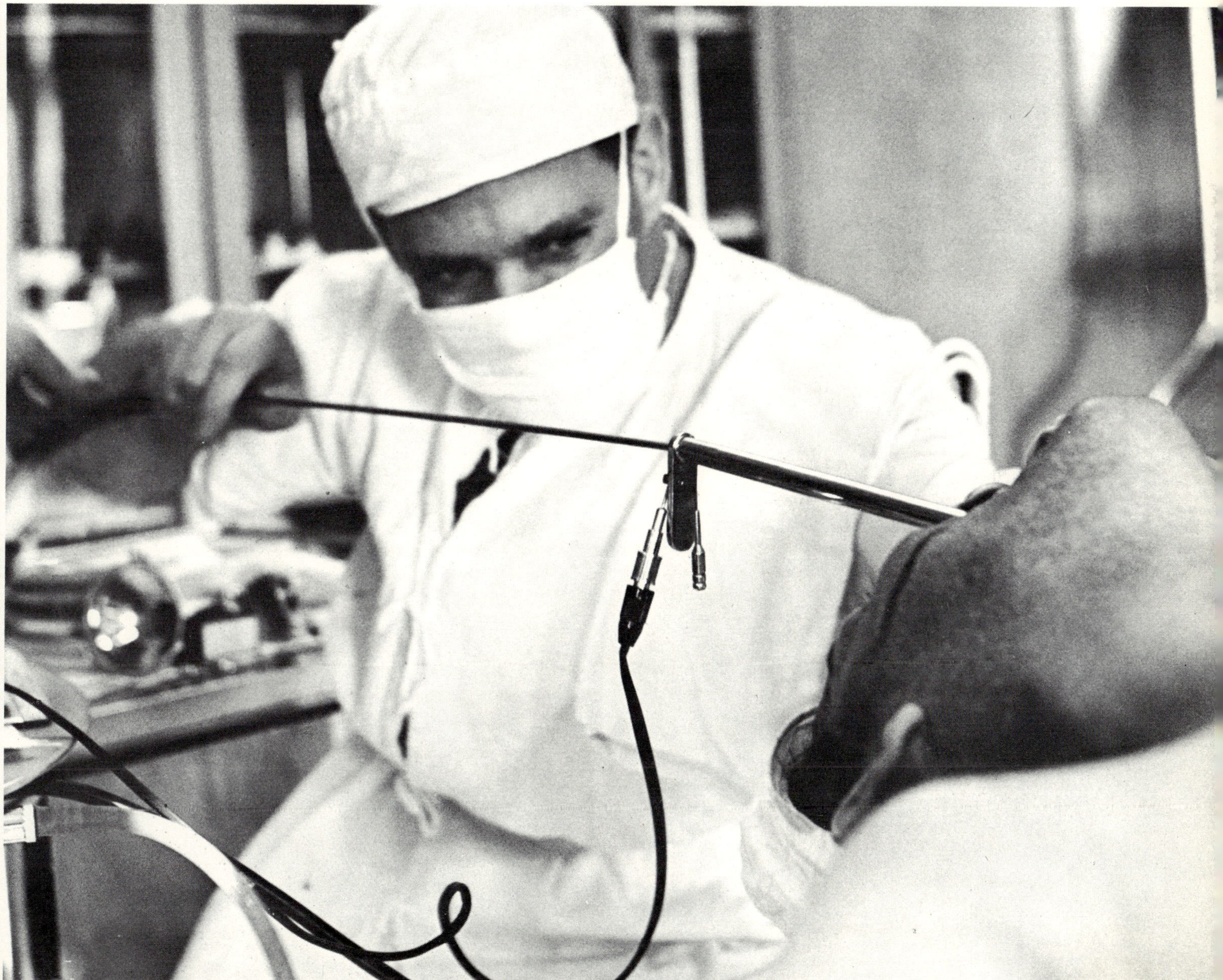

Peering into a patient's lung through an illuminated bronchoscope, the anesthesiologist inserts a flexible tube that will be used to wash out secretions.

A Blockade on Pain's Path

Anyone who has ever applied an ice pack to a painful sprained ankle has employed, in crude form, one of the anesthesiologist's most useful and sophisticated techniques, regional (sometimes called "local") anesthesia. This is a sharpshooting approach to the control of pain, numbing a particular area of the body without affecting other areas.

The anesthesiologist most usually achieves this effect, not by chilling the surface of the body, but by drugging a nerve inside the body. An injection of a substance like procaine shuts down the selected nerve, blocking the pathways that transmit certain pain signals to the brain.

This technique, long used by dentists to block off the nerves around teeth, finds increasing application in cases ranging from painful childbirth to major amputations. Among its chief advantages is safety. Because local anesthetics do not affect the brain, there is little risk that they will interfere with breathing and heart action, as general anesthetics often do. They also give the patient a ringside view of his own operation. Awake and pain-free, he may trade jokes with the surgeon as an appendix is removed or a broken leg is set.

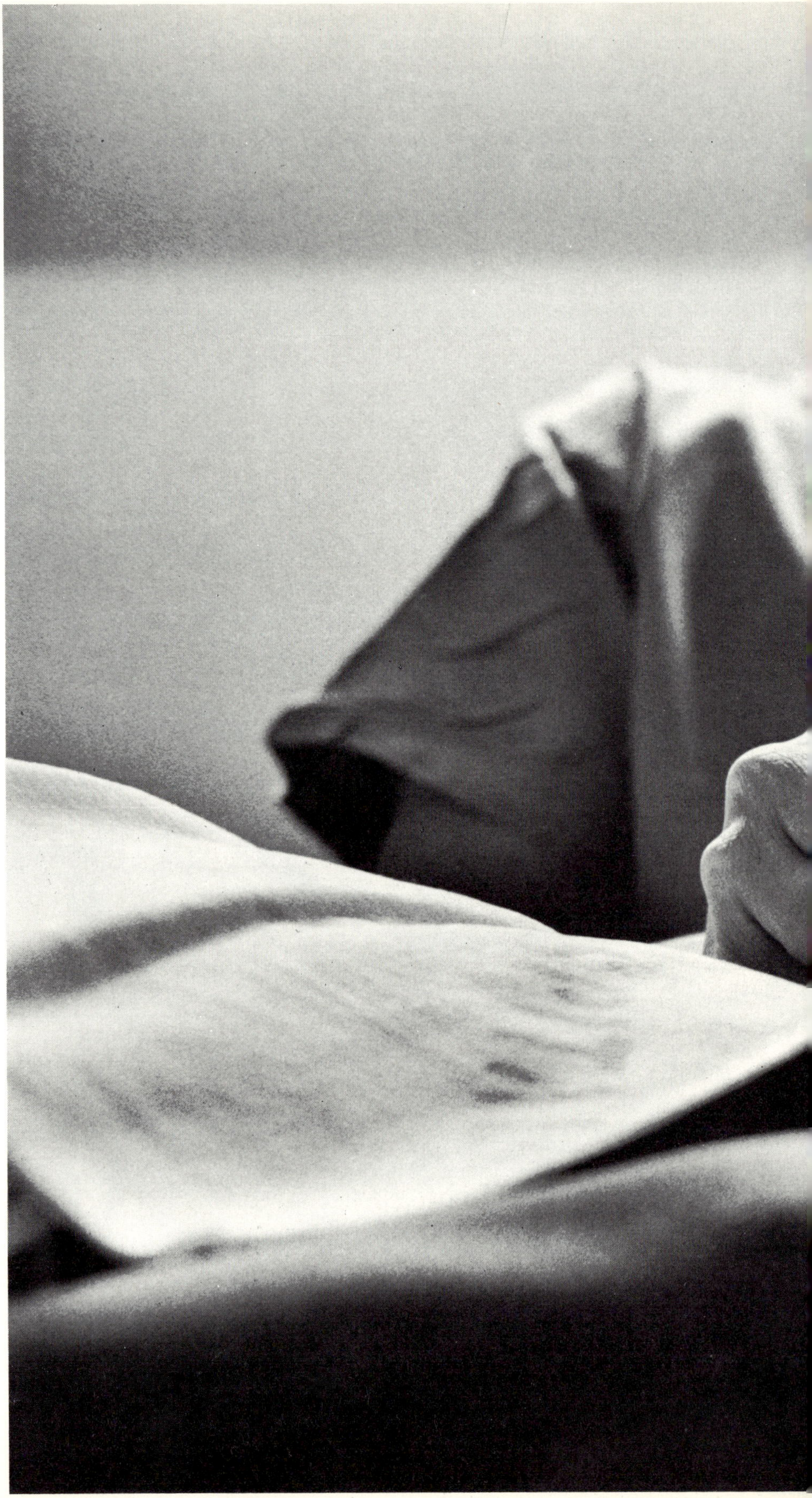

A NEEDLE IN THE NECK
Relieving persistent pain spasms from a healed arm fracture, Dr. Y. R. Lee of Cook County Hospital injects procaine to deaden a main interconnection of nerves in the neck. The drug stops "echoing" nerve signals, initiated by the injury, that cause painful blood vessel spasms.

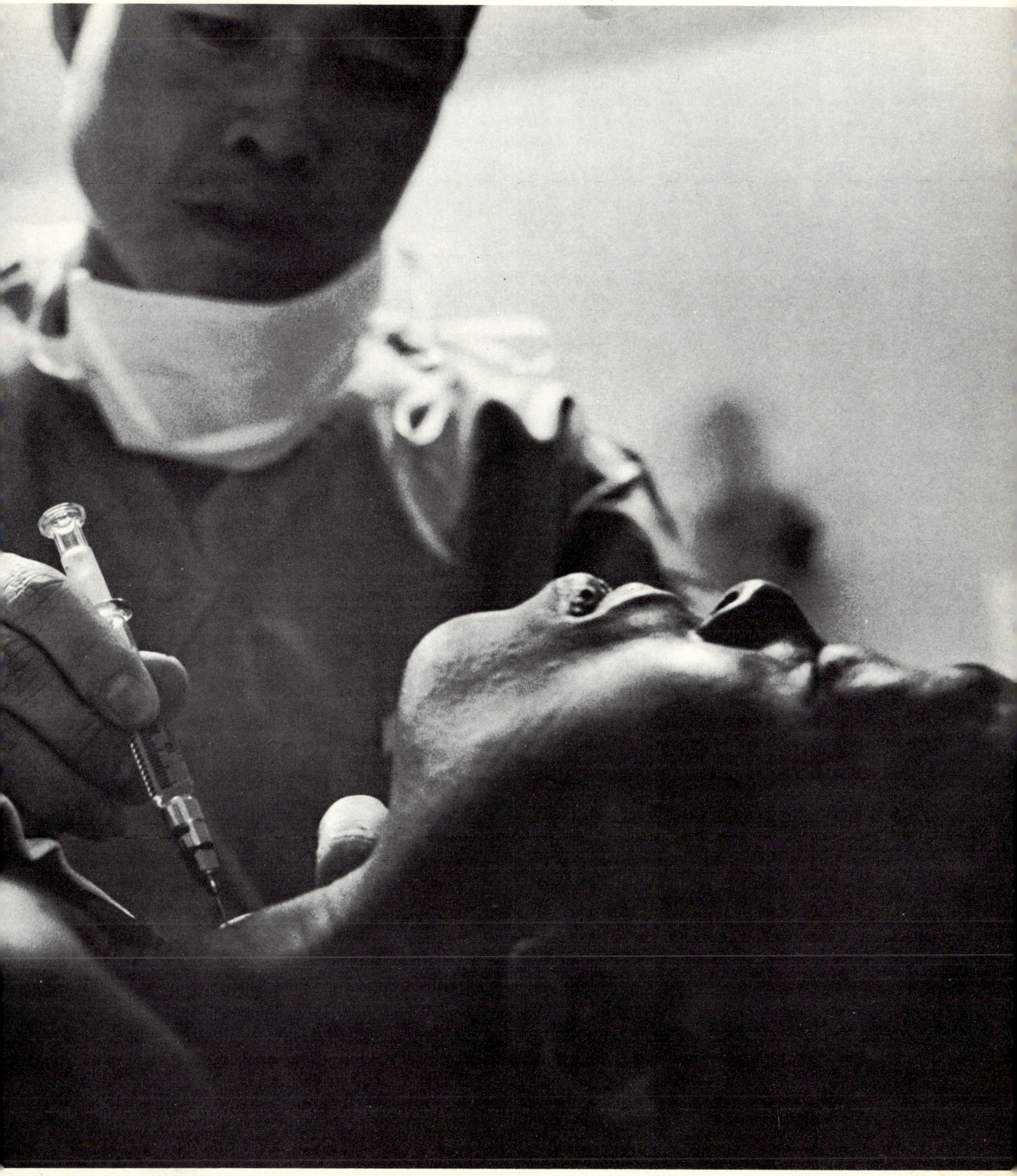

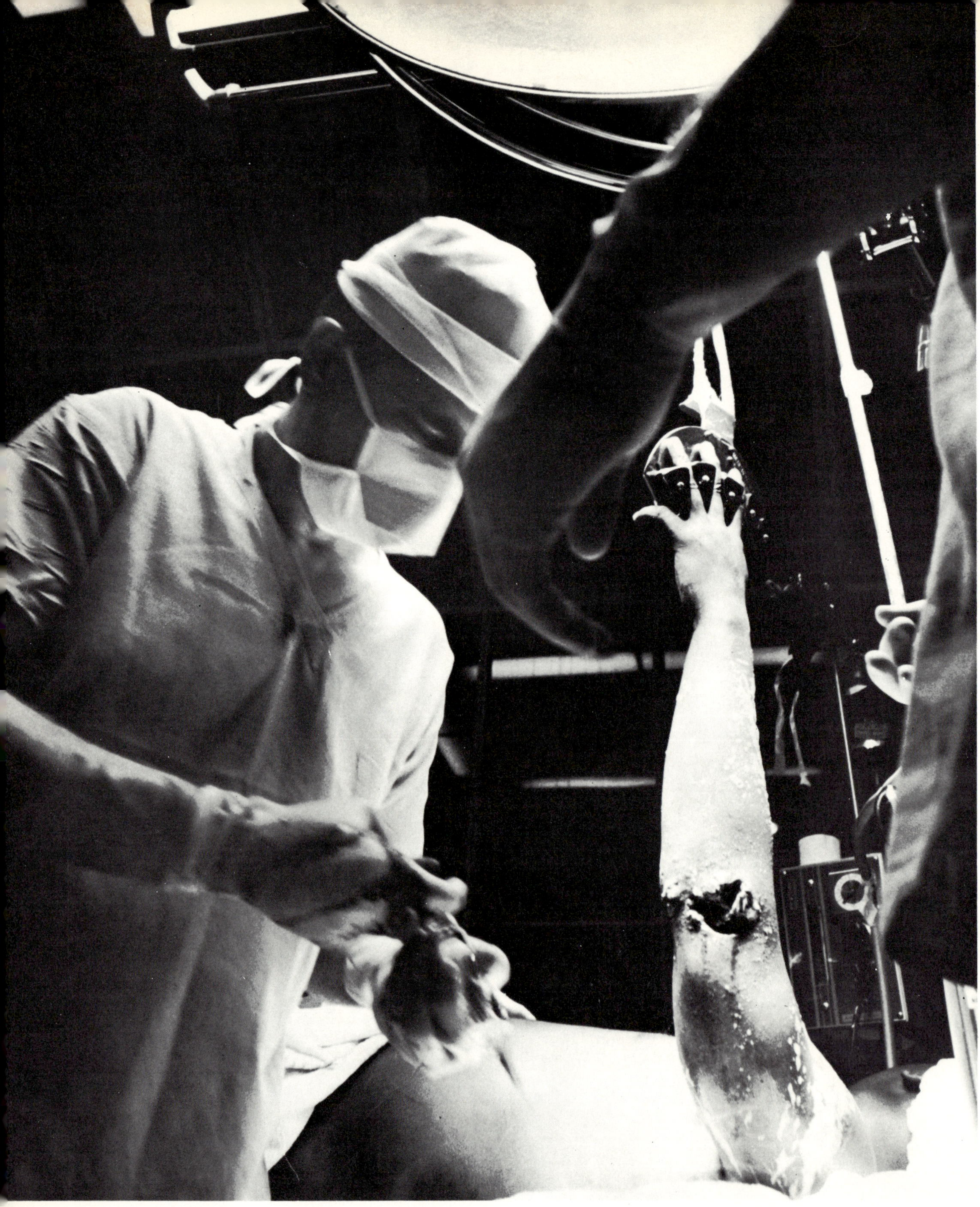

A MANGLED ARM
His badly gashed left arm suspended overhead, an accident victim is readied for emergency surgery. The anesthesiologist at left has just injected a local anesthetic drug into the brachial plexus, a nerve network located below the shoulder, thus blocking all sensations from the badly injured arm.

A Man for All Emergencies

In the emergency room, the anesthesiologist meets a severe test of his drugs and skills. He is often confronted with serious and painful injuries, like those shown on these pages—cases requiring immediate action to limit suffering and preserve life. He must decide quickly on an anesthetic procedure, although this choice may be complicated by the patient's injuries as well as by lack of information on the patient's previous reactions to drugs.

Recognizing these uncertainties, the emergency room anesthesiologist braces himself for adverse, and possibly dangerous, drug effects. If such distress signs appear, he must be ready with counteracting drugs, which work to offset the effects of the anesthetic. He may use ephedrine to offset shock and low blood pressure, pentothal for convulsions, neostigmine to reverse the effects of curare. For the most serious emergency of all—heart stoppage—the anesthesiologist is ready to use any of 15 different stimulant drugs at his disposal.

A BLISTERED FACE
A face covered with second-degree burns presents a difficult problem to the anesthesiologist. In this case, unable to inject a pain-killer directly into the blistered skin, he relieved the man's suffering by setting up an apparatus to drop cyclohexanone, a local anesthetic, into a vein of the foot.

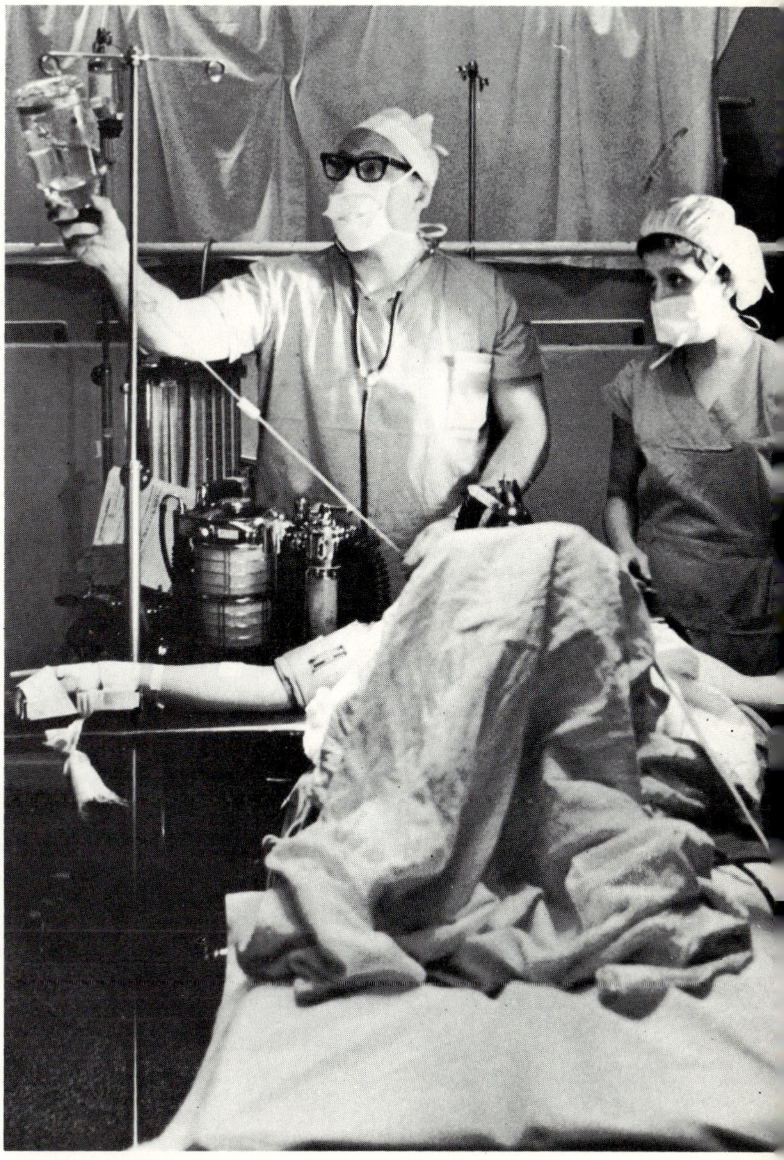

A BULLET-PIERCED BODY
A woman victim of a gunshot wound breathes cyclopropane through a face mask while an anesthesiologist prepares a bottle of saline solution to combat shock, caused by loss of blood. The elevated position of the woman's legs is an antishock measure to assist the flow of blood to the brain.

Drugs for Incurable Agonies

There are in the United States today several million people who are in torment—infants gasping for breath because of respiratory disorders *(opposite);* adults wracked by asthma *(below);* people of all ages slowly wasting with cancer. Once their only hope for relief lay in narcotic drugs, or brain surgery for the removal of the pain center—or death. In recent years, however, anesthesiologists have brought pain-killing drugs and techniques out of the operating room to make life bearable for a number of these sufferers from chronic pain.

Today many hospitals maintain clinics where anesthesiologists provide oxygen for victims of lung ailments and inject doses of anesthetic drugs to block nerves such as those that trigger the excruciating facial pain of trigeminal neuralgia. An effective technique often used to dull the pain of terminal cancer is the alcohol nerve block: corrosive alcohol, injected into the nerve, so damages it that the passage of sensation may be blocked for months at a time.

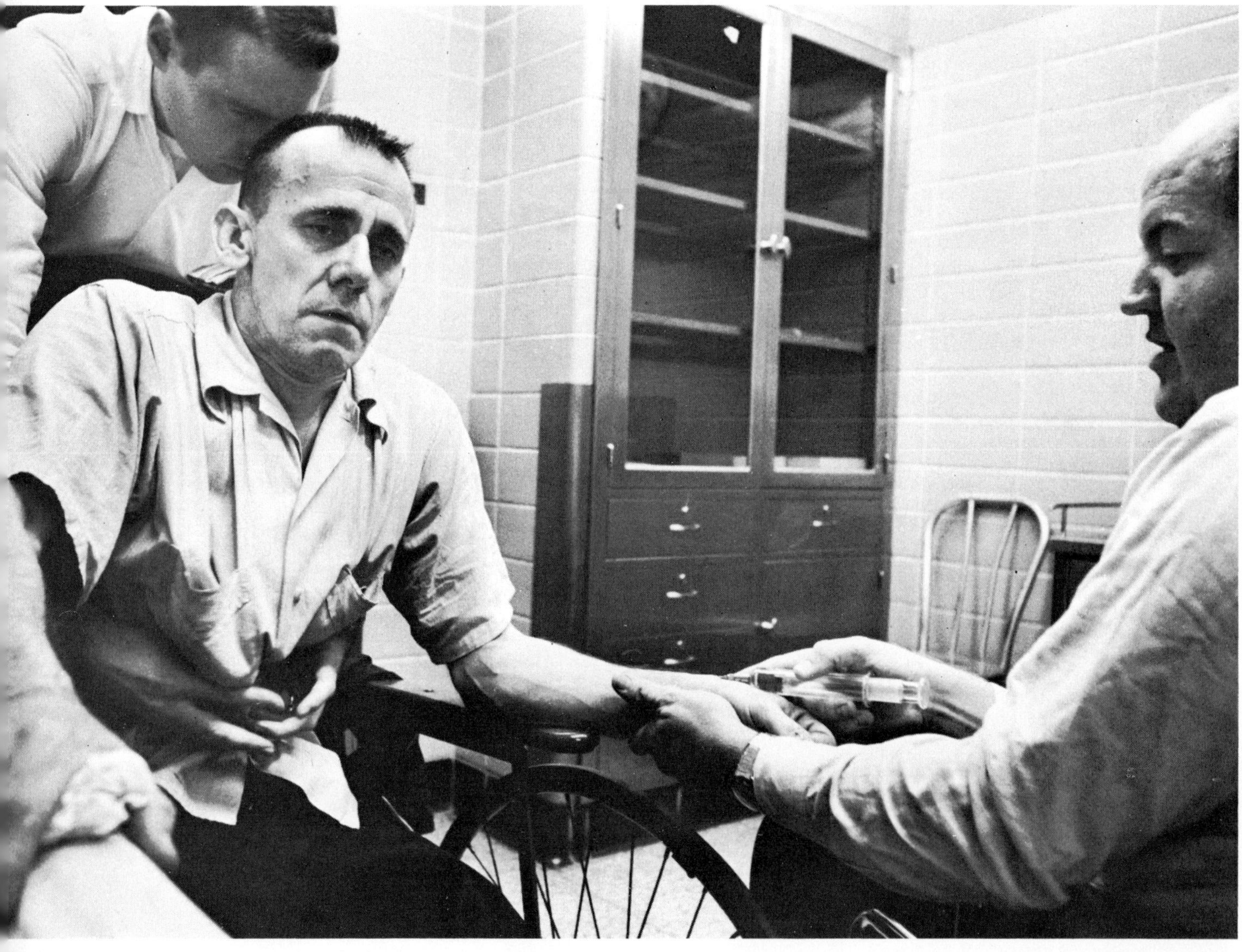

RELIEF FOR AN ASTHMATIC

Gasping for breath, his face contorted with pain, the victim of a severe asthma attack is wheeled into a Chicago clinic. Here Dr. Alon Winnie will give him an injection of aminophylline, a drug that relaxes bronchial muscles and may bring relief for one or two hours. Since asthmatics often become drug resistant, anesthesiologists switch drugs to find the most effective remedy.

SLEEP FOR A SICK BABY

This two-day-old baby, suffering from a defective heart and labored breathing, will be given around-the-clock treatment in an incubator at Cook County Hospital. An anesthesiologist is using a stethoscope to check breathing and heartbeat, both of which are assisted by humidified, oxygen-enriched air that is continually pumped into the body through a nasal tube

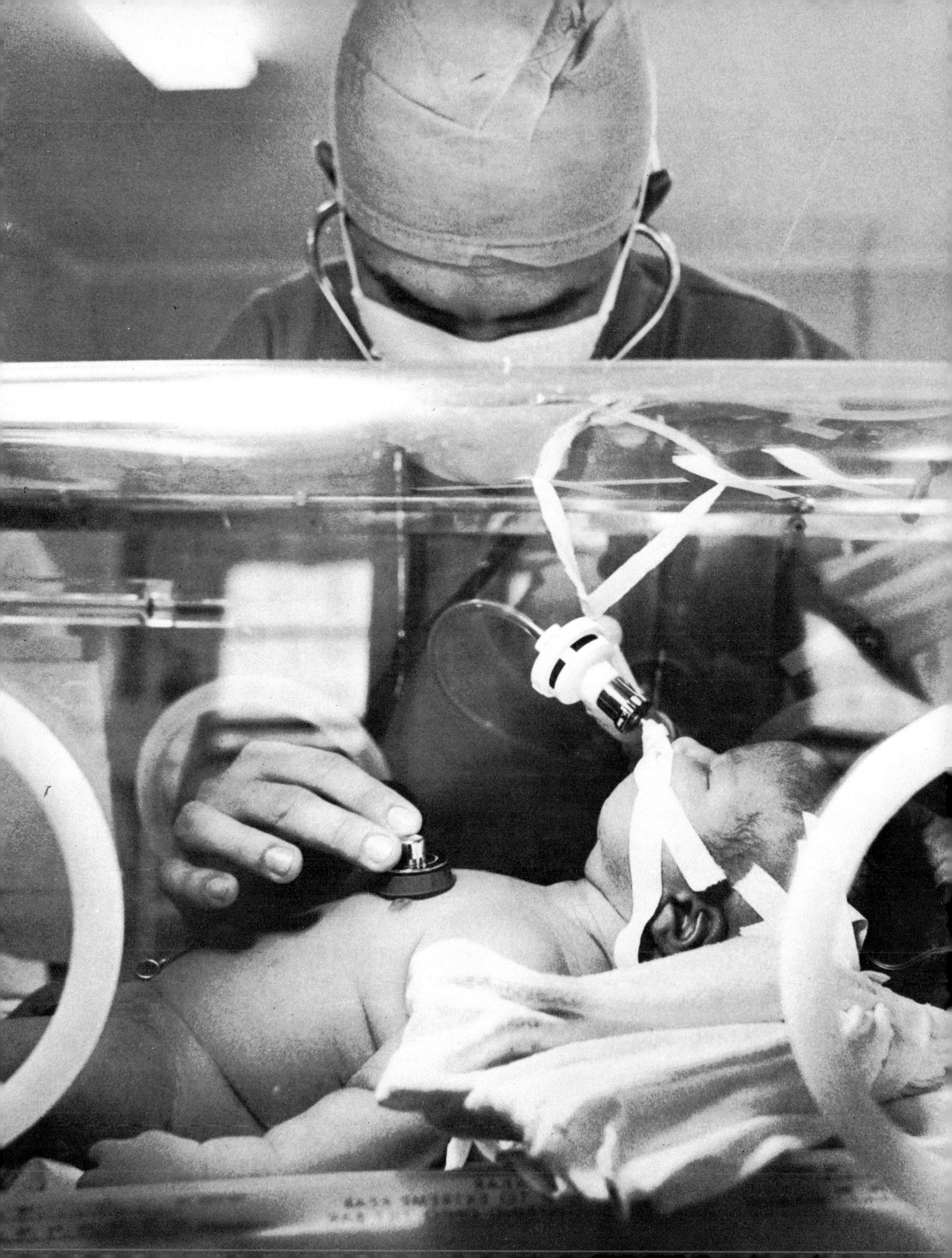

A Test of Men and Machines

How far the anesthesiologist has now come from the ether-pourer of a century ago may be judged by this picture showing part of the equipment he uses to keep a patient alive during open-heart surgery. This complex, five-hour operation calls for the heart and lungs to be stopped while their work is taken over by the anesthesiologist's heart-lung machine *(right)*, which pumps oxygen-enriched blood through the body. While the surgeon repairs or replaces portions of the silent, blood-free heart, the anesthesiologist monitors the gauges of his machines, ready to administer anesthetics, oxygen, blood fortifiers, blood thinners, blood substitutes or muscle relaxants as needed.

The surgeon's last task is to reopen the veins and arteries that restore blood to the newly mended heart. It is now that the anesthesiologist's most delicate work begins. Like a mechanic tuning an engine, he monitors the rhythm of the heart, administering stimulants to speed it up or sedatives to slow it down. Only when the anesthesiologist has adjusted the heart to a firm, steady beat can he and the other specialists of the operating team relax in the satisfaction of their hard-won victory over disease.

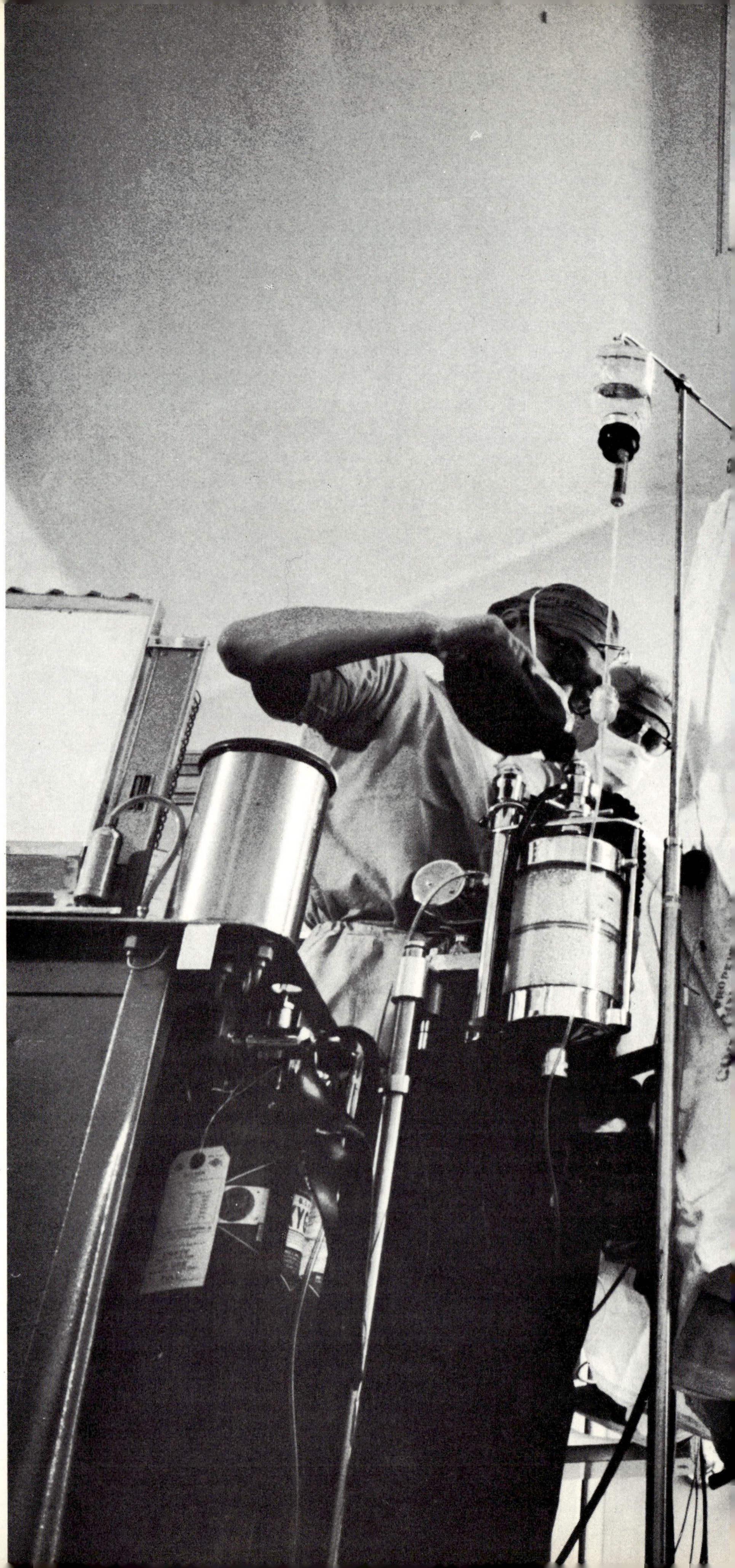

A STAND-IN FOR LUNG AND HEART
In this view of the anesthesiologist's position during open-heart surgery, the heart-lung machine at the right has become an extension of the patient, breathing for him and circulating his blood. It also receives drugs through connections to the machine shown at left and blood additives from solutions hanging on either side.

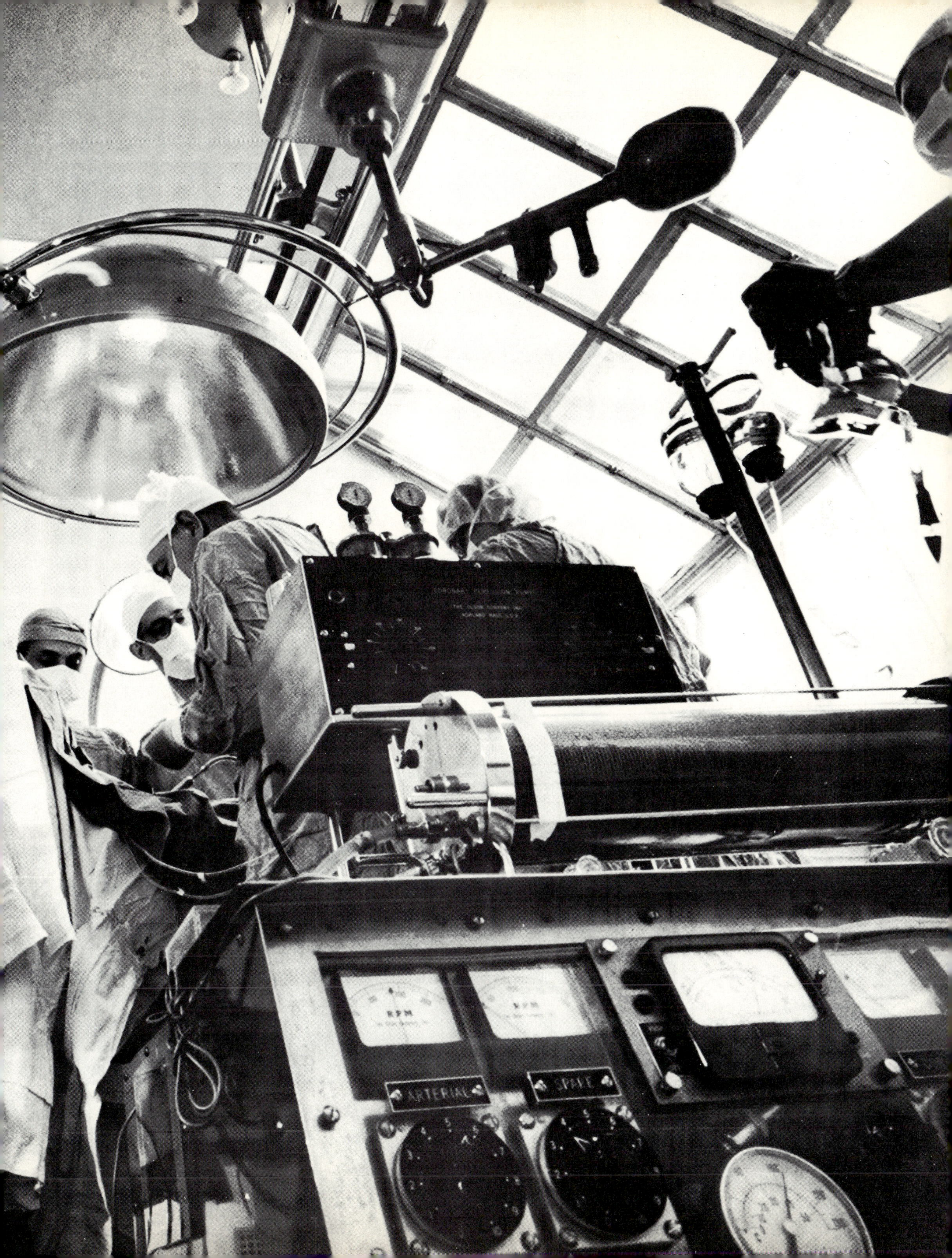
RPM
RPM
ARTERIAL
SPARE

4

Help for the Heart

A heart attack is often signaled by a sharp pain in the left arm, as shown in this reenactment of a seizure suffered by a commuter on a train. Heart diseases afflict about 15 million Americans; drugs help most of them, but there are no cures.

OF ALL THE BODY'S ORGANS, the heart is perhaps the most vital. Men can survive the loss of half their intestines, half their lungs, half their kidneys, even half their brains. But nobody ever survived with half a heart. Not surprisingly, heart disease ranks with infectious disease as a principal cause of death. In the United States, where infectious disease is being increasingly controlled, diseases of the heart and its blood vessels kill more people than all other diseases put together.

Yet despite the critical importance of the heart, little can be done for its ills. Surgery can now repair some heart defects, but the drugs that give relief in heart ailments are few—and most of the effective medicines have been known for a long time. Of the four "heart drugs" most commonly used today, one was introduced into medicine in the 18th Century, another was discovered in the 19th Century, while the other two are some 50 years old. With all its sophisticated knowledge, modern pharmacology has not yet managed to improve on these venerable remedies, nor has it discovered drugs that can cure other heart diseases that are outside the province of the four veteran drugs. It is unfortunate but true that aside from new drugs that alleviate high blood pressure, "heart drugs" are little better now than they were in 1920.

Both the shortcomings and the achievements of the heart drugs are worth examining for the light they cast on virtually all remedies. Few drugs offer complete cures. Many effective ones have been used (and misused) for years. Almost all are unsatisfactory in some respect. Yet without them, millions now enjoying useful lives would be dead.

The four heart drugs came into the pharmacopoeia by different routes —from the lore of folk remedies as well as from scientific research. They won prized places in the drug list for their remarkable ability to relieve pain and save lives. And yet only one among them can—sometimes—literally cure the disorder for which it is prescribed.

To understand the role of the four drugs in diseases related to the heart, we must take a quick look at the organ itself and at the blood-circulating system of which it is a part. The function of the blood is to carry food and oxygen to the tissues of the body and at the same time remove waste products. It circulates through a network of pipes (the blood vessels), powered by a pump (the heart). Both pipes and pump are subject to disease, but the consequences are likely to be acutely serious when the pump is affected. Serious damage to a vessel may or may not be dangerous, depending on where in the body the damage occurs; serious damage to the heart is always dangerous and often fatal.

One of the commonest heart disorders is somewhat misleadingly called "congestive heart failure." The term does not mean that the heart fails to beat, but that its pumping capacity has become inadequate for the body's needs. Congestive failure can be produced by damage to the heart's valves, which makes them leaky, or by damage to the heart muscle, which makes the pump weak. Whatever the cause of congestive failure, it limits the heart's ability to drive enough blood through the vessels to meet the body's needs.

The body attempts to cope with the problem of diminished blood supply by using several compensating mechanisms. When any muscle is chronically overworked the body responds by enlarging that muscle. Thus the heart, which consists primarily of muscles, grows larger so that it can pump harder. More significant is another compensating action designed to economize on the limited blood flow. Tiny muscles in the blood-vessel walls contract the blood vessels to cut down the movement of blood to almost all parts of the body except the heart and brain —thereby attempting to ensure that these two absolutely essential organs will receive the oxygen they need. However, this measure can be costly: the sluggish flow to the rest of the body can produce many kinds of damage, owing to decreased oxygen supply and inadequate removal of wastes. One of the most serious consequences can result from decreased blood flow through the kidneys. These organs eliminate excess salt from the body by filtering out the sodium that makes up part of the salt compound. But with lowered blood flow, the kidneys excrete sodium less efficiently. And since the kidneys are geared to maintaining a fixed proportion of sodium to water in the blood, excess salt in the body means excess water, too.

THE DISCOVERER OF DIGITALIS, William Withering, studies a foxglove plant, source of this powerful heart stimulant. An English physician of the 18th Century, Withering was led to his discovery by his study of plants, an interest that began when he gathered wild flowers for his wife and that eventually made him one of the leading botanists of his time. This expertise enabled him to pick out foxglove as the key ingredient in an old wives' remedy for the condition called dropsy *(opposite)*. Only much later was the true value of foxglove's digitalis learned; it can help dropsy because it alleviates congestive heart failure, one cause of dropsy.

As a result, the body's tissues become waterlogged—a condition called edema, or "dropsy." The excess water can amount to 30 pounds or more of extra weight for the body to carry around, with a proportionately greater strain upon an already inadequate heart. When edema affects the lungs, the effect is worse, for waterlogging cuts down the flow of oxygen into the blood just when oxygen is already in short supply.

To reduce the excess sodium (and therefore the excess water) the physician often prescribes a "low sodium" or "salt free" diet. He may also attack the problem by means of a diuretic drug, which stimulates the kidneys to step up their excretion of sodium. But diets and diuretics, though they may eliminate the excess water, do not—in a very literal sense—go to the heart of the matter. The heart remains incapable of performing its duties; the body's tissues may still be starved for oxygen. To correct this situation, the doctor will almost certainly prescribe some preparation of digitalis.

From potion to prescription.

The story of digitalis is one of the most fascinating in the history of pharmacology. This drug was long an old wives' remedy; it was first prescribed by a physician for heart trouble nearly 200 years ago. Nevertheless a century and a half passed before its effects and proper use were understood. The halting progress of digitalis from potion to modern prescription illustrates how inadequate knowledge of pharmacology can nullify the value of even an effective drug.

In 1775, an English physician named William Withering was asked his opinion of a folk remedy esteemed, not for its effect on the heart, but for its ability to relieve the swelling of dropsy. The recipe, he was told, "had long been kept a secret by an old woman in Shropshire, who had sometimes made cures after the more regular practitioners had failed." The medicine, like many of the period, was a complicated concoction, with more than 20 different ingredients. Withering, however, was sophisticated enough to recognize that many of the components were merely window dressing. From his knowledge of botany, he suspected that the active principle of the mixture was to be found in only one of the ingredients—the leaves of the foxglove, whose pretty purple flowers dot English gardens in early summer. Accordingly, he began to treat dropsical patients with a tea made with foxglove leaves. In many cases it did indeed relieve them of excess fluid by markedly increasing urine output.

Withering studied the drug for 10 years. He learned to obtain leaves of uniform potency by gathering them at a particular stage of the plant's growth, and he determined the most effective dosage. In 1785, he published his observations. His book, *An Account of the Foxglove and Some of its Medical Uses,* is a classic of painstaking scientific investigation.

A remedy misunderstood

Unfortunately, the book was ahead of its time. Its basic trouble was one that has beset many studies beside Withering's: lack of information on precisely what the drug did in the body. Withering had carefully catalogued most of the foxglove's externally observable effects: increased urine flow, nausea, purging, disorders of vision and a slowed pulse. ("It has," he noted, "a power over the motions of the heart to a degree yet unobserved in any other medicine.") But neither he nor his successors for generations afterward had either the knowledge or the techniques to determine the effects of the drug inside the body—and therefore the diseases for which it could best be used.

From the drug's diuretic effect, Withering himself deduced that it acted on the kidneys—though he warned that it would not produce diuresis under all conditions. Some later physicians were less cautious: they used digitalis, as the drug came to be known, as a "remedy" for all forms of edema, and sometimes—following the ancient tendency of doctors and laymen alike to make too much of a good thing—for totally unrelated conditions. Used thus promiscuously its effects were so uncertain that many physicians stopped using it entirely.

By 1855, at least one basic fact had become clear: digitalis did not act directly on the kidneys; its virtues, whatever they might be, lay in what Withering had called its "power over the heart." A French physiologist, Edme Vulpian, thought he knew the nature of the power: digitalis, he said, benefited the patient with an enlarged heart by improving the "tone" of the heart muscle—that is, by increasing its ability to contract—thereby reducing the size of the organ. He concluded, therefore, that the time to use the drug was *after* the heart had become enlarged—but that course of action was rather like trying to lock the door when the horse was halfway out of the stable. Vulpian was confusing cause and effect. In congestive failure, the heart is not inadequate because it is enlarged; it becomes enlarged because it is inadequate.

A CRUEL CARTOON, by the 19th Century English artist Thomas Rowlandson, lampooned dropsy and consumption, widespread diseases in Rowlandson's day. The enormous paunch that he drew on the gentleman is a symptom of dropsy, or edema, an accumulation of body fluid sometimes caused by congestive heart failure. For this form of dropsy, a remedy, digitalis, had earlier been discovered by William Withering *(opposite),* but the drug was improperly used until recent times. No cure for consumption, or tuberculosis, suffered by the wraithlike lady in the cartoon, was available until the introduction of streptomycin in 1947.

Pharmacologists continued to puzzle over the drug but made little progress until the beginning of the 20th Century. Then a number of investigators evolved a new theory: digitalis influenced not the size or the "tone" of the heart, but, as Withering had written more than a century before, "the motion of the heart," particularly the rate of the heartbeat.

Scientifically, this was a little closer to the truth. But therapeutically, it led to the use of digitalis only for a condition called delirium cordis, which affects the heart's rhythm, but *not* for congestive failure, the major cardiac condition for which it is now considered essential.

It was not until the 1930s that the real secret of digitalis' power began to be revealed. During that decade, experiments on animals and on isolated bits of heart muscle showed that the drug's main action is directly on the muscle. It causes the muscle to contract more forcefully and therefore to pump blood more effectively. This finding explained all the observations that had previously blurred the picture. The more vigorous a heart is, the more slowly it beats, because each beat is more efficient. With an adequate flow of blood through the kidneys, sodium—and therefore water—is excreted more efficiently. Finally, with the heart no longer overloaded, its size may subside toward normal.

The explanation of digitalis' action in the body also put it into its proper place in the doctor's armory against disease: it is now the specific drug—what doctors call the "drug of choice"—for all cases of congestive failure. After long fumbling, medicine could make full use of the genius of Withering, not to mention the mother wit of the anonymous old woman in Shropshire.

Digitalis merely increases the vigor of the heart muscle, and this change will not, of itself, relieve every type of heart disorder. To do an effective pumping job, for example, the heart must contract not merely vigorously, but also rhythmically. Rhythm is essential because the heart must perform an enormous amount of work. It can handle this load only if each of its various chambers and each fiber of its muscles contract in precisely the right sequence and at the right time, just as a group of men can hoist a heavy weight only if they pull together on the rope. If some pull "out of step," their efficiency is cut. The same thing happens if the heart becomes "arrhythmic," with some of its parts contracting out of sequence with the rest. The condition, called cardiac arrhythmia, can constitute a mild and harmless nuisance or can so impair the heart's efficiency as to bring death within minutes.

Pulses from a pacemaker

The heart gets out of step when its electrical control system goes awry. The heart's contractions are normally kept in rhythm by a network of specialized muscle fibers, which conduct electrical impulses to the rest of the heart on signal from a bit of tissue called the "pacemaker." By this means, the organ maintains a rhythm of about 70 beats per minute when the body is at rest.

In some types of arrhythmias, the timing network has been damaged by disease, causing it to emit abnormal impulses. More commonly, however, arrhythmia stems from damage to the heart muscle itself. When irritated or injured, a portion of that muscle begins to act as an independent source of timing signals, sometimes much more rapid than the normal heartbeat; abnormal beats have been clocked at rates up to several hundred a minute. The rapid signals can override the signals of the pacemaker, throwing the heart's motions into disorder.

Long before the detailed mechanisms of the heart's timing system were understood, their ailments were being effectively treated with drugs. Digitalis, the oldest of the heart drugs, can slow the rapidity of an irregular heart, but it does not make an irregular heart regular. In most cases, the drug of choice is quinidine, which works quite differently. It depresses the electrical activity and irritability of the heart muscle, reducing or abolishing the independent impulses that are throwing the heart into turmoil.

Powdered bark for "rebellious palpitation"

Like digitalis, quinidine was used centuries ago but its action was long misunderstood before it assumed its proper role in medicine. As its name suggests, it is related to quinine. Both drugs are derived from the bark of the cinchona tree, and both are similar chemically.

As early as 1749, a Parisian physician named Jean-Baptiste de Sénac reported that he had used powdered cinchona bark to cure "rebellious palpitation" of the heart, but his report passed unnoticed. The drug was not forgotten, however. A century or so later, chemists had learned to purify quinidine and to separate it from quinine, used for malaria.

Credit for rediscovering the antiarrhythmic effects of these drugs seems to belong not to a doctor but to a layman anonymous as Withering's old lady from Shropshire. One day in 1912, a patient whose name does not appear in the published medical records called at the Vienna office of Dr. Karl Wenckebach, and complained of an abnormal heartbeat. Wenckebach examined him and said that he could promise no cure. The patient thereupon declared flatly that he could cure himself.

When Wenckebach expressed disbelief, the man announced that he would return next morning "with a regular pulse." He did. On questioning him, the doctor found that the patient had dosed himself with quinine. Later, experimenters compared the efficacy of quinine and its nearly identical twin, quinidine. The latter proved the better of the two —it is effective in smaller doses and thus side effects are less serious.

The histories of digitalis and quinidine, from their beginnings in foxglove leaves and cinchona bark to their use in modern medicine, have certain features in common. The third important heart drug—more precisely, a group of related drugs—has a history differing at almost every point. These drugs, called nitrites, are not natural substances, extracted from leaves or bark, but products of chemists' ingenuity. The medical significance of nitrites was discovered by physicians—no anonymous old ladies or obstreperous heart patients played a part. Their proper use was worked out, not generations after their original discovery, but within a few years—and they have been used for the same purpose ever since.

That purpose is the relief of an extremely painful and relatively common form of heart trouble called angina pectoris. Its cause is always some interference with the heart's own blood supply—usually resulting from the condition called atherosclerosis, in which fatty deposits may narrow the walls of the coronary arteries and thereby reduce the flow of blood (and thus of oxygen) to the heart. The heart itself cannot feel pain. But its frantic signals for more oxygen can produce what is called "referred" pain in other parts of the body. Particularly characteristic is pain traveling down the left arm to the little finger and a sensation of pressure or strangling, as if the chest were being compressed in a gigantic vise (the term "angina pectoris" is Latin for "strangling of the chest").

The nitrites, which provided physicians with their first effective weapon against angina, came into medicine as part of the great scientific upsurge of the mid-19th Century. A new understanding of chemical theory, in particular, spurred chemists to build hundreds of new compounds; no less assiduously pharmacologists studied the effects of those newly synthesized compounds on animals and human beings.

Amyl nitrite vs. angina's agony

One of these new substances was a volatile liquid called amyl nitrite. First synthesized in 1844, it was studied by several investigators, who reported that the fumes of amyl nitrite produced flushing of the face and a widening of the tiny blood vessels called capillaries. In 1867 these reports were brilliantly used by Thomas Lauder Brunton, a 23-year-old Scottish medical student. Brunton had the insight to suspect that such a method of increasing blood flow might counteract angina pectoris and ease its pains. He tried amyl nitrite on some of his patients and it worked.

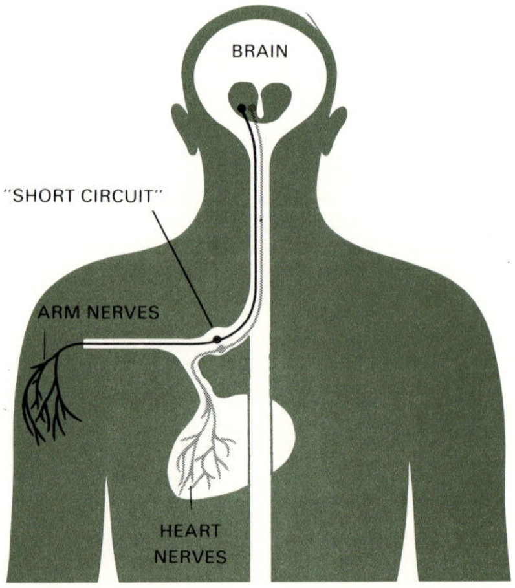

THE TORTUOUS PATH OF PAIN in heart ailments, including the very painful angina pectoris, causes the victim to feel not only chest constriction but also an ache in his left arm *(seen here from rear)*. The misplaced or "referred" pain arises because the stricken heart signals the brain that it needs more oxygen. This strong message travels along a nerve close to another nerve path—one used for arm-pain signals—and at one of several points a "short circuit" may occur: the oxygen signals excite the adjacent nerve, making it send arm-pain signals to the brain. Treatment with nitroglycerin alleviates the oxygen lack causing the pain.

In 1879, twelve years later, another British doctor, William Murrell, discovered that nitroglycerin worked equally well. The two drugs are chemically similar, as their names suggest, but how they relieve angina remains a puzzle. For many years it was thought that, as Brunton believed, they did so simply by widening the coronary vessels. More recently, however, some scientists have come to suspect that their effect may be more subtle, and that they act, not by stepping up the heart's *supply* of oxygen but by reducing its *need* for oxygen. But again, how they do this—if they do it at all—is unknown.

Disorders that involve the coronary arteries, as angina does, are particularly dangerous because these blood vessels supply the heart itself. Other diseases of the blood vessels, affecting less vital parts of the body, are usually less serious. So long as they remain restricted to a particular organ or region, their effects may be unpleasant or even disabling, but are seldom fatal. This is not true, however, of one blood-vessel disorder that affects the entire arterial system simultaneously. It is called shock.

Shock usually stems from a relaxation of the muscles that regulate the diameter of the arteries. Normally, these muscles shunt blood to various tissues, as needed, by constricting arteries or permitting them to open wider. Occasionally, however—generally as the result of poisoning or severe injury—all the muscles relax at once, so that vessels throughout the body are wide open. The result resembles the situation in an apartment building when all the water faucets are opened at once. The water pressure in the building drops sharply, so that water does not gush from the faucets but merely trickles out. In shock, blood pressure falls sharply, and blood merely trickles through the wide-open circulatory system, supplying insufficient oxygen and removing too few wastes.

A drug to transmit "orders"

Because shock threatens all the body's tissues at once, it is very serious indeed. The physician can often combat it by administering a drug that will constrict some of the arteries and thus raise the blood pressure. One common drug of this sort is nor-epinephrine. This substance is, in fact, one of the body's own hormones—one of the regulatory chemicals that transmit "orders" from the nerves to the tissues. There are other drugs that work in similar fashion, but all of these drugs—including nor-epinephrine—are still far from satisfactory (for one thing, they tend to constrict too many of the arteries, thus sometimes hampering circulation instead of helping); and pharmacologists and physicians are still searching for better compounds.

With all their shortcomings, antishock drugs are superior to the other circulatory drugs in one important respect: they can, in some cases, actually correct the disorder for which they are used. The others, immensely valuable though they are, can at best relieve some of the symptoms of disease or abolish some of its secondary effects; they cannot cure the disease itself. Digitalis can strengthen the beat of a weakened heart and cut down edema in the body—but it cannot restore the heart's original strength. Quinidine can sometimes restore a normal heartbeat—but it cannot remove the injury or irritation that produced the abnormality. And the nitrites, though they rapidly relieve the pain of angina, cannot remove the atherosclerotic deposits that constrict the coronary vessels and cut the heart's blood supply.

The limitations of "heart drugs" are unfortunately typical of drugs in general—"kidney drugs," "liver drugs" and "nerve drugs." Indeed, with the important exception of the drugs that cure infection, no class of drugs is of much use in treating the fundamental causes or processes of disease. Drugs can relieve pain and discomfort (as the nitrites do in angina); they can limit or prevent some of the effects of disease (as quinidine does for arrhythmias); they can even at times counteract disease to the point of restoring a semblance of normal functioning (as digitalis does in congestive failure). Beyond this, however, the body must heal itself—if it can. When it comes to curing disease, modern physicians and pharmacologists, for all their skill and science, are little better off than the great 16th Century French surgeon Ambrose Paré, who often said, after a successful case: "I treated him—God cured him."

Keeping the Body's Balance

Although human beings look reasonably solid, 65 per cent of their weight is actually liquid, and keeping that fluid balanced in quantity and composition is one of the most subtle ways in which drugs help the body. The job is a vital one because almost all processes in the body take place in some kind of liquid solution. Water is the basic ingredient of protoplasm, the jellylike substance that makes up the bulk of every body cell. A salty solution of warm water, laden with nutrient chemicals, bathes and nourishes these cells, and water also makes up the liquid part of the blood.

A relatively minor change in the body's fluid content can result in severe illness or death. To keep the composition of its watery world stable, the body performs a skillful balancing act. During every second of a human lifetime, vital organs juggle nutrients and wastes as dexterously as a circus performer. Their balancing act is governed by signals transmitted by two tireless systems that work automatically, even in sleep: the autonomic nervous system, which transmits nerve impulses from the brain; and the circulatory system, which carries chemical messengers to the vital organs. When the body's skillful jugglers slip, drugs can restore the balance.

THE BODY'S CIRCUS ACTS
Balancing like circus performers, bodily devices control fluids essential to life. The autonomic nervous system and circulatory system *(top figure)* send nerve impulses and chemicals to organs *(red, in bottom figure)* that juggle gases, salts and acids. The balancing organs are the pituitary, the lungs, the kidneys and, capping the kidneys, the adrenals.

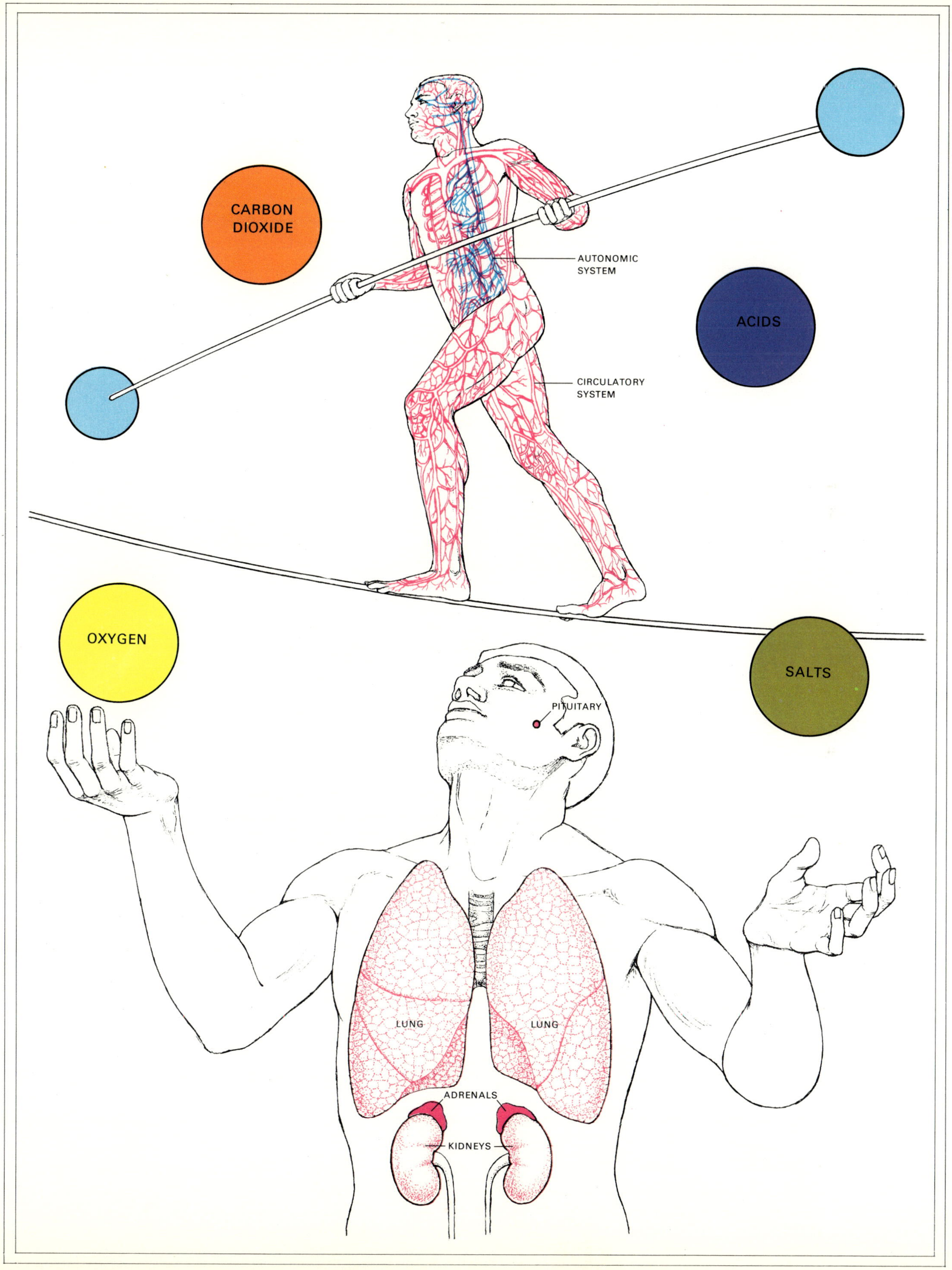
CARBON DIOXIDE
AUTONOMIC SYSTEM
ACIDS
CIRCULATORY SYSTEM
OXYGEN
SALTS
PITUITARY
LUNG
LUNG
ADRENALS
KIDNEYS

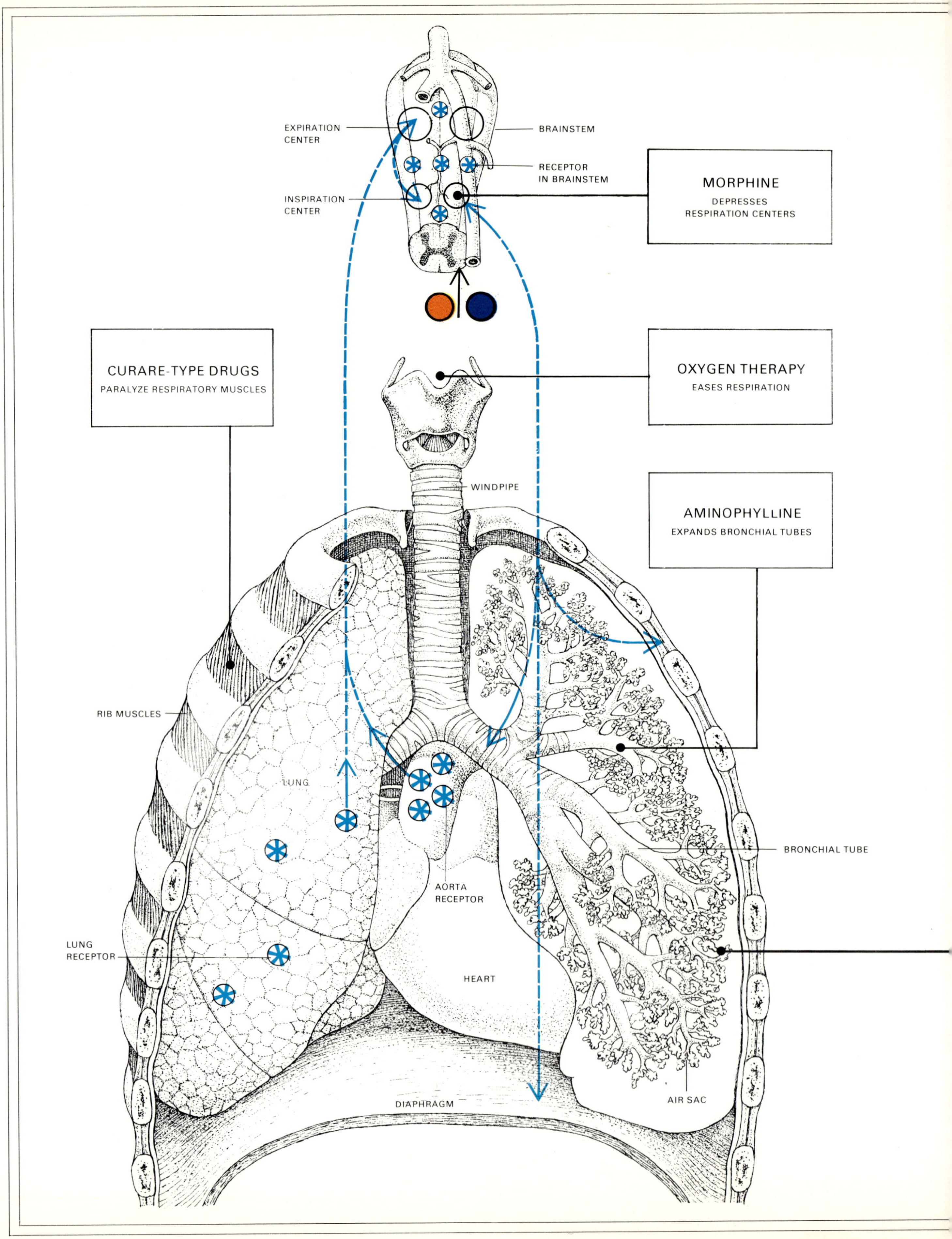

EXPIRATION CENTER
BRAINSTEM
RECEPTOR IN BRAINSTEM
INSPIRATION CENTER
MORPHINE
DEPRESSES RESPIRATION CENTERS
CURARE-TYPE DRUGS
PARALYZE RESPIRATORY MUSCLES
OXYGEN THERAPY
EASES RESPIRATION
WINDPIPE
AMINOPHYLLINE
EXPANDS BRONCHIAL TUBES
RIB MUSCLES
LUNG
BRONCHIAL TUBE
AORTA RECEPTOR
LUNG RECEPTOR
HEART
AIR SAC
DIAPHRAGM

Juggling Gases in the Lungs

The first of the body's fluid-balance acrobatics—respiration, the juggling of oxygen and carbon dioxide in the blood—is one in which drugs may be called on to assume a leading role. The performance begins as oxygen is rhythmically sucked down the windpipe and sent through the branching bronchial tubes to the millions of microscopic, gossamer-thin air sacs that make up the lungs *(opposite)*. The air sacs—so tiny that a lineup of 5,000 of them would measure only an inch, but so numerous that their combined surface area is half the size of a tennis court—are entwined by minute blood vessels, or capillaries *(detail below)*. It is in the sacs that the actual juggling takes place: oxygen moves from air sac into capillary blood while carbon dioxide simultaneously moves the other way.

The oxygen is sought by the blood's red cells, which are made up largely of hemoglobin, an iron-rich compound with a great affinity for oxygen. United with hemoglobin, the oxygen is carried to the rest of the body; eventually it is freed and delivered to individual body cells. After the cells use the oxygen to burn fuel in energy-generating reactions, they release the waste product carbon dioxide. It dissolves in the blood liquid and goes back to the air sacs—there to be exchanged for fresh oxygen.

To control this juggling, two brainstem centers normally adjust the rate of breathing. But occasionally trouble arises because the lungs' air sacs become abnormally rigid (as in emphysema) or the bronchial tubes abnormally constricted (as in asthma). At such times drugs of several types *(described in boxes on the drawings)* can intervene in several ways to keep up the vital exchange of oxygen and carbon dioxide. Drugs can be used either to expand the tubes and thus to ease breathing, or to put a temporary stop to breathing during lung surgery.

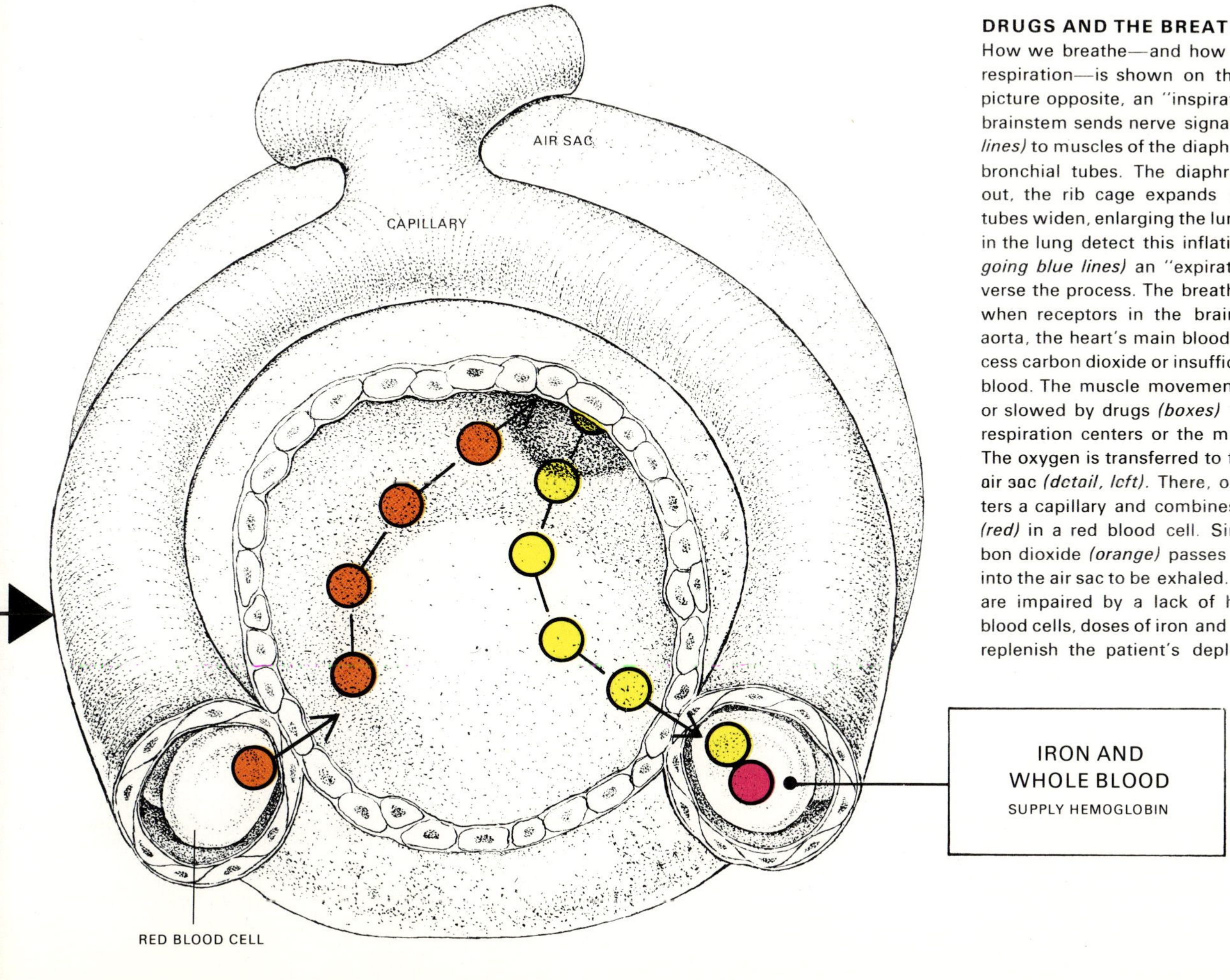

DRUGS AND THE BREATH OF LIFE

How we breathe—and how drugs can control respiration—is shown on these pages. In the picture opposite, an "inspiration center" in the brainstem sends nerve signals *(downward blue lines)* to muscles of the diaphragm, rib cage and bronchial tubes. The diaphragm then flattens out, the rib cage expands and the bronchial tubes widen, enlarging the lung. Nerve receptors in the lung detect this inflation and signal *(upgoing blue lines)* an "expiration center" to reverse the process. The breathing rate increases when receptors in the brainstem and in the aorta, the heart's main blood vessel, detect excess carbon dioxide or insufficient oxygen in the blood. The muscle movements can be stopped or slowed by drugs *(boxes)* that act upon the respiration centers or the muscles themselves. The oxygen is transferred to the blood from the air sac *(detail, left)*. There, oxygen *(yellow)* enters a capillary and combines with hemoglobin *(red)* in a red blood cell. Simultaneously, carbon dioxide *(orange)* passes from the capillary into the air sac to be exhaled. If these processes are impaired by a lack of hemoglobin or red blood cells, doses of iron and blood transfusions replenish the patient's depleted bloodstream.

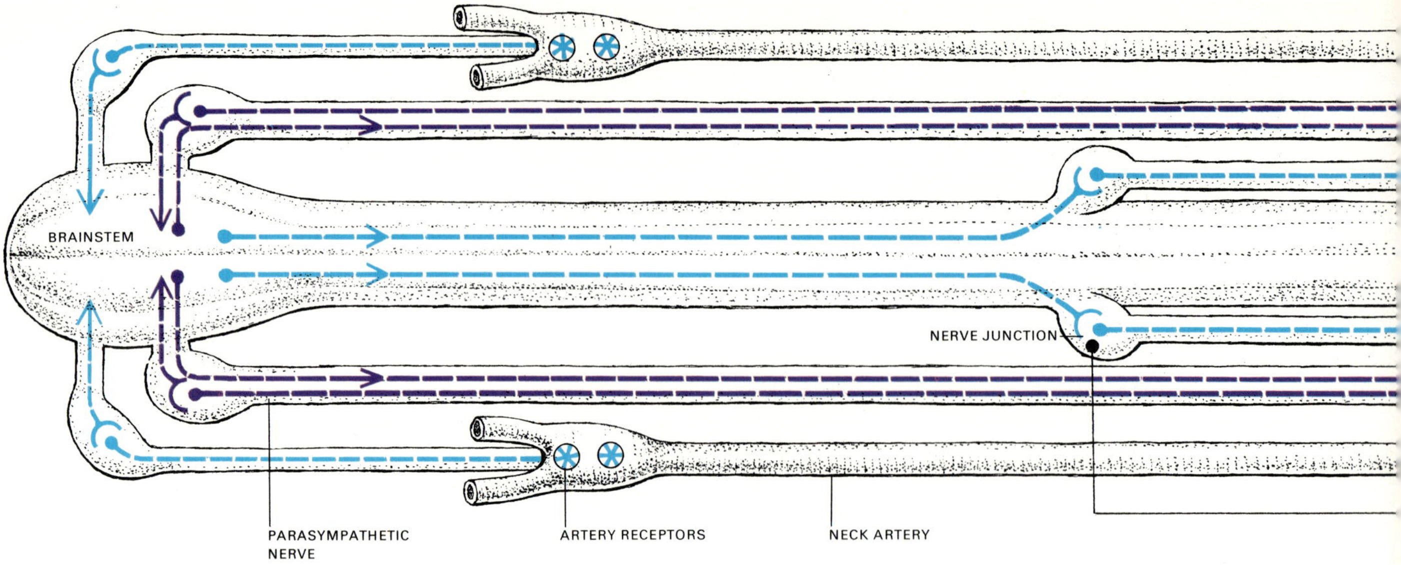

A Pump to Move the Fluids

The body must balance not only the composition of its fluids, but also their constant motion. Blood flows through arteries, veins and capillaries; plasma, the liquid part of the blood, constantly seeps through capillary walls, carrying nutrients to body cells and returning wastes to the bloodstream. All of this motion is powered by the body's pump, the heart, and sustained with the help of drugs when illness strikes. The heart is instructed to pump fast or slowly, powerfully or gently, by means of nerve signals.

Two different sets of nerves send signals to the heart: the sympathetic nerves *(blue lines)*, which speed up the heartbeat; and parasympathetic nerves *(purple lines)*, which slow it. Both sets are part of the autonomic nervous system, so called because it works automatically, without conscious intervention from the brain, to control organs that must operate constantly whether we are thinking about them or not. If we depended on conscious control rather than the autonomic system, the heart would not beat nor the lungs breathe when we were asleep or unconscious.

When the power or the rhythm of the heart is affected by cardiovascular diseases, drugs can be used to regulate the heart's functions. In congestive heart failure, for example, the heart's pumping capacity fails to meet the needs of the body, but the drug digitalis acts directly on heart muscle to increase the force of its contraction. Another drug, quinidine, reduces the muscle's electrical activity, suppressing the signals that cause the erratic heartbeat called an arrhythmia. Epinephrine stimulates the heart's tiny "pacemakers"—the bits of nervelike muscle tissue that spark and regulate the heartbeat—to speed circulation in a patient suffering from shock. And in cases of high blood pressure, circulation can be lowered by drugs that block nerve impulses to the heart, either by reducing the amount of a chemical messenger that stimulates the heart muscle, or by affecting the so-called ganglia junctions within the nerve system itself.

MECHANICS OF A HEARTBEAT

The heart is a powerful muscle normally controlled electrically but affected at several points by drugs *(described in the boxes)*. Ordinarily it is regulated by the brainstem *(opposite)* that coordinates signals from receptors *(left)* in the aorta, and the neck arteries that are attuned to blood pressure. When blood pressure is low or the carbon dioxide level high, the brainstem sends a faster heartbeat signal along the spinal cord via sympathetic nerves *(blue)*; a slower beat is called for over parasympathetic nerves *(purple)*. Normally, the heart begins to contract for a beat when a tissue "node" called the first pacemaker *(red, left)* generates an impulse *(dotted red arrows)* that spreads through the two upper chambers of the heart—the atria—and triggers a second pacemaker. In turn, the second pacemaker transmits the impulse down conductive tissue within the septum separating the two halves of the heart. The impulse spreads *(red arrows)* around the two lower chambers, the ventricles, causing them to contract and thus to pump blood out of the heart.

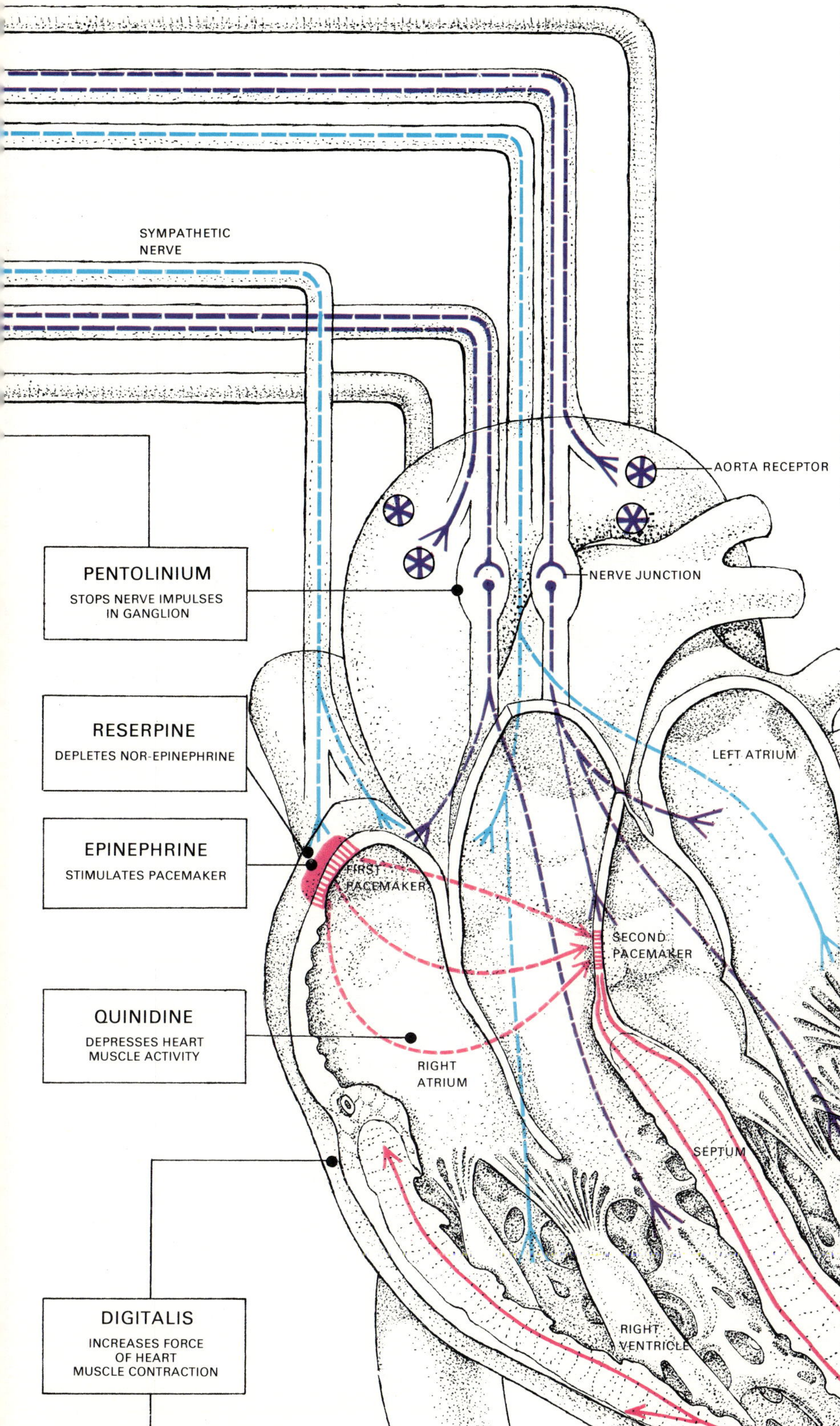

Highs and Lows of Blood Pressure

A number of drugs can be used to control one important factor in maintaining fluid balance: the pressure of the blood in the arteries. If the pressure is too low, only a trickle of fluid may reach the body cells; if pressure is consistently too high the heart may weaken from overwork.

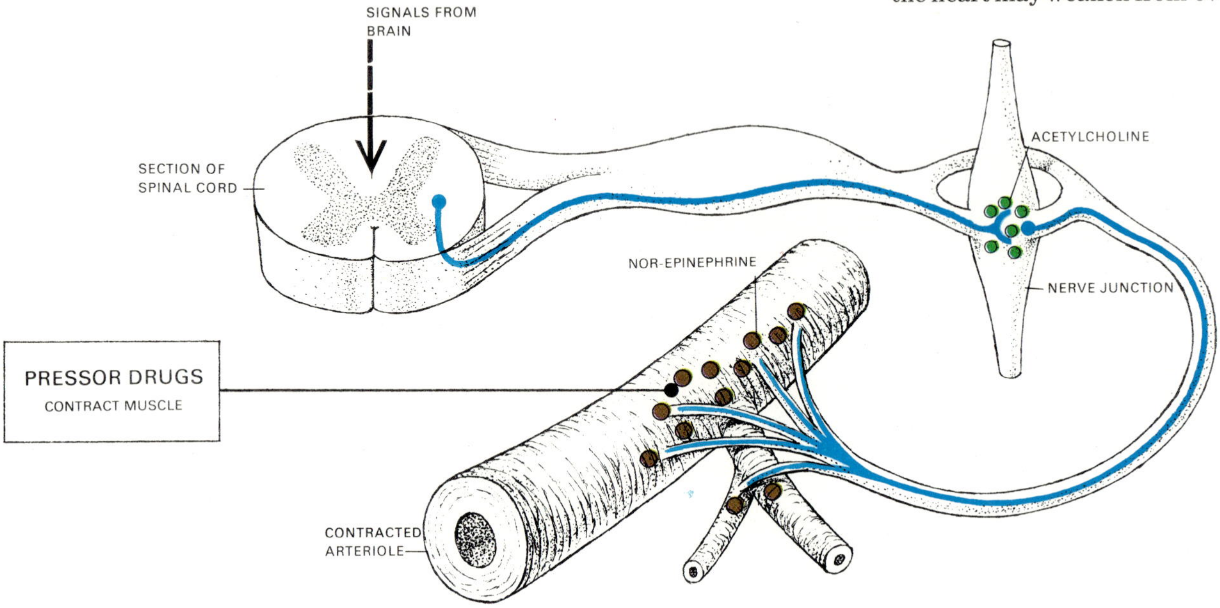

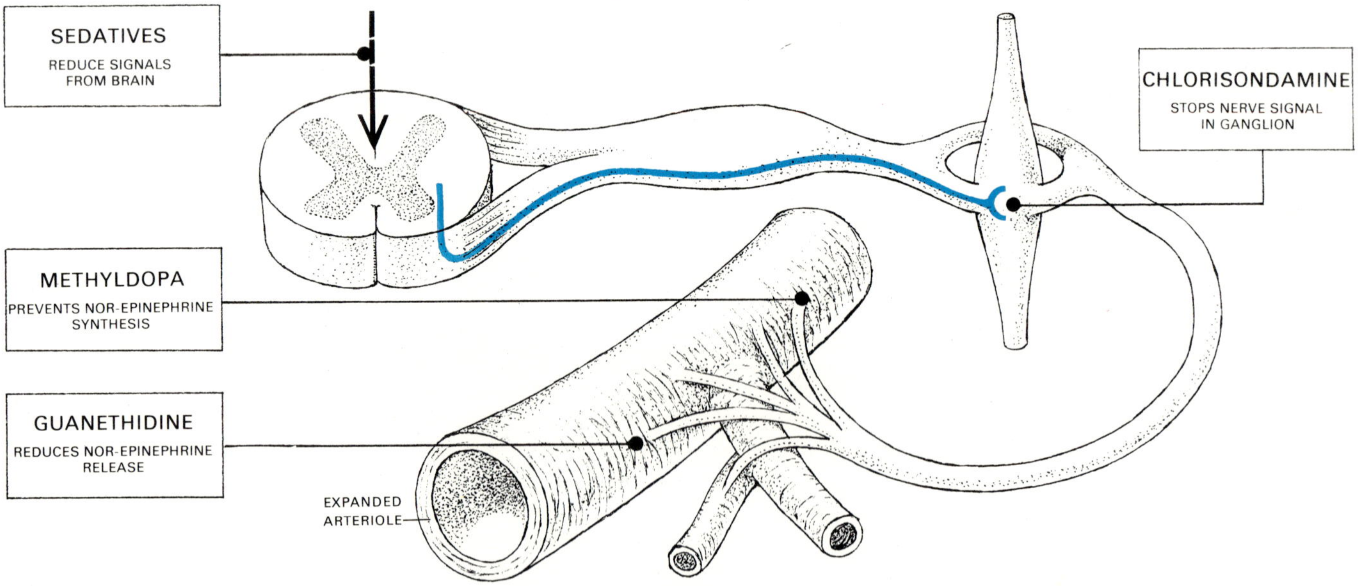

TO CONTRACT AND EXPAND VESSELS

An arteriole contraction *(top)* begins when the brain sends an electrical signal down the spinal cord and along a nerve *(blue line)* to a nerve junction. At the junction the nerve releases a chemical messenger, acetylcholine *(green)*, that stimulates a second nerve *(blue line)* to transmit the signal to the muscular wall of the vessel itself. There, another messenger, the chemical nor-epinephrine *(brown)*, signals the arteriole muscle to contract. If illness causes any of these chemical messengers to fail, "pressor" drugs, such as epinephrine, can be used to signal the contraction directly and thus raise the pressure of the blood. If a decrease of blood pressure is called for, the arterioles can be widened *(bottom)* by a variety of drugs. Sedatives cancel the original contraction signal coming from the brain to the nerves, drugs like guanethidine reduce the amount of messenger released at the nerve endings, and the drug methyldopa prevents the formation of the messenger in nerves.

Both high and low blood pressure can usually be traced to the smallest of the arteries, the arterioles. If the arterioles contract too much or if an excess of fluid is forced through them, the blood pressure soars. On the other hand, if the vessels expand too much or the volume of fluid is abnormally low, the pressure goes down. Ordinarily autonomic nerves and chemical messengers control the arterioles and the amount of fluid. But when these regulators fail, drugs can take over the job of regulating the vessels or can act in other ways to solve circulatory pressure problems.

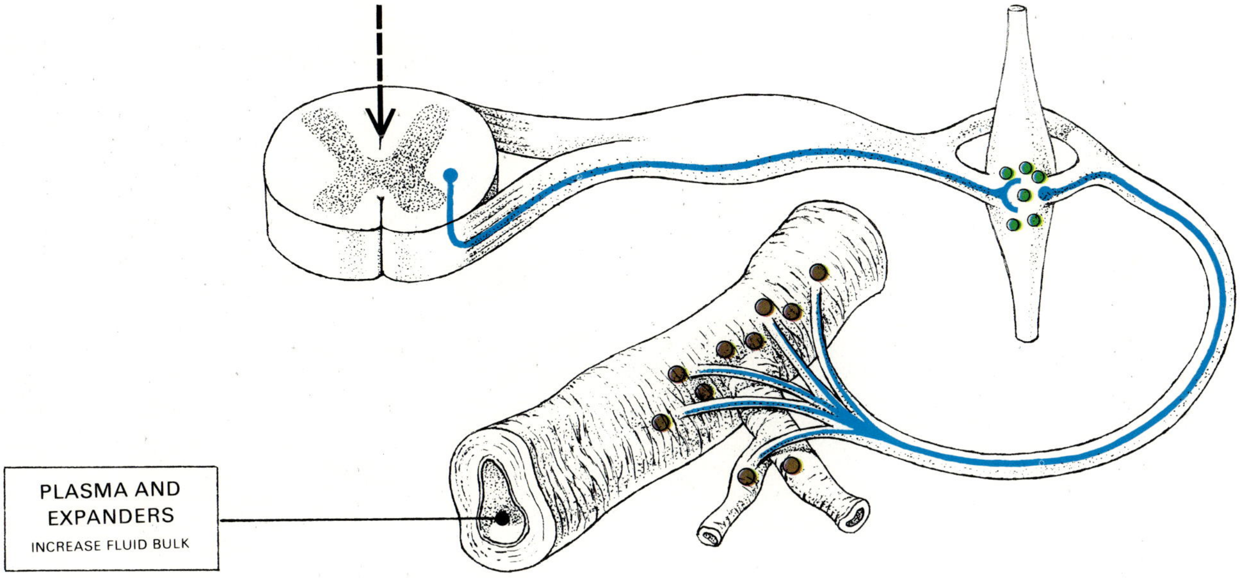

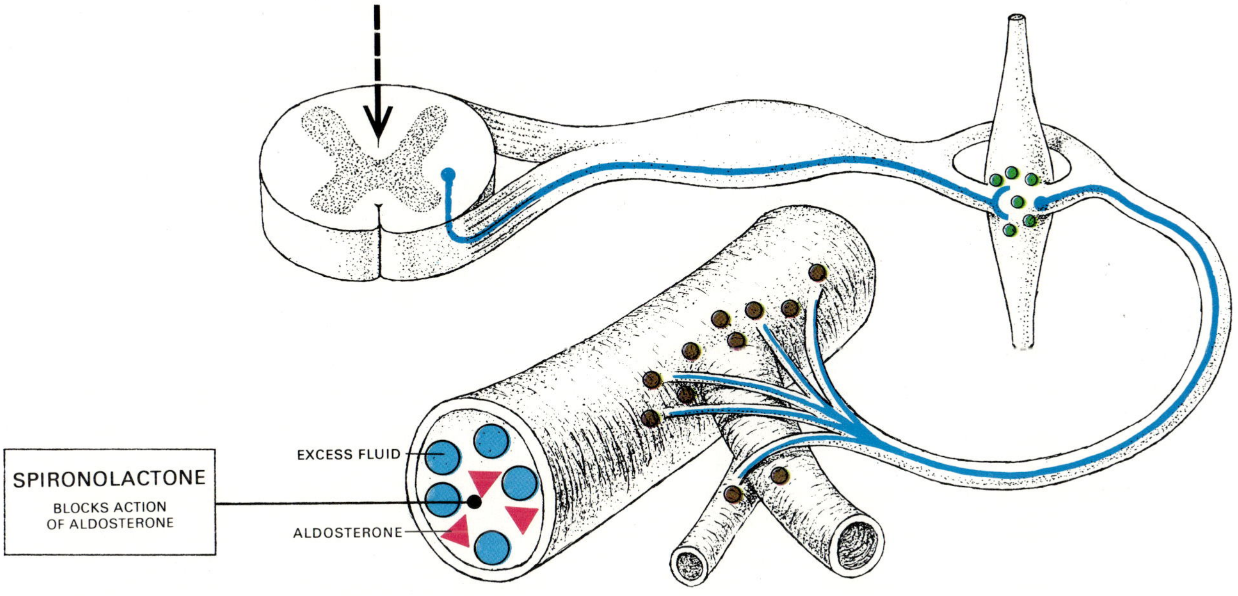

TO INCREASE AND DECREASE FLUID

While some drugs regulate the diameter of the arterioles, others change the amount of fluid within them. If there is too little fluid—the condition called shock *(top)*—the arteriole walls lose tension and become flabby; then, when a nerve *(blue line)* releases nor-epinephrine *(brown)* to make the muscle contract, it cannot. To restore the vessels to their normal diameter, the patient will be given a plasma transfusion or a drug that expands the fluid volume. An overstretched vessel *(bottom)*, however, can be as dangerous as a flabby one. In one form of high blood pressure the vessels swell with excess fluid *(blue circles)* because an oversupply of the hormone aldosterone *(red triangles)* circulates in the bloodstream. The unwanted aldosterone forces the kidneys to return excess salt and water to the blood vessels—but a drug, spironolactone, acts to reduce the effects of aldosterone. In this indirect way, the drug decreases the amount of fluid and lowers the blood pressure.

Fluid Balance in the Kidneys

Drugs help to maintain fluid balance even in the body's excretions—the acid or alkaline wastes that are eliminated by the kidneys. These twin organs get rid of the wastes in the form of urine. Urine actually passes through two stages. At first, it contains not only acids and alkalies, but

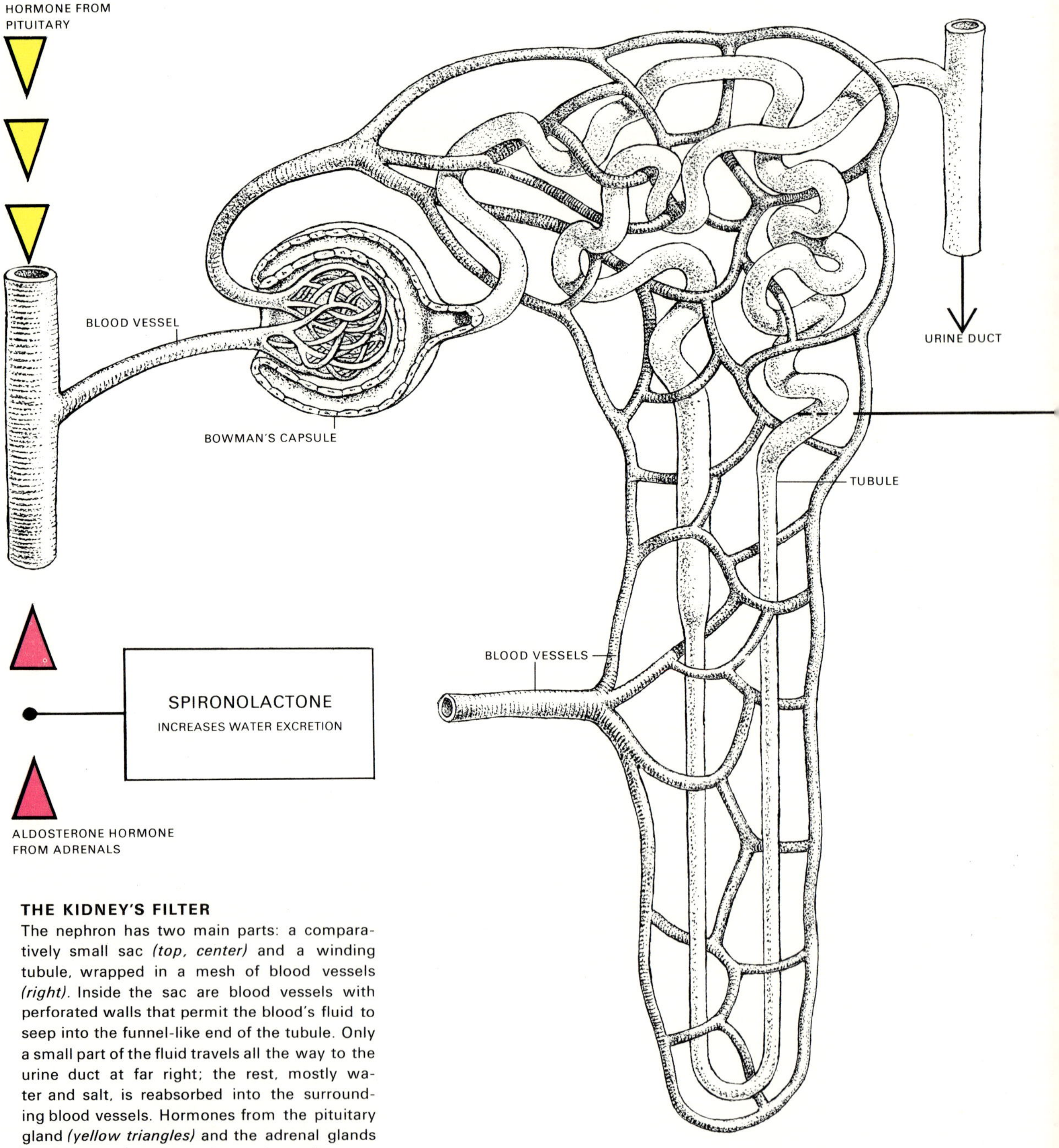

THE KIDNEY'S FILTER

The nephron has two main parts: a comparatively small sac *(top, center)* and a winding tubule, wrapped in a mesh of blood vessels *(right)*. Inside the sac are blood vessels with perforated walls that permit the blood's fluid to seep into the funnel-like end of the tubule. Only a small part of the fluid travels all the way to the urine duct at far right; the rest, mostly water and salt, is reabsorbed into the surrounding blood vessels. Hormones from the pituitary gland *(yellow triangles)* and the adrenal glands *(red triangles)* regulate the reabsorption process. One of them, the adrenal hormone aldosterone, can be blocked by the drug spironolactone if too much salt and water is being reabsorbed.

also important salts and water that the body needs; the kidneys must excrete the wastes, but reabsorb almost all the water and salts.

The kidney performs this juggling act in over a million tiny filters called nephrons *(opposite)*. Blood enters the nephron bearing water, acids, alkalies and salts, and dribbles through a half-inch-long tubule *(cross section below)*. There, most of the salts and water are reclaimed and returned to the blood. The nephrons filter about 180 quarts of water a day; they reclaim all but two of them. In fact, a common kidney problem arises when these hardworking organs work *too* hard. In some diseases, such as heart failure, too much salt and water are reabsorbed into the blood, expanding its volume and bloating the patient's tissues. For this condition, called dropsy, diuretic drugs are used to increase the excretion of salt and water.

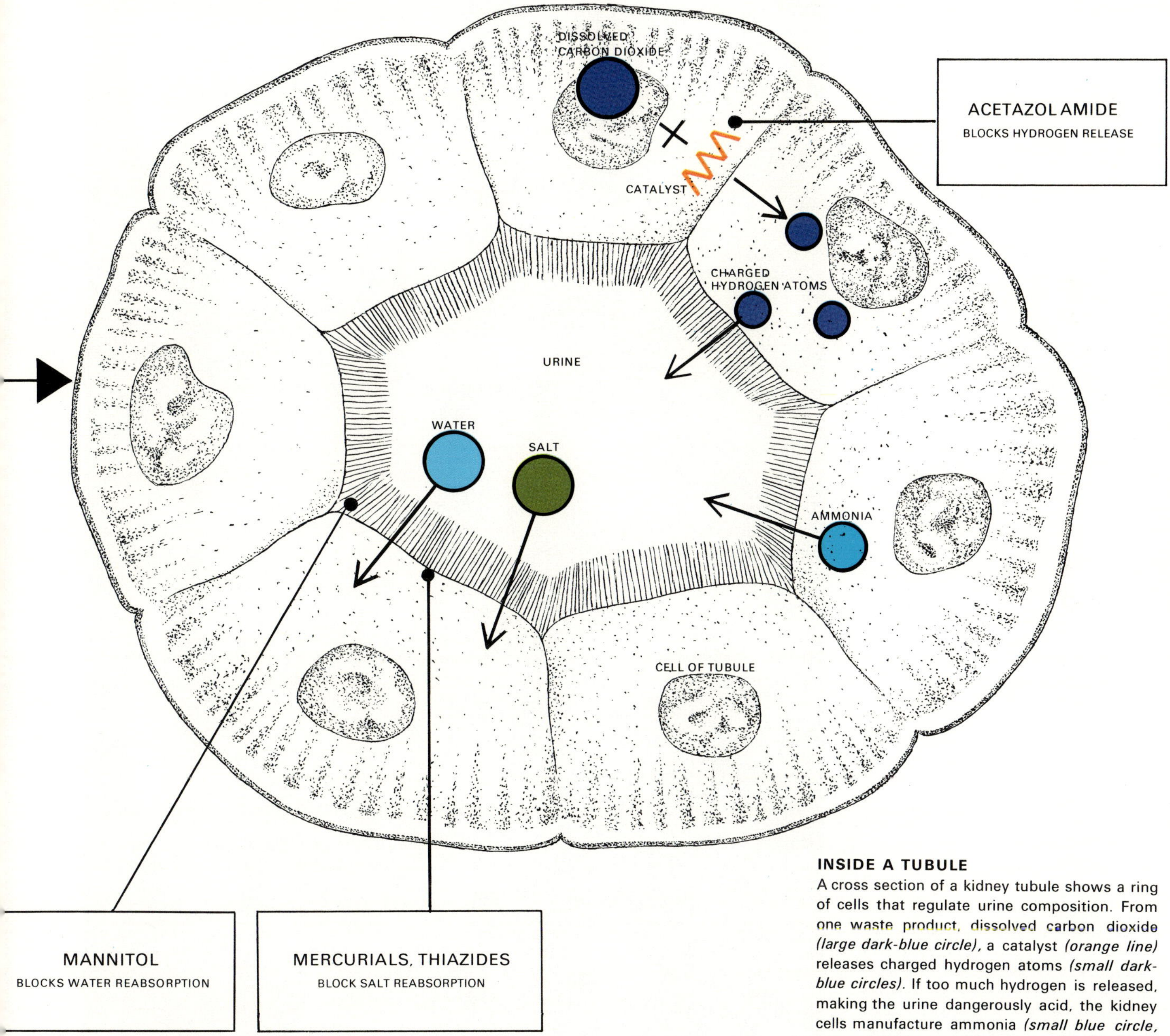

INSIDE A TUBULE
A cross section of a kidney tubule shows a ring of cells that regulate urine composition. From one waste product, dissolved carbon dioxide *(large dark-blue circle)*, a catalyst *(orange line)* releases charged hydrogen atoms *(small dark-blue circles)*. If too much hydrogen is released, making the urine dangerously acid, the kidney cells manufacture ammonia *(small blue circle, lower right)* to neutralize the acidity. The cells also reabsorb salt *(green)* and water *(pale blue, at left)* from the urine. But if too much salt and water are already present, the drugs called diuretics may be used. One, acetazolamide, blocks the hydrogen-releasing catalyst; a number of others stop the reabsorption of salt and water.

5

Battling Deadly Microbes

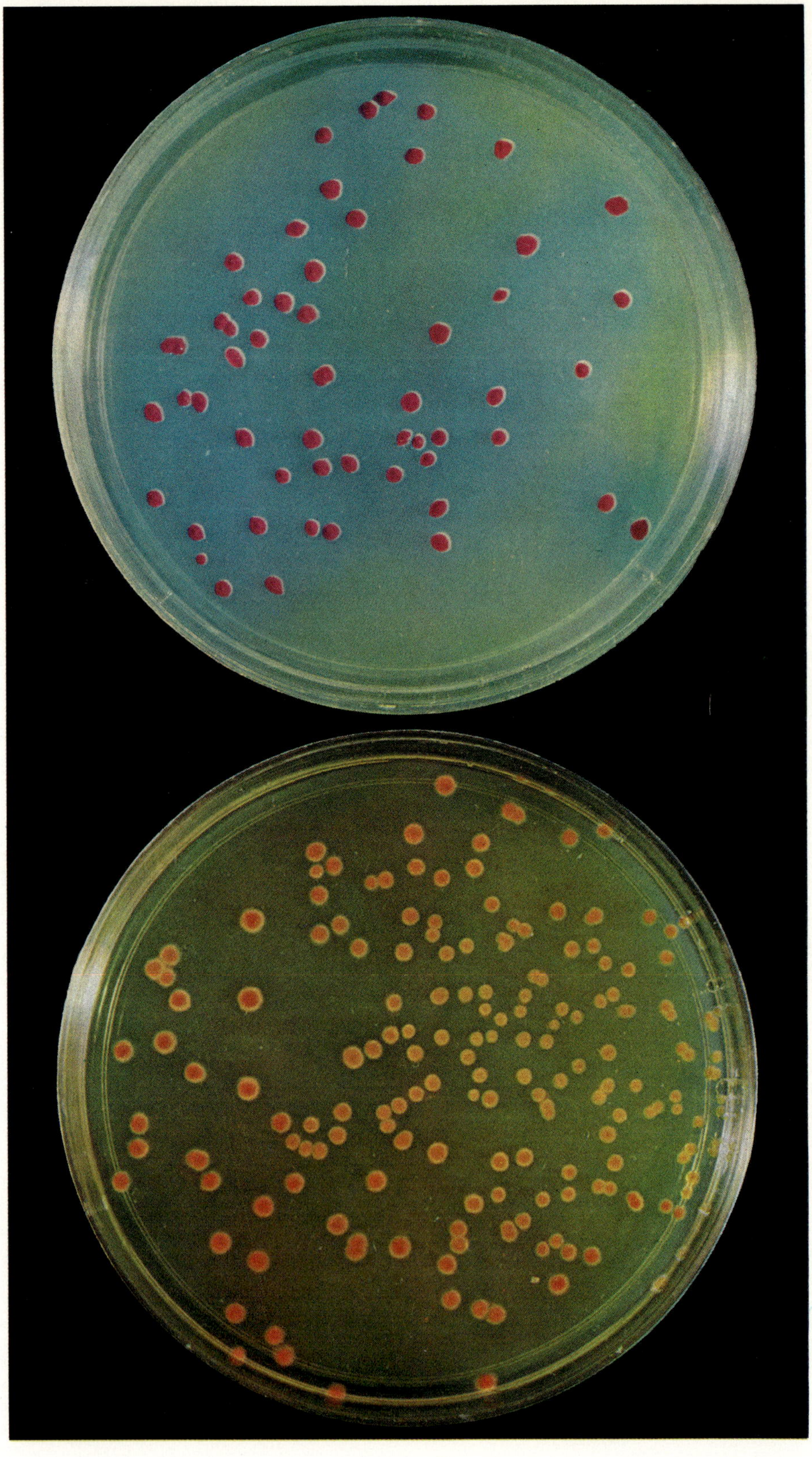

Antibiotics that attack useful bacteria can do harm as well as good. For example, two strains of *Escherichia coli* bacteria—one of which *(bottom)* causes diarrhea—coexist in the intestines. Normally, the harmless strain *(top)* keeps the other in check. But antibiotics may destroy the beneficial germ, permitting the harmful one to proliferate.

IN 1935—not a particularly unhealthy year in this country—infectious diseases such as pneumonia and tuberculosis killed 233,881 Americans. Thirty years later, with a considerably larger population, the death toll from this group of diseases had dropped to 77,963.

These two figures reflect a major triumph of drug science—indeed, its greatest triumph to date. In the treatment of infectious disease, as in no other important branch of medicine, the physician can offer not only relief but also cure. Thanks to modern drugs, the doctor can, more often than not, attack the root causes of infectious disease.

The triumph of the anti-infection drugs is a case study in modern scientific progress. Their discovery, like most scientific discoveries, came about through a combination of inspiration, luck and hard work in solving the problems of basic research. After experiments proved that the drugs worked, barriers remained to their successful use in medicine. The widespread use of these drugs required the solution of a different set of problems—notably, how to produce the drugs in quantity and at a reasonable price. And though scientific genius played a role in discovery and application, the drugs did not spring from the insights of a few towering intellects; dozens of pharmacologists, physiologists and physicians played their parts; so did hundreds of chemists, engineers and technicians. So, for that matter, did a British policeman, a dust mote wafted onto a culture dish of bacteria, and a rotten cantaloupe in a fruit-dealer's bin.

The drugs that resulted from this work include both the antibiotics, such as penicillin and streptomycin, and such other chemicals as quinine and the sulfa drugs. (Vaccines, though they have played an important role in the fight against infectious disease, are not discussed here because they do not themselves combat infection but prevent infection by fortifying the body's natural defenses against it.)

These drugs have not solved all the problems of infectious disease. A whole class of infectious organisms, the viruses—responsible for such diseases as influenza, encephalitis and the common cold—has thus far resisted the triumphant advance of modern pharmaceutical chemistry. Other organisms have shown an unnerving talent for "learning to live with" drugs that once were lethal to them. In the long fight against infectious disease, science has by no means won the war—but it has unquestionably won a series of major battles.

In this war, as in all wars, strategy is based on understanding the nature of the enemy—in this case, parasites. Infectious disease is a special case of parasitism. Victims of body lice, tapeworms and tuberculosis all suffer from the same problem: they are hosts to organisms that they would be better off without. The physician's job is the same in all three cases: to get rid of the parasite without getting rid of the patient.

The job is relatively easy in the cases of the louse and the worm, because these organisms are visible and vulnerable. The larger creatures that infest the human skin can usually be spotted by a casual inspection, and intestinal worms can be detected with little greater difficulty.

Even the earliest civilizations were aware of these organisms and of the role that they played in disease. Thousands of years ago, with only the crudest trial-and-error techniques, men developed drugs to remove such unwanted visitors.

These parasites are vulnerable even to crude drugs because their large size requires the support of correspondingly complex structures and living processes. Each of these relatively big parasites maintains itself by the interplay of a large number of physical and chemical reactions, and a drug that sufficiently disrupts almost any of these reactions can kill the parasite. In the words of the German chemist Gerhard Domagk, one of the great names in the field of anti-infection drugs, "the more highly developed an organism, the greater the number of targets it offers for [chemical] attack." In fact, the whole history of man's war against parasites demonstrates that the bigger they are, the easier they fall.

Pinpointing a tiny target

The germs that cause such diseases as TB are much smaller and tougher targets than either lice or worms. Until the invention of the microscope in the 17th Century, they were completely invisible and indeed unknown. Even after they could be seen, their role in disease was not clarified for some 200 years. At that time, the latter part of the 19th Century, medicine possessed only two major germ killers: quinine for malaria and ipecac for amoebic dysentery, both derived from plant sources. These two were joined by a third in 1910, when the German chemist Paul Ehrlich synthesized the first man-made anti-infection drug, arsphenamine (also called salvarsan and "606"), to treat syphilis.

Significantly, both malaria and amoebic dysentery are caused by protozoa, the largest and most complex of the disease germs, while the organism that causes syphilis is a spirochete, which is smaller and less complex. A successful assault on still smaller and simpler microbes, such as pneumonia bacteria, had to wait for another quarter century.

In retrospect, this long delay seems strange, for hints of the coming victory over bacteria kept cropping up. As early as 1917, researchers noticed that certain synthetic compounds called sulfonamides could destroy bacteria. Unfortunately, this work was not followed up. In 1928, another hint was supplied by one of the most famous accidents in scientific history. A culture dish in the hospital laboratory of a British bacteriologist, Alexander Fleming, was accidentally contaminated with a mold of the genus *Penicillium*. Fleming noticed that bacteria within the area of contamination died off, and concluded that the mold contained a destructive chemical, which he called penicillin. He predicted that pencillin might be useful in fighting disease, but it turned out to be extremely difficult to extract from the mold, and Fleming ("from lack,"

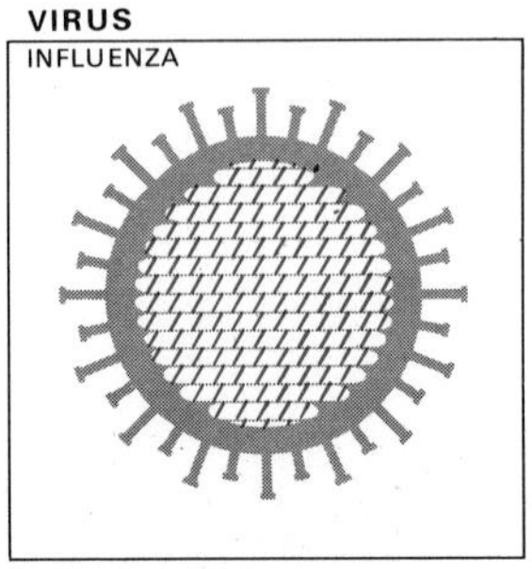

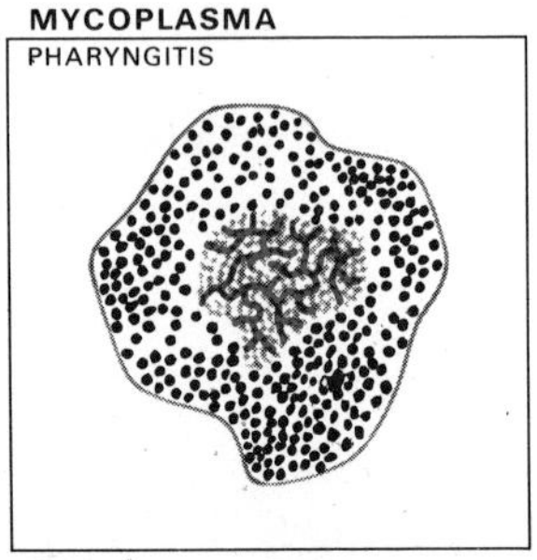

THE TOUGHEST MICROBES for drugs to kill are simple structures like the influenza virus and the mycoplasma that causes pharyngitis, a throat infection. Smallest and simplest of all microbes is the flu virus *(right)*—a strand of protein and genetic material wound up like a ball of twine and covered with protein and fatty material. The prickly surface spines enable the virus to attach itself to the slippery lining of the body's respiratory tract. In the slightly more complex mycoplasma microbe *(far right)* the genetic material is clumped in the protein, which is surrounded by a membrane of triple thickness. Both the mycoplasma and influenza microbes are so simple they ordinarily cannot exist on their own. When they invade body cells, they must rely on the cells for essential life processes; as one result, nearly all drugs that kill viruses and mycoplasma kill the host cells as well.

he later said, "of sufficient chemical assistance") went on to other work.

No lack of chemical assistance hampered the man who was to strike the first effective blow against the bacteria that cause disease. Gerhard Domagk worked for the great German chemical trust, I. G. Farbenindustrie, as the head of its laboratory in pathology. In 1935, after studying the antibacterial effects of a number of dyestuffs, he reported that a recently patented red dye called prontosil could cure mice infected with streptococcus bacteria. Administered to a baby who was dying of "strep" infection, prontosil effected a complete cure.

Domagk's discovery put antibacterial drugs "back on the agenda." So wrote a group of French investigators who followed his lead and discovered that the curative effects of prontosil were actually due to another chemical compound, sulfanilamide, which was formed when the dye was broken down in the body. In scores of laboratories, chemists began tinkering with the sulfanilamide molecule, producing sulfapyridine, sulfadiazine and some 6,000 other "sulfa" drugs. And as the drugs piled up, so did the medical reports on their beneficial effects.

In 1938, the hunt for bacteria-killing drugs took a new turn when an Australian pathologist and a German refugee chemist teamed up at Oxford University for "a systematic investigation of the chemical and biological properties of the antibacterial substances produced by bacteria and moulds." H. W. Florey and Ernst Chain began with the penicillin that Fleming had laid aside in 1929. After working out a way of partially purifying the drug, they were able to confirm Fleming's findings on penicillin's extraordinary ability, even in minute concentrations—one part in 50,000—to kill a variety of bacteria.

A temporary triumph

It was fortunate that penicillin was potent, for it was still fiendishly hard to extract from the mold that made it. By 1940, after two years' labor, the Oxford group had managed to accumulate enough of the crude preparation to treat just five patients. Two died despite the drug. The first successful case was an Oxford policeman dying of bacterial "blood poisoning." The course of his disease was reversed by penicillin—part of which the researchers had salvaged from the urine of other patients who had received the drug—but his life could not be saved. He died when the supply of the drug was exhausted.

This dramatic temporary victory over disease was encouraging but tantalizing, in wartime desperately so because of the need to treat infected battle and bombing wounds. Florey and Chain grew the mold only in small flasks—and it required the contents of 300 flasks to treat a single patient for half a day. Quantity production would have required acres of laboratory glassware—and war-torn Britain, pounded by the

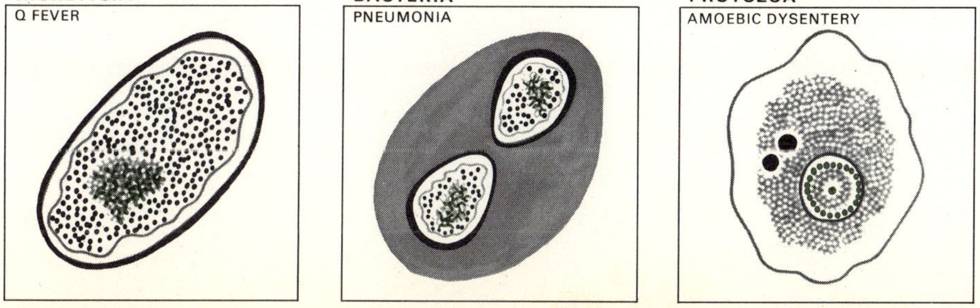

VULNERABLE MICROBES, relatively easy for drugs to kill, are complex organisms usually capable of living independently of body cells. For example, the rickettsia *(far left)*, which causes Q fever, is enclosed by a rigid wall as well as by a membrane. When the microbe invades body cells, some of its life processes go on independently and can be disrupted without killing the body cells. Still more complex is the twin pneumonia bacterium *(center)*, enclosed by rigid walls and carbohydrates. Pneumonia bacteria live outside body cells, and penicillin cuts through the carbohydrates and the cell wall to destroy them. The amoebic dysentery protozoa *(near left)* also lives outside the body cells, taking nourishment, in the stage shown here, from its food vacuoles *(black dots)*. Its highly organized nucleus *(circle containing green genetic dots)* can be disrupted by drugs like emetine.

nightly air raids of the Luftwaffe, was no place for that sort of project.

The Oxford researchers went to America. There they were put in touch with the laboratory of the U.S. Department of Agriculture at Peoria, Illinois. One of the laboratory's specialties was research in fermentation—a biochemical process which, like penicillin production, is carried out by molds. The laboratory's expertise proved invaluable. A new method of feeding the *Penicillium* mold increased the yield of the drug 10 times. Even so, the first 18 months produced only enough penicillin for 200 patients.

The summer of 1943 finally saw the solution of the production problem. Luck played a part, in the form of a new, high-yielding strain of *Penicillium,* which turned up on a moldy cantaloupe in a Peoria market. American ingenuity was also involved; three pharmaceutical companies, working in an almost new area of technology (now called biochemical engineering), developed a way of growing the mold in enormous vats. Over the next 18 months, penicillin production multiplied some 1,500 times. By the end of the war, there was enough for every wounded soldier who needed it, and for every civilian, too.

Penicillin and sulfa drugs dealt a body blow to many infectious diseases. For example, in bacterial pneumonia (one of the commonest infections in industrialized countries) the death rate had been about 30 per cent. Sulfa drugs cut the figure to an estimated 10 per cent and penicillin to 5 per cent or less. Not all such diseases responded to these drugs, but year by year new drugs were developed to widen control over infections. One of the most dramatic of these achievements was that of Selman A. Waksman at Rutgers University.

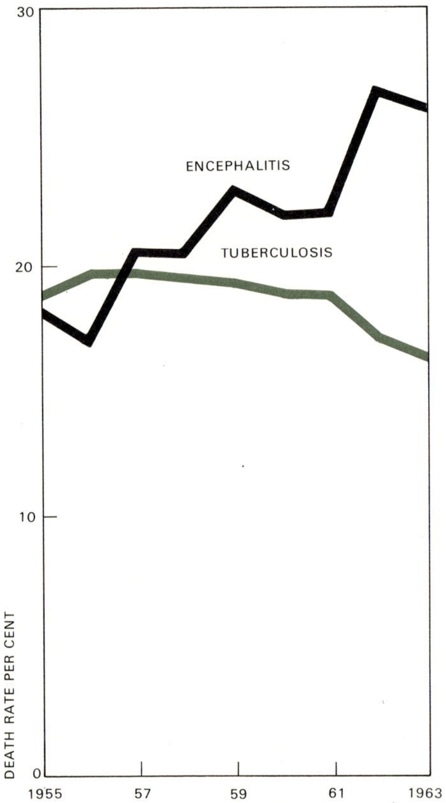

THE IMPORTANCE OF DRUGS is indicated by this graph of the U.S. mortality rate from encephalitis and tuberculosis during the years 1955 to 1963. During this period, research failed to yield drugs that would conquer viruses, and the mortality rate of the viral disease encephalitis climbed steadily. At the same time, the mortality rate from bacterial diseases such as tuberculosis steadily declined, thanks to effective antibacterial drugs like streptomycin and aminosalicylic acid, together with improved health measures.

Lifesavers from the soil

An expert on microorganisms that live in the soil, Waksman had been struck by the fact that the tuberculosis bacillus is rapidly destroyed when buried in soil. To seek the reason, he began hunting in 1939 for an anti-TB substance in cultures of soil bacteria. Like Florey and Chain before him, Waksman was turning the hunt for anti-infection drugs in a new direction. He was looking for a bacteria-killing chemical derived, not from a mold, but from bacteria themselves; in effect, he planned to use bacteria to kill bacteria. After five years, during which he and his associates studied no less than 10,000 species of soil bacteria, he produced the first antituberculosis drug: streptomycin, extracted from a bacteria group called *Streptomyces*. Subsequently, *Streptomyces* contributed half a dozen other drugs, including the tetracycline compounds, the first "broad-spectrum" antibiotics that attack dozens of bacterial species of widely different types.

These great discoveries of the 1940s and 1950s have given physicians a well-stocked arsenal of weapons—but only against bacteria. For the most part, viruses resist treatment by drugs. Vaccines have drastically reduced the incidence of viral diseases, such as smallpox, polio and measles. But these diseases have not been wiped out, and to an unvaccinated individual they are as dangerous as they ever were. And there are neither vaccines nor drugs effective against other important viral diseases, such as encephalitis and the all-too-common cold.

One reason for this lack of progress is that viruses were, until quite recently, almost impossible to study in the laboratory. Another is the fact that they are extremely simple in structure. Even the least complicated bacterium can survive only by carrying on several hundred chemical reactions, any one of which might be blocked or misdirected by a drug. A virus probably makes do with only a dozen reactions or so—and not one of them, as yet, is vulnerable to drugs.

A dangerous placebo

If more people understood that viruses are largely invulnerable to all known drugs, a serious health problem might be avoided. This problem arises from the overuse of antibiotics. Many persons, believing that antibiotics can cure any infection, press their doctors for a dose of penicillin for virus ailments like influenza or the common cold. And some doctors are unwise enough to yield to the pressure, in effect using the antibiotic as a placebo. The patient may or may not benefit from the "placebo effect"—but any benefits he gains may be heavily outweighed by his becoming allergic to the drug, so that future treatment with it will be dangerous, even fatal (some 300 people die each year from allergic reactions to penicillin).

The phenomenon of sensitization does not mean that a drug is toxic. So far as is known, no one has ever been harmed by his first treatment with penicillin; indeed, the fatal dose of the drug is so high that it has never been determined. But for a sizable number of people—perhaps as many as 10 per cent of the population—treatment with penicillin results in an allergy to the drug, so that subsequent doses will produce reactions ranging from intolerable skin rashes to death.

There is another hazard arising from overuse of antibiotics that is especially relevant to the "broad-spectrum" tetracyclines, which can cause harm because they kill some but not all bacteria. Normally, the body contains a great variety of species of bacteria. These bacteria usually hold one another in check; no one species can multiply sufficiently to cause any harm. But if an antibiotic eliminates most of the competing species—and no drug can eliminate all of them—the survivors may undergo explosive multiplication, producing a dangerous "superinfection." This condition is particularly dangerous if the surviving microbes are resistant to anti-infection drugs. Nowadays, this is often the case. Drug resistance has become a problem to physicians, a danger to their patients and a perennial challenge to pharmacologists.

Drug resistance develops because microbes, like people, vary in their response to drugs: some can survive a dose that others rapidly succumb to. Moreover, microbes transmit this resistance to their descendants. Thus drugs that weed out the "unfit" (i.e., vulnerable) strains of microbes subject the species to a kind of unnatural selection. Carried on

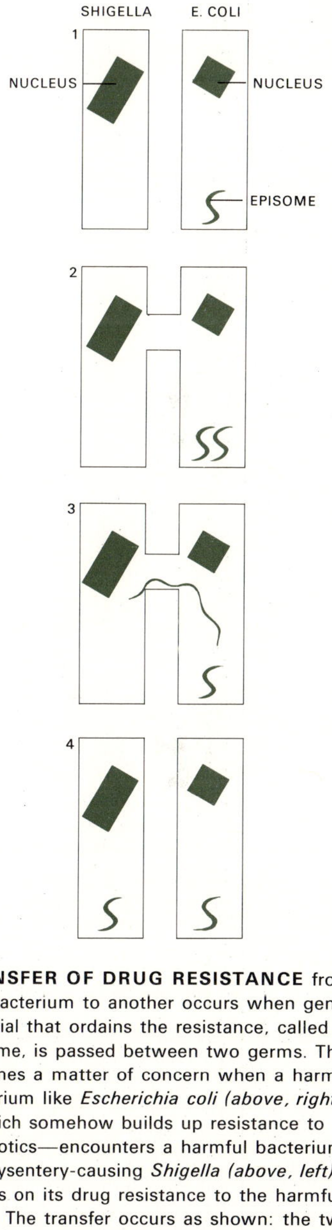

TRANSFER OF DRUG RESISTANCE from one bacterium to another occurs when genetic material that ordains the resistance, called an episome, is passed between two germs. This becomes a matter of concern when a harmless bacterium like *Escherichia coli (above, right)* —which somehow builds up resistance to antibiotics—encounters a harmful bacterium like dysentery-causing *Shigella (above, left)* and passes on its drug resistance to the harmful germ. The transfer occurs as shown: the two bacteria, only one of which has an episome, meet (1) and a passageway apparently forms between them (2); the episome duplicates and crosses the passageway (3), endowing the *Shigella* with resistance to antibiotics (4).

over several generations (a generation in microbes may last less than an hour) this evolutionary process may produce strains that cannot be affected by any medically practicable doses of the drug. The use of streptomycin, in fact, has produced strains of harmful bacteria that literally cannot live *without* it.

In the unending war between drug makers and microbes, the invention of an effective drug is only one small victory; the microbe always strikes back, somehow, so that total conquest of an infectious disease remains tantalizingly out of reach. Witness the case of malaria, which by rights should be well under control. It is not.

Malaria has been afflicting man with its violent cyclical chills and fever for as long as we have any record, and almost certainly long before records were made. Closely related species of the parasite infect both men and apes, and the common ancestor of these strains is thought to have plagued the common ancestor of the higher primates. The disease was formerly widespread in nearly all the moist tropical and temperate areas of the world, and even today threatens nearly a billion people. Though its commonest forms are seldom directly fatal, they are grievously debilitating; in the poverty-stricken countries where they are endemic, the disease drains off an enormous amount of human energy that could otherwise go toward improving the standard of living.

AN ANTIMALARIA STAMP, issued by the West African republic of Sierra Leone in 1962, commemorated an international campaign to wipe out the infectious disease. Conceived by the World Health Organization, the campaign was aimed mainly at the malaria-spreading *Anopheles* mosquito, depicted on the stamp under a globe bearing the Health Organization's symbol. Success was striking at first—malaria mortality dropped 50 per cent in 10 years—but progress later slowed, partly because both mosquito and disease organism developed resistance to the drugs used against them.

"Miraculous results in Lima"

The first chemical blow against malaria was probably struck by some anonymous but sharp-witted Peruvian Indian medicine man, who discovered that the powdered bark of the cinchona tree could sometimes put a fever-ridden warrior on his feet. Certainly by about 1630 the Spanish conquerors of Peru knew of the bark's effects ("it has," wrote a Spanish monk in 1633, "produced miraculous results in Lima").

By the end of the 17th Century, the drug—variously called Peruvian Bark, Jesuit Powder or Cinchona—was in fairly general use as a cure for and a preventive against the violent periodic fevers that were eventually recognized as symptoms of malaria. (It was also used for other types of fevers, which it, like aspirin, can relieve though not cure.) Unfortunately, the bark—or, more specifically, its active principle, quinine—was sometimes ineffective, often toxic and invariably expensive. But for some 300 years quinine remained the only useful antimalarial drug.

During the years between the two World Wars, several synthetic antimalarials were developed, chiefly by German chemists, spurred by their country's lack of quinine during World War I. Ironically, the chief beneficiaries of this research were not the Germans but Allied troops in World War II. Hundreds of thousands of them were dosed with the synthetic drug quinacrine (Atabrine), first prepared in Germany from a derivative of coal tar. (Quinacrine—like quinine itself—can both cure malaria and, if taken regularly, prevent its symptoms.) But quinacrine did not wipe out malaria. Of the Allied troops who invaded Sicily during the war, more were hospitalized with malaria than with battle wounds.

Allied researchers set up a large-scale program for turning up newer and even better antimalarial drugs, in the course of which they screened more than 18,000 compounds. Among the discoveries was chloroquine, whose molecule resembles those of quinine and quinacrine. Soon after the war it became the standard drug for almost all types of malaria.

A drug to kill a disease carrier

Meanwhile, a quite different drug, the potent insecticide DDT, had opened up what seemed to be an even more effective means of abolishing the disease: that is, wiping out the mosquitoes that transmit the malaria parasite, rather than attacking the parasite after it has entered the body. In the United States, DDT and chloroquine together nearly eradicated malaria (as late as 1935, it had attacked some 100,000 Americans annually). In 1955, with similar successes chalked up in the U.S.S.R. and other European countries, the World Health Organization started a world-wide program to conquer malaria.

The results have been impressive. In scarcely more than a decade, the annual toll of a quarter of a billion malaria cases had been cut by 44 per cent; the annual death toll of some two million had been chopped in half. The "side effects" of the program have been equally extraordinary. In parts of Cambodia, land values in formerly malarial areas have doubled now that it is relatively safe to work there; in Ceylon, rice cultivation is up tenfold as a result of the elimination of malaria.

But progress is slowing down. None of the malaria drugs are as effective as they once were. Mosquitoes are rapidly becoming drug resistant: more than a quarter of the mosquito species that transmit malaria from man to man can now withstand DDT—and most other available insecticides as well.

Even worse, the malaria parasite is showing itself quite as adaptable as the mosquito, its insect partner in disease. In 1960, two American geologists working in South America came down with a malaria that proved to be unaffected by chloroquine. At first, the experts did not believe it—but before long, similar resistant strains of malaria microbes had turned up on the other side of the world, in Thailand, Cambodia and Malaya. And in the fall of 1965, American troops in Vietnam began coming down by the hundreds with chloroquine-resistant malaria. As one expert put it, "the world's number one anti-malaria drug had been knocked out of the box."

What is true of malaria seems to be true of most other infectious diseases. Even with adequate supplies of drugs, and adequate medical facilities for administering them—which only a minority of the world's people possess—man's unwanted microbial guests can at best be contained, not eradicated. Total victory over infection, if it can be achieved at all, will require a greater scientific breakthrough than that embodied in the work of Fleming, Domagk and Waksman. The microbes of disease have been on earth far longer than man and, despite all our science and skill, they promise to be with us for quite a while to come.

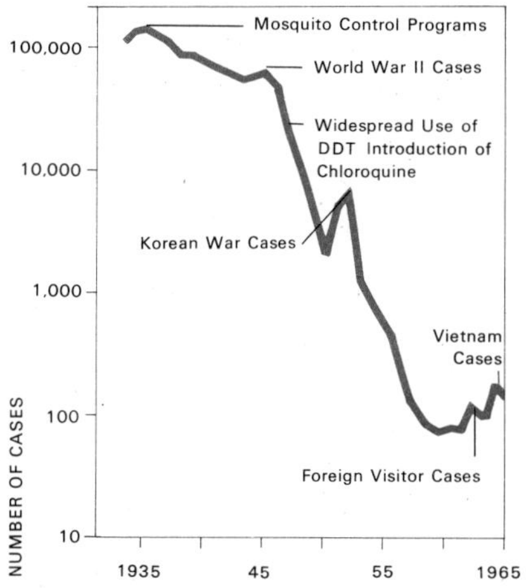

THE UNEVEN DECLINE OF MALARIA, which doggedly resists total eradication, is shown in this graph. In the early 1930s, when more than 100,000 cases of malaria were reported in the U.S. annually, mosquito control programs resulted in a modest decrease. Then returning World War II veterans brought in additional cases, causing the graph to rise slightly. After the war new drugs—notably chloroquine and the insecticide DDT—produced a sharp drop. This progress, in turn, was interrupted by the return of Korean War veterans with malaria. Later, the decline resumed—to be reversed again in the 1960s by an influx of foreign visitors and Vietnam veterans.

When Natural Defenses Fail . . .

Every moment of every day the human body is attacked by germs—viruses, bacteria and other microbes that can trigger infections as trivial as a cold or as dangerous as meningitis. Yet nearly every invasion is repelled by the body's defenders, sometimes working alone, sometimes reinforced by drugs.

How this defense system operates is only now being explained. The findings of immunologists like the Nobel Prize winner Sir Macfarlane Burnet of the Australian Academy of Science *(opposite)* have shown that one basic mechanism supports all defensive action. It is the human body's ability, developed over millions of years of evolution, to preserve its own individual quality—the special genetic characteristics that make its cells uniquely its own. The body automatically recognizes the alien quality of genetically different cells, such as disease germs, and tries to protect itself against them by placing physical obstacles, such as skin, and antiseptic secretions, such as tears and mucus, in their way. If germs pass these barriers, the body calls upon special cells and chemicals to destroy them. But even these defenses may fail. Then drugs are needed, either to augment the body's own protective powers or to provide weapons that the body does not possess.

AN ALIEN MONSTER REJECTED
The chimera of Greek myth, a freakish blend of lion, goat, serpent *(opposite)* could not normally be encountered among humans. For, as immunologist Sir Macfarlane Burnet explains, the human body refuses to be a chimeric mixture; it rejects alien species, such as germs that invade it, destroying them with scavenger cells *(white)* and chemicals *(colored circles)*.

DRUGS AGAINST ACNE

The figure at left symbolizes how drugs help repair damage caused by acne, as shown in the skin section at center. Standing alongside is Marion B. Sulzberger of the U.S. Army Medical Research Unit in San Francisco, who pioneered acne studies. The skin's outer layer is represented by the light pink areas, which overlie a layer of pigment *(orange)*. In the darker pink layer at the left are a skin-cooling sweat gland *(blue line)* and black hairs. In healthy skin *(bottom hair)* a shielding lubricant called sebum flows up the hair shaft from sebaceous glands *(gray-green)*. In acne *(middle and top hairs)*, these glands enlarge and the outer skin layer thickens, blocking the sebum. A blackhead—hardened sebum—forms at the surface, and bacteria *(purple ovals)* cause infection *(red)*. To treat severe cases, Sulzberger applies drugs *(white symbol, top right)* that unclog the sebum outlet, and he gives antibiotic pills *(top left)* to kill bacteria.

The Skin: Shield against Germs

The body's first line of defense is its skin—17 square feet of wrapping, no more than 3/16 inch thick, that acts as a physical barrier to mechanical injury and as a shield against germs.

The skin is actually a single organ, but it performs a variety of functions. It filters out dangerous ultraviolet rays from the sun, prevents internal tissues from drying out in the air or getting soggy in the rain, cools the body by evaporation from the sweat glands, and eliminates waste products through the pores. It is also a factory, producing vital body chemicals: its cells help make vitamins and exude a protective oil called sebum.

At the nose, mouth and anus skin turns inward to become a modified "inner" skin that lines the respiratory and digestive tracts. There, its cells produce another protective secretion, mucus, that contains an antiseptic, lysozyme, also present in tears. However, the skin's own defensive materials can fail and then drugs are needed.

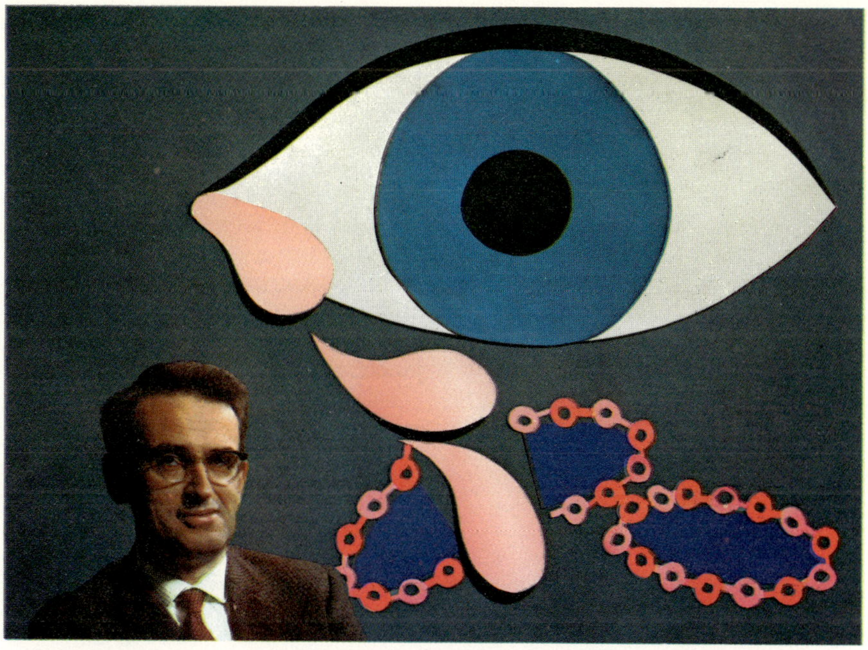

THE BODY'S OWN ANTISEPTIC

The germ-killing qualities of the liquids secreted by the eyes and the bronchial tubes are due to a natural antiseptic, lysozyme. Britain's D. C. Phillips *(above)*, A. X. North and C. F. Blake have found how lysozyme dissolves bacteria *(above, purple)* despite their protective walls made of two types of sugar (represented by two shades of pink rings). Lysozyme breaks chemical bonds between the sugars and destroys the cell walls. Tear ducts surrounding each eye supply lysozyme to protect these organs. In a bronchial tube *(cross section below)*, antiseptic is released by mucus cells *(yellow)* and circulated by hairs on the bronchial cells *(pink with black nuclei)*. If bronchial infection occurs despite the lysozyme, the resulting cough can be controlled with dextromethorphan, tested by Hylan Bickerman *(below, center)* of Columbia University.

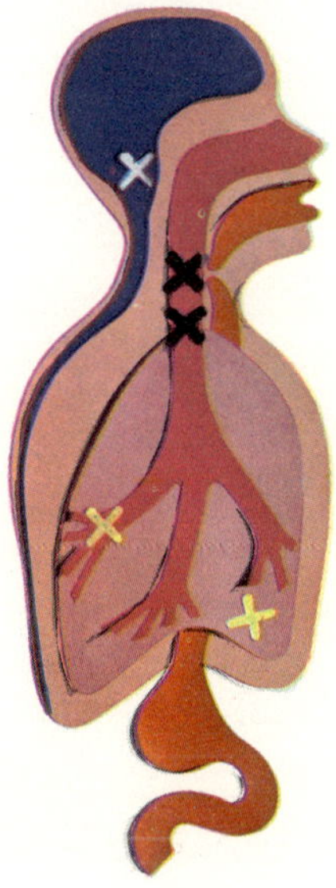

REMEDIES FOR COUGHS

Drugs that have been developed to control coughs resulting from infection of the bronchial tubes act in the three areas shown above. Some opiates prevent the brain's "coughing center" *(white cross)* from stimulating a cough. Other sedatives keep the nerves in the lungs and bronchial muscles *(yellow crosses)* from alerting the coughing center. Expectorants *(black crosses)* stimulate the flow of soothing fluids and mucus that fights infection in the upper respiratory area.

Chemical Defense against Viruses

Despite the skin barrier, some invading germs do enter the body. Then the inner defenses take over. The fastest to mobilize is an antivirus chemical called interferon, which is released by the tissue cells within an hour after a virus invasion.

Interferon acts indirectly, taking advantage of a quirk in virus reproduction. An invading virus cannot multiply until it enters a body cell, where it can safely shed its outer jacket, thus freeing the genetic molecules inside. Then the molecules reproduce so wildly—up to 10,000 times in seven hours—that they seize control of the infected cell. They force the cell to make jackets for the newly reproduced virus molecules, which then become ready to attack other cells in the body.

When viruses are inside cells, they are safe from most direct drug action, for drugs powerful enough to kill the virus generally kill the cells. Interferon, released by the infected cell, does not protect that cell, but prompts defensive action by nearby cells; it stimulates the adjacent cells to produce a protein that prevents virus molecules from reproducing and spreading infection. Scientists now hope to boost interferon production artificially with drugs such as statolon (described below), which has shown promise in tests on animals.

STATOLON'S STIMULATION

Experiments by Samuel Baron *(above)* of the U.S. National Institutes of Health show how the drug statolon can stimulate the production of virus-blocking interferon in animals. In the panel at left is a mouse infected with a large dose of encephalomyocarditis virus, represented as a red ring and orange spiral in its brain. The mouse responds to the infection by making interferon *(purple chain)* and protective protein *(green)*—but not enough of either to save it from death. In contrast, a second mouse *(center)* is saved if its tail is injected with statolon. The statolon injection stimulates this mouse to produce interferon and protein *(right)* quickly—so soon that it can fight off a virus attack even when infected with an amount of the virus that would prove fatal to its littermate. Statolon has not yet been tested on humans, but the principles that make it work on animals hold out hope that they can apply equally well to people.

INTERFERON'S INTERFERENCE

The late Alick Isaacs *(above)* of Britain, discoverer of the antivirus agent interferon, explained how it acts on human cells *(yellow, with light blue nuclei)*. Starting at bottom: (1) the left-hand cell is invaded by a virus, shown as a circular jacket of protein *(red)* enclosing a spiral of genetic molecules *(orange)*; (2) the virus sheds its protein jacket, thus releasing its genetic matter, which reproduces. Immediately, the infected cell begins to create interferon *(purple chain)*, which leaves the damaged cell and surrounds an uninfected neighbor; (3) stimulated by interferon, the neighbor cell manufactures a protein *(green chain)* that prevents viruses from reproducing inside it; (4) the combination of interferon and protective protein has blocked the multiplication of viruses inside the neighbor cell. But the unprotected cell, forced by the virus to manufacture jackets for viral progeny, has burst, releasing the new viruses it has clothed.

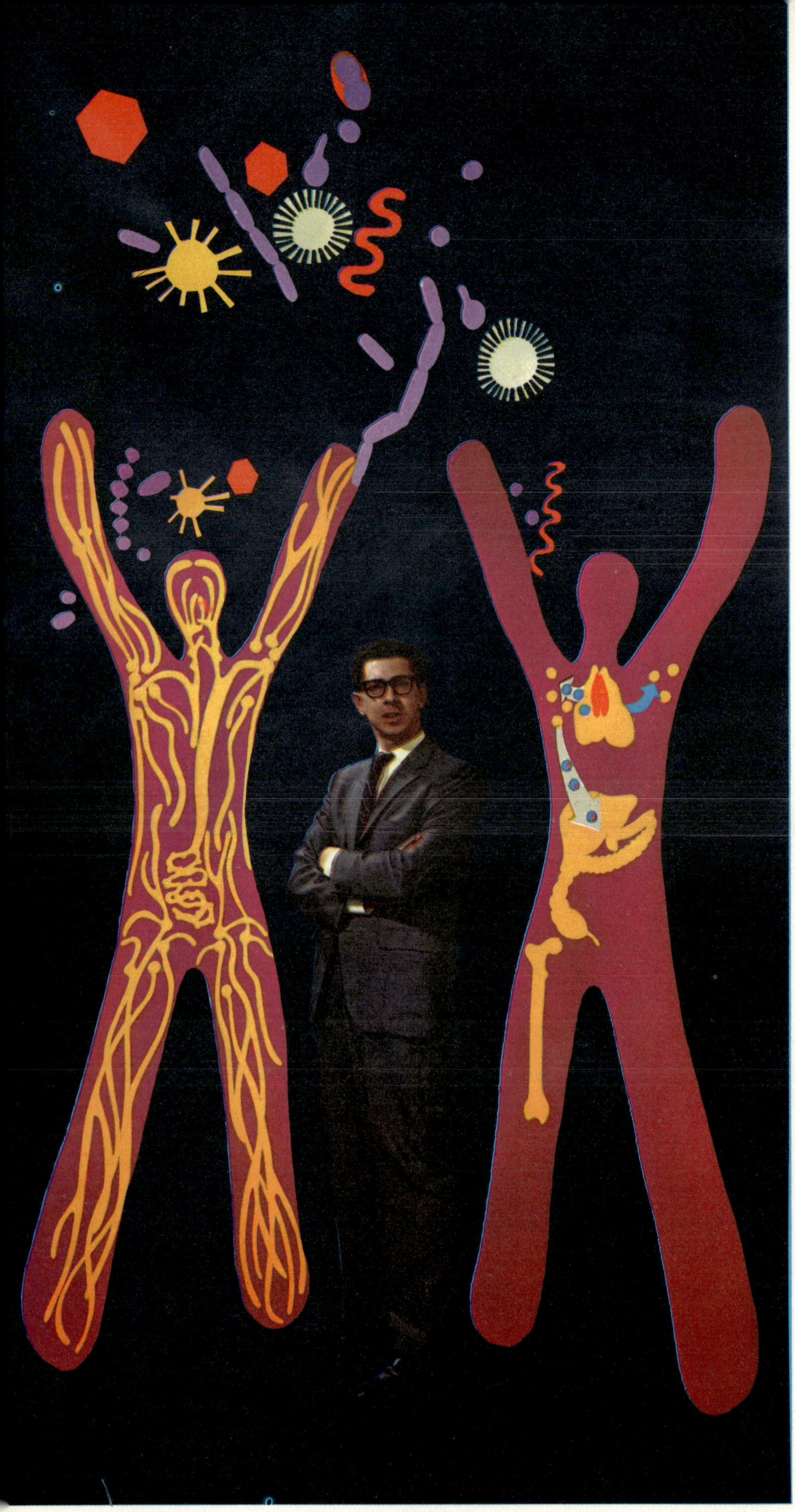

A NEW ROLE FOR THE THYMUS

British immunologist Jacques Miller *(left)* has explained the thymus' function. In the figure to his left is the lymph vessel network that drains off germs. To his right are regions rich in defense cells: bone marrow, abdominal organs, lymph nodes and the thymus. This gland is large in childhood *(yellow)*, when it supplies special cells *(white arrow)* and a hormone *(blue arrow)* that later stimulates the cells to defensive action. In adult life, the thymus contracts *(red)*.

NEWFOUND CAUSE OF FEVER

Barry Wood *(opposite)* of Johns Hopkins University has demonstrated that infectious fevers start when phagocytes—the white blood cells with the stringy black nuclei—engulf bacteria *(purple and gray)*. Phagocytes secrete a chemical *(red drops)* that enters lymph vessels *(yellow, far right)*. The chemical resets the brain thermostat *(pale pink, far right)* to raise the body temperature, an action that can be offset by aspirin *(the white molecular symbol)*.

White Cells Enter the Fray

If the body's frontline defense is overcome, allowing germs to establish a beachhead in body tissues, infection sets in. The infected area becomes inflamed and swollen as blood vessels expand to bring up blood-borne reserve troops. These defenders are white scavenger cells called phagocytes, which squirm out through the blood vessel's walls to engulf and digest microbes in the surrounding tissue. As the phagocytes counterattack the invaders, they release a chemical that causes fever. Fever seems to aid the body's defense forces, but how it does so is unknown—as is the mechanism by which ordinary aspirin, that common and reliable drug, reduces fever.

The debris of dead microbes and phagocytes is drained away by the body's intricate network of lymph vessels. Other parts of the lymphatic system—the tonsils in the throat and the thymus gland beneath the breastbone—were once thought to be useless. Now it is known that the tonsils are especially rich in disease-fighting phagocytes, and that during childhood the thymus manufactures special cells that later will develop into defenders against infections.

SAPPING A WORM'S ENERGY
The panels behind Dr. Ernest Bueding of Johns Hopkins, an authority on diseases caused by worms, show how drugs *(white symbols)* damage these parasites *(green)*. At the top of the left panel a cell *(pink)* of a whipworm absorbs glucose *(blue drops)* and turns it into energy *(yellow streaks)* with its metabolic machinery *(gray)*. The second cell is being treated with cyanide dye. This bars glucose and makes the cell use up reserve nutrients *(blue dots)*. At top of the central panel, dichlorophen permits glucose to enter a tapeworm's cell, but it scissors off a coupling essential to energy production. At bottom of the panel an antimony drug acts like a monkey wrench to upset the metabolism of a fluke's cell. The panel at upper right shows a roundworm's muscle *(pink and brown)*. A nerve ending *(gray, with yellow insulation)* normally releases acetylcholine *(red dots)* to activate the muscle. Mecamylamine and piperazine drugs block this action, thus paralyzing the worm.

Drugs to the Rescue

The germs of some infections may thrive in spite of all-out efforts by the body's defenders. Though the white blood corpuscles do valiant work in relieving infection, they cannot grasp and dissolve all the bacteria of certain strains, such as those that cause pneumonia and tuberculosis. And phagocytes have little effect upon large parasites, the infective agents of the major diseases that trouble the world today: malaria attacks nearly a billion people, and worm infestations even more.

To fight infections, doctors depend upon drugs such as the sulfonamides, whose application to medicine in the year 1935 marked the dawn of mod-

CRACKING A WALL
Penicillin demolishes bacteria *(purple)* whose cell walls consist of sugar joined to sugarlike molecules *(pale blue and lavender)*. Jack Strominger of the University of Wisconsin has found that these sugars are held together by connecting links *(aqua Z-shapes)* manufactured in a membrane *(pink)* inside the cell wall. The drug *(white symbol)* halts this manufacture, and the wall bursts *(right)*.

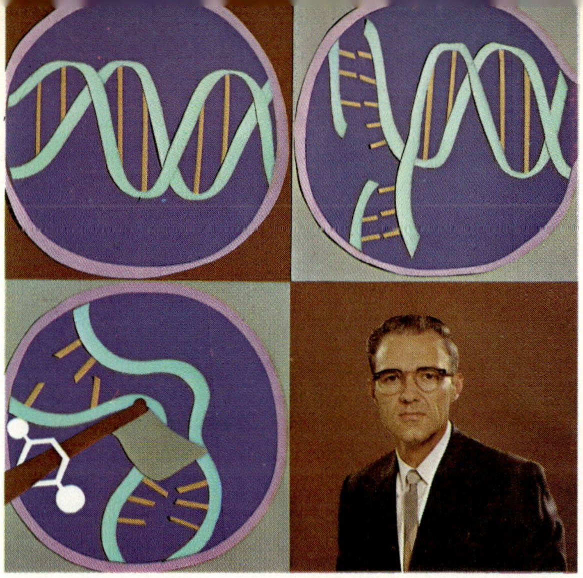

SPLITTING A SPIRAL
A bacterium's genetic material resembles a spiraling rope ladder *(top left)* with rungs that separate when the germ reproduces *(top right)*. Gene Brown of M.I.T. showed how sulfa drugs *(white symbol, bottom left)* put an ax to the spiral by blocking the germ's production of folic acid, a chemical necessary for the formation of new rungs. Unable to reproduce, the germ soon dies off.

DISTORTING A CODE
Germs build proteins according to a genetic "code," represented by triplet combination of four letters H, G, D and O in a specific order *(top row)*. Protein components *(colored rectangles)* link up in order by the code—G with H, D with O *(bottom row)*. Dr. Luigi Gorini of Harvard has demonstrated that streptomycin *(white symbol, at right)* forces germs to transpose the code's order as if seen through the wrong glasses, depriving their cells of needed proteins.

BLOCKING A PROCESS
The manufacture of the rungs in a germ's genetic "ladder" can be compared to the making of a wooden rung: from tree to log, plank, board and rung. Sulfa drugs disrupt first stage, as shown by the white molecule acting on a bacterium *(purple and lavender)* between tree and log. Pyrimethamine, studied by G. H. Hitchings of Wellcome Research Laboratories, acts at second stage. It attacks the malaria parasite *(purple and pink)* between log and board.

ern drug science. In the 1940s the arsenal of drugs was enormously expanded when scientists learned how to make bacteria-killing chemicals from molds, and the age of antibiotics arrived.

At first, scientists did not know how these drugs kill germs. Then in 1940 the British biochemist D. D. Woods discovered that all the sulfa drugs work against bacteria by blocking folic acid, a vitamin the germs need to make their genetic molecules. More recently, the action of some antibiotics has been found to be extremely diverse and ingenious. A sampling of their masterful attacks is visualized in the backdrops above.

Antibodies That Cinch the Victory

Drugs can kill some germs, but ultimately the battle against infection is won by the body itself. After an infection has set in, the body calls into action two extraordinary chemical defenders called antibody and complement. Their role was first accurately analyzed between 1928 and 1950 by Michael Heidelberger of New York University *(opposite)*, who with F. E. Kendall and Elvin Kabat determined the chemical nature of the antibody and demonstrated the existence of the complement—so called because it aids or complements the action of an antibody.

The antibodies offer a more precise defense against infection than the interferon that blocks virus reproduction *(page 106)*. While interferon acts against most viruses, an antibody effective against one type of germ will not act against another type. Each antibody is tailored to interlock with and neutralize a specific molecule of a germ. This unique

molecule, called an antigen, is frequently found on the germ's surface.

Every one of the thousands of species of germs bears different characteristic antigens. It is, in fact, the antigen on a germ that signals the body to recognize the germ as an alien invader. Thus signaled, the body begins to manufacture an antibody to neutralize the invader. In a lifetime, the body makes thousands of types of antibodies against the myriad antigens that attack it.

CATCHING AN INTRUDER
To the left of Dr. Michael Heidelberger are yellow figures representing the body's genetically similar cells and, in orange, an alien invader. Defenses against the invader are shown along a blood vessel *(pink)*. At top left, bacteria *(lavender)* and viruses *(orange)* infect the tissues. Specialized cells *(aqua sphere)* secrete chemicals that help phagocytes leave the vessels to engulf bacteria *(center)*. Then antibody *(red dots)* and complement *(green)* destroy remaining germs. Formula at far left represents a mathematical statement of the quantitative relationship between antibody and antigen.

FACTORIES FOR ANTIBODIES

In stylized backdrops, the body's antibody producers surround Gustav Nossal, Director of the Walter and Eliza Hall Institute of Medical Research in Melbourne. Dr. Nossal has proved that antibodies are manufactured in plasma cells *(blue with pink nuclei)*, made in lymph nodes. When a germ reaches a node *(top left)*, its antigen, symbolized by a tan half-figure, stimulates plasma cells to grow and develop "factories" *(black dots)* and "canals" *(black networks near Dr. Nossal's feet)*; these, in turn, release antibodies *(red dots)*. The antibodies travel in lymph *(yellow)* and blood *(pink)* to reach the site of infection. There *(upper right)* they meet and neutralize the antigen they have been formed to fit *(interlocking orange and tan half-figures)*.

Immunity: The Body's Memory

One of the body's most powerful defenses against infection is its immunological memory—a memory that can be acquired naturally, through exposure to disease, or artificially, through the action of certain drugs. Once an invading germ has been repelled by antibodies, the body never forgets. If the microbe ever attacks again, the body remembers its earlier battle and produces appropriate antibodies to counter the antigen—and these new antibodies are produced much faster the second time than the first, so fast that the victim may not even be aware of the second invasion. In this way, an initial victory over some diseases—chicken pox, for instance—often leaves the victim with a lasting "natural immunity" against future attacks.

The victims of certain infections, however, never acquire natural immunity. Colds and influenza represent the best known failures of the body's memory, but these lapses are hardly surprising. The common cold is not a single disease; its symptoms can be produced by as many as 100 different germs, each of which has a different antigen. And the influenza virus is particularly insidious because it constantly mutates, thus changing its antigen.

To combat a number of infections that may cause damage before natural immunity is gained, artificial immunity is often produced by a special class of drugs, the vaccines. Vaccination introduces weakened germs into the body to trigger the development of antibodies. Thereafter the body can re-create the antibodies as needed to protect itself against future attacks by the same type of germ.

A BENIGN SHOT

Posed before a symbolic backdrop of a vaccine "shot" are Harry Meyer *(left)* and Paul Parkman of the U.S. National Institutes of Health, who developed a German measles vaccine. This is expected to protect pregnant women from German measles, which could harm their unborn babies. The new vaccine uses the mechanism common to most vaccines. German measles viruses are grown in the laboratory. Then they are rendered harmless, although they still bear their antigens. An injection of this weakened strain *(red beaded rings enclosing orange spirals)* is shot into a healthy body. In the body, antibodies *(red balls)* form against the antigen—and the body will remember how to make those antibodies if the same infection strikes again.

REMEMBERING AN INVADER

The body knows how to make antibodies to fit a specific germ, says James Gowans of Oxford University, because the blood's lymphocyte cells *(blue with magenta nuclei)* learn the code for that virus' antigen and remember it for up to 15 years. This memory is indicated here by a picture of an adult *(bottom)* "remembering" an antigen-antibody match formed as a child *(top)*.

Flaws in Prenatal Defenses

An unborn baby's prime protection against microbes and overly potent drugs is the placenta that surrounds the fetus in its mother's womb. The placenta separates blood vessels of mother and fetus by a fluid and tissue "barrier," which ordinarily prevents germs and large molecules in the mother's blood from reaching the fetus. But the system is not foolproof: harmful germs or molecules do occasionally get through the barrier to the fetus' body. Among them are the German measles virus and drugs like thalidomide that can interfere tragically with a fetus' development.

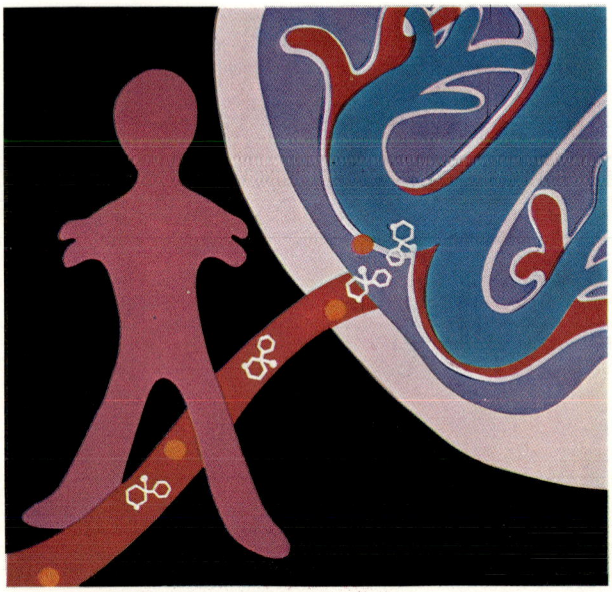

A DRUG BREACHES A BARRIER
Babies with incomplete and malformed limbs have been born to women who took thalidomide at the stage of pregnancy during which arms and legs develop. This antinausea drug *(white molecular symbol)* proved able to cross the barrier *(purple)* between the mother's blood vessels *(red, lower left)* and the baby's *(red and blue, upper right)*. Though the molecules of some protective maternal antibodies *(orange dots)* also cross the barrier, they do not neutralize thalidomide, because antibodies protect against microbes but not against drugs.

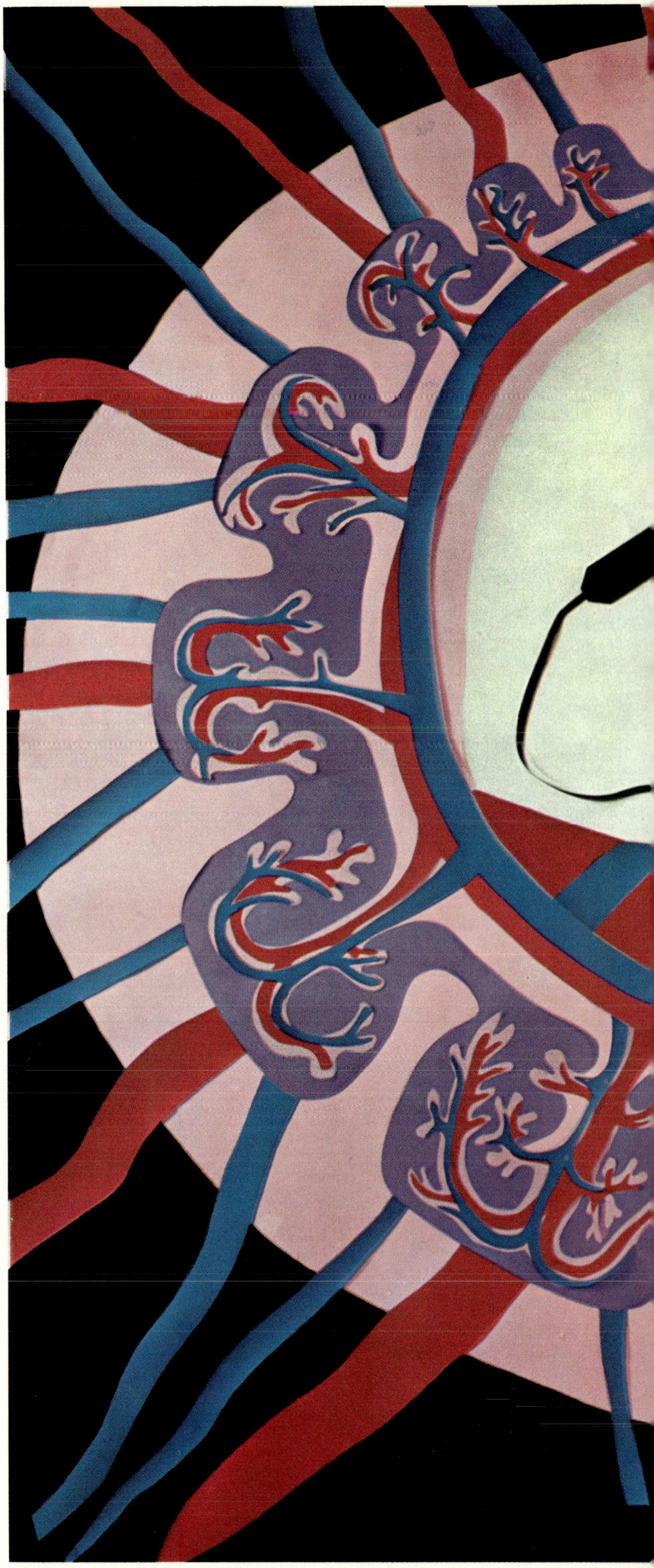

TESTING A FETUS' DEFENSES
Because of the protection given to an unborn baby by the fluid and tissue barrier *(purple)* that separates the baby's and the mother's blood, the belief has been that the fetus had no need to make antibodies and could not do so. Arthur Silverstein of Johns Hopkins University has disproved this by injecting antigens into living sheep and monkey fetuses; the unborn mammals, he found, could produce antibodies if they had to. Since the barrier is leakier than was once thought, this discovery points to new methods of prenatal protection.

When the Body Attacks Itself

Some of man's most pernicious ailments can be fought only by using drugs to counteract the body's own defenders. These ills arise when the defenders err, attacking not harmful invaders but innocuous or beneficial substances—even part of the body itself. Rheumatic fever, which is generally preceded by a streptococcus infection, may occur because the antigen of streptococcus bacteria resembles a substance in the heart muscles; the antibody designed to neutralize the germs also attacks the heart.

A common example of harm done by defenders is allergy. An allergic person reacts to harmless antigens. Hay fever, for example, occurs because the body produces an unneeded antibody against pollen antigens.

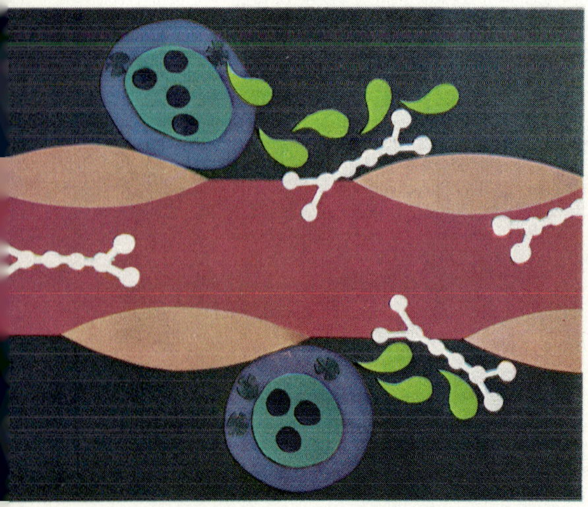

ATTACKING AN ALLERGY
Hay fever occurs when the chemical histamine *(yellow-green drops)* is released by special cells *(purple and blue)* in response to pollen antigen. The histamine coats the cells *(in pink)* lining the blood vessels, causing fluids to seep from tissue cells, eyes and nose. But an antihistamine drug *(white)*, taken in time, will coat the linings first, temporarily blocking the histamine.

BACKGROUND OF A SNEEZE
Lawrence Lichtenstein *(right)* and David Levy of Johns Hopkins, developers of a hay fever test, pose before sneezing profiles. The center panel shows how a special cell *(purple and blue)* releases histamine *(yellow-green drops)* when antigen *(green hemispheres)* from pollen *(yellow)* unites with an allergy victim's antibody *(red)*.

6

The Drug Hunters

Preparing darts for hunting, a Peruvian Indian dips them in curare, a paralyzing poison sometimes used to kill humans as well. It is also one of the great prizes of the quest for new drugs; in minute quantities, it relaxes muscles during surgery.

THE REVEREND EDWARD STONE, an 18th Century English clergyman and amateur pharmacologist, sought new drugs according to a rule. God in His wisdom, Stone believed, had provided for man's well-being by placing the cures for diseases in close proximity to their causes. For example, the "agues and intermitting disorders" (malarial fevers) that abounded in swampy districts ought to be cured, or at least alleviated, by some plant growing around marshlands.

In 1763 the Reverend Stone made a discovery that seemed to him to prove conclusively that his idea was correct. On rambling walks around his parish town he learned that the countryfolk of the region often treated fevers with a decoction made from the bark of the willow, a tree common in marshy locations. He sampled a bit of willow bark and was pleased to find that it had the same "extraordinary bitterness" as quinine—at that time the only available antimalarial and fever-reducing drug, and a terribly expensive one. Stone, who had a local reputation as a healer, treated some 50 fever-stricken patients with the willow-bark mixture, and it reduced the fever and relieved pain in every case.

In a letter to the Royal Society of London for Improving Natural Knowledge, Stone simultaneously proclaimed the virtues of the willow tree and the confirmation of his concept of pharmacology: "As this tree delights in a moist or wet soil, where agues chiefly abound, the general maxim, that many natural maladies carry their cures along with them, or that their remedies lie not far from their causes, was so very apposite to this particular case, that I could not help applying it; and that this might be the intention of Providence here, I must own, had some little weight with me." Stone's case histories were persuasive, and willow bark became a standard item in the physician's arsenal of drugs. Even more important, chemists later got around to isolating the bark's active principle and then to synthesizing a number of related compounds, which are called salicylates, from the Latin *salix* (willow). One of them was acetylsalicylic acid, better known as aspirin, which has become the standard fever-reducing drug both in the hospital pharmacy and the home medicine chest.

The Reverend Stone's discovery (or more accurately, rediscovery, for the virtues of salicylate-containing plants had been known in antiquity) was a classic case of a useful conclusion reached from faulty premises. First, the salicylates cannot do what he expected them to do; they are not antimalarial drugs. The ailments for which they are most useful are not the "agues" emanating from mosquito-ridden swamps but the colds, grippes and influenzas that afflict mankind regardless of topography. Second, there is no necessary connection between the bitter taste of a drug and its physiological effects; morphine, which will not help fever of any kind, is just as bitter as quinine. Nor, for that matter, is there any evidence that the Almighty is as provident of man's pharmacological requirements as the clergyman believed; otherwise we might expect to find a cure for tetanus in the horse dung where tetanus bacteria are commonly found.

Yet Stone's notion, for all its fallacies, bears a crude resemblance to the theory behind what is now called the "rational" approach to pharmacology—one of the two basic methods of discovering new drugs. Though most of his assumptions were wrong, his fundamental procedure was, and is, perfectly valid: decide what you want to do to the body, then figure out what sort of drug ought to do it. In principle, the rational approach is the ideal path to drug discovery. Because it allows the pharmacologist to progress directly to his goal, it is quick and cheap —and in addition possesses the combination of intellectual precision, economy and dexterity that the scientist calls elegance.

But for all its efficiency and elegance in theory, the rational approach is almost impossibly difficult in practice. To alter the body rationally requires exact knowledge of the body's biochemical processes and of the ways these processes can be modified by a specific kind of drug molecule. Though modern knowledge of these matters is infinitely greater and more sophisticated than the primitive learning of the Reverend Stone, it is very seldom sufficient to lead pharmacologists along the straight, rational path to an effective drug.

Trial, error—and luck

Because of this ignorance, nearly all advances in modern pharmacology, from 19th Century anesthetics to the contraceptive pill of the 1960s, have come through the second method of discovering drugs—the empirical, or trial-and-error, approach. The empirical pharmacologist is a scientific detective who collects clues, sifts through evidence and fits together seemingly unrelated facts, until finally he can track down a useful remedy. Some of his discoveries seem to be nothing but happy accidents, but recognizing the significance of an "accident" always demands acute observation and broad knowledge. More often, chance plays only a small role in the search for a new drug, and success depends on careful preparation and hard work.

The drug seeker does not start blindly. He draws on his up-to-date understanding of biochemistry for leads to chemicals that are known to influence important bodily functions. Then he looks for new members of that chemical family. His search is far more extensive than any ancient hunt for hidden pirate treasure. He penetrates unmapped jungles seeking new plants, soil organisms and even witch doctor remedies that may be useful. He collects the venom of deadly snakes and dredges the ocean bottom for strange sea creatures that produce unusually potent compounds. He methodically examines the synthetic chemicals pouring out of laboratories and refineries. From this study of hundreds and even thousands of different substances may come one or two promising compounds (10,000 substances were tested in the five years of research that led to streptomycin). But even then the pharmacologist's search is not ended; he may still have to alter the molecular structure of his discovery in order to fashion a drug that can be used on humans.

Expeditions to the remote corners of the world and meticulous screening of vast numbers of materials make trial-and-error drug searches very expensive. But this approach has been enormously productive, repaying its cost many times over in benefits to mankind. Until knowledge of biochemistry advances far beyond its present state, the laborious trial and error of the empirical approach remains the best method of finding new drugs.

In his search, the modern pharmacologist draws on four main sources for the materials he will scrutinize. He may look to the traditional lore of folk medicine for remedies worth trying. Or he may, more directly, seek physiologically active compounds among plant chemicals, animal substances or man-made synthetics. Each of these four sources offers special possibilities and poses special problems for the drug hunter, and each is worth separate consideration.

The pharmacologist seeking new drugs knows that mankind has been engaged in the same search, though in a crude way, for thousands of years. Folk medicine—the accumulated findings of generations of medicine men, priest-magicians, "wisewomen" and plain quacks—has piled up an enormous haystack of nonsense, in which careful search can sometimes find a sharp needle of scientific truth. It was folk medicine—the traditional family remedy of willow-bark tea—that enabled the Reverend Stone to reach a useful conclusion from irrational premises, that helped William Withering to the discovery of the heart drug digitalis and that put morphine and quinine (among other valuable drugs) into the pharmacopoeia.

Nor is the scientific adaptation of folk medicine wholly a thing of the past. One of the most successful recent examples is the discovery of the tranquilizer reserpine, which owes its present use to a couple of shrewd Indian chemists who noted that snakeroot, or rauwolfia—the natural source of modern reserpine—had long been used by folk practitioners in their country to treat insanity. Another instance of folk-medicine investigation, though it ended in far less of a pharmacological success, reveals some of the stranger-than-fiction adventures experienced by determined drug hunters in search of new remedies from old sources. This tale includes an elixir of youth, an Oriental prince and an ancient manuscript found in a ruined temple.

Rejuvenation from a jungle creeper

As recounted in an American medical magazine a few years ago, "the story begins with a 1932 report by an Englishman in Siam (now Thailand) that elderly natives got a new lease on life by eating the root of the *kwao* vine, a jungle creeper of the bean family." Chemical studies by Thai and German scientists showed that the root contained a strong estrogen—a substance akin to certain female hormones—which, in the case of elderly women at least, could indeed be expected to have some rejuvenating effect.

In 1948, British and Australian researchers interested in estrogens turned up the earlier reports. Their curiosity piqued, they mounted an expedition to Thailand. With the aid of a Thai botanist, Prince Lakshnakara Kashemsanta, the expedition brought back some hundreds of pounds of *kwao* root, as well as a pamphlet by a Thai civil servant describing its virtues. The pamphlet, in turn, was based on an ancient Burmese medical treatise inscribed on palm leaves, which had been found in a temple wrecked by lightning. *Kwao,* it declared, "was well known in both Thailand and Burma, and was reputed to make old people young. One patient was said to have reached the age of 280."

When the researchers purified the active principle of *kwao,* they found that it was quite as potent, both in the test tube and in patients, as any known estrogen that could be given by mouth. But the investigation ended in an anticlimax: *kwao* also produced side effects that made it "unsuitable for use in medicine." Moreover, when its molecular structure was worked out, the drug turned out to be chemically as well as pharmacologically akin to known drugs, and not, as had been hoped, a completely new chemical species of estrogen.

Clearly, even when folk medicine turns out to be right, it is sometimes not quite right enough. But the possibility of even this much gain has sent pharmacological explorers into remote regions of the globe to consult with medicine men and witch doctors.

Clues from Christian converts

One of these hunters of exotic drugs is Dr. Bruce W. Halstead, Director of the World Life Research Institute of Colton, California. Halstead has spent many months on journeys through the South American jungles studying the remedies of Indian witch doctors. For safety's sake, he collaborates only with practitioners who have been converted to Christianity and are therefore less likely to take hostile action against a visitor. Halstead's contacts with the world of the witch doctor are medical missionaries in South America, many of whom he has known for years. When he gets word that a knowledgeable native has embraced Christianity, he sets off on a journey that begins at a California jetport and may finish on muleback along a jungle trail. With luck, a single one of Halstead's expeditions may find a dozen or more promising herbs in the witch doctors' pharmacopoeia.

Among the potentially useful substances turned up in this manner are an oral contraceptive and several digitalislike preparations. All of these, Halstead notes, are prescribed by the witch doctors for purposes that make good medical sense—the contraceptive as a contraceptive, the heart drugs for a weakened heart. Halstead respects the sharp observations and shrewd reasoning of folk practitioners, and feels that pharmacologists who neglect this source of information may miss valuable bets. Indian snakeroot, he recalls, was "laughed out of the office" of one important drug-company official. Another company, with fewer prejudices, took the trouble to investigate it—and ultimately marketed millions of dollars worth of reserpine.

Such valuable folk remedies are, of course, the exception. The actual

PHYSOSTIGMA VENENOSUM BALFOUR

COFFEA ARABICA

MEDICINAL BEANS containing alkaloids—plant substances noted for their powerful effect on body processes—are the sources of two important drugs. One is physostigmine, obtained from the Calabar bean—fruit of the tropical vine *Physostigma venenosum* Balfour *(top)* which once supplied poison to West African tribes. Physostigmine's influence on nerve transmission and muscle action makes it useful for control of glaucoma, a serious eye disease. Another alkaloid is caffeine, contained in coffee beans, the seeds of *Coffea arabica (bottom).* Caffeine is used in headache drugs and to counteract barbiturate poisoning.

effect of a native drug may turn out to be precisely the opposite of the witch doctor's claim. One remedy, supposed to relieve headaches, proved instead to induce a violent, though brief, headache. Halstead suspects that the plant may owe its reputation as a cure to the fact that when the drug-induced headache subsides, the patient is likely to feel relieved to have only his original—and relatively mild—headache again. The principle is the same as that of the old joke about the man who explained why he hit his head with a hammer: "It feels so good when I stop."

Concentration on the witch doctor's kit of medicines narrows the pharmacologists' search by providing a group of preselected substances. But such a selection, limited by the folk practioners' rough-and-ready methods of gathering and processing materials, omits a great many compounds that might be valuable. This drawback can be avoided by examining different groups of materials selected, not from folklore, but from knowledge of their chemical activity. One drug hunter, Dr. Robert F. Raffauf of the Philadelphia drug firm of Smith Kline & French, specializes in plant compounds, particularly the alkaloids, that are known for their powerful effects on man. The drug potential of these substances can be seen from the fact that they include (among many other useful compounds) caffeine, quinine, morphine and reserpine—as well as a deadly poison called coniine, the active ingredient of the hemlock that Socrates swallowed.

Raffauf's office carefully scans reports on alkaloid-containing plants (about one plant species in 10) and when a new one turns up, he, like Halstead, hits the trail. He himself often performs the first step in the drug-screening process right in the jungle; by means of a chemical reagent he can determine with considerable accuracy whether the plant he has plucked does in fact contain an alkaloid. Later, in his Philadelphia laboratory, Raffauf leads the teams of scientists who analyze and test the substances he has collected. His new discoveries include one alkaloid that lowers blood pressure in animals (though not, in its present form, in human beings) and several potential pain-killers.

Drugs from the ocean's depths

The pharmacologists who study animal rather than plant products have come up with even more promising substances. Certain compounds manufactured by marine animals, for example, seem to act exactly like medicinal drugs, effectively guarding their makers against biological enemies or disease.

One of the most unusual of these is produced by the lowly sea squirt, *Ascidia nigra*, which makes an antibiotic that apparently protects it against external parasites. Even when a sea squirt is cut or scraped, it does not contract an infection, as do similar but unprotected species. The sea squirt's antibiotic seems to have a "broad-spectrum" action, killing many different kinds of microbe. In this respect it resembles the valuable tetracycline drugs, but its usefulness to medicine remains to be established.

ERYTHROXYLON COCA

RAUWOLFIA SERPENTINA

MEDICINAL LEAVES AND ROOTS that are rich in alkaloid compounds provide two powerful drugs with greatly differing properties. Cocaine, extracted from the leaves of *Erythroxylon coca,* a shrub native to the Andes Mountains *(top),* is widely used as a local anesthetic for operations on the nose and throat. Reserpine is an alkaloid obtained from *Rauwolfia serpentina (bottom),* a shrub found in the Indian subcontinent. Prized for many centuries as a folk remedy against insomnia and insanity, it was introduced in the United States in the 1950s to combat high blood pressure and mental illness.

An even richer source of potential drugs is the sea cucumber, a distant relative of the starfish. This sluggish bottom dweller secretes a substance, holothurin, that can kill fish in concentrations diluted down to one part per million. The poison is thought to explain why the sea cucumber, an otherwise toothsome morsel, is seldom if ever bothered by piscine predators. Holothurin contains one substance resembling digitalis, as well as other compounds that affect the peripheral nerves.

The hunt for drugs in plant and animal substances involves hundreds of pharmacologists in laboratories and field expeditions throughout the world. The pharmacologists who screen man-made chemical compounds are no less industrious. Every one of the hundreds of new substances concocted each year in the laboratories of academic and industrial chemists is characterized by some sort of physiological activity, and there is always the chance that the activity may turn out to be just what the doctor would like to order.

Exploiting this source of new drugs is especially easy for some drug companies. Lederle Laboratories, for example, has easy access to a copious supply of newly synthesized compounds; its parent corporation, American Cyanamid, manufactures chemicals ranging from fertilizers to shampoos. A company rule requires that every new chemical synthesized in any American Cyanamid division be listed in the "CL (Cyanamid Laboratory) File," for possible pharmacological screening. One product, a chemical used in the manufacture of rubber, turned out to be a possible antitubercular drug.

Even after such a substance has been found, the drug seeker's work has barely begun. He has turned up something of promise, no more. At this point its origin is of little importance. Whether it came from an old woman's herb garden, a tropical jungle, an animal's bloodstream or an industrial laboratory, it must undergo long study before it is finally used to allay suffering or set aside as worthless.

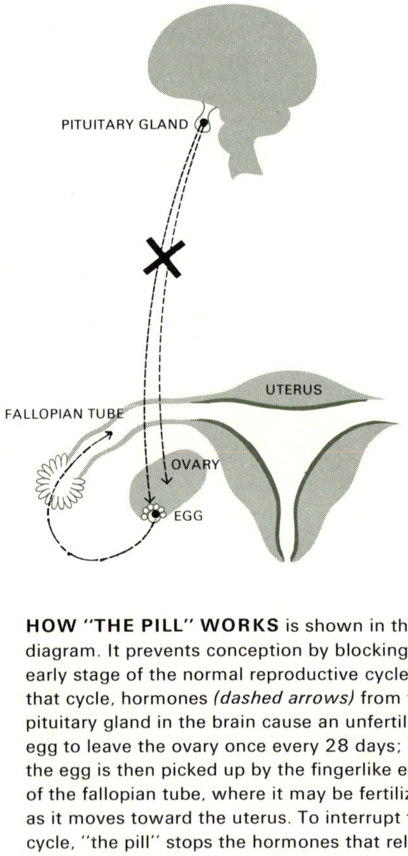

HOW "THE PILL" WORKS is shown in this diagram. It prevents conception by blocking an early stage of the normal reproductive cycle. In that cycle, hormones *(dashed arrows)* from the pituitary gland in the brain cause an unfertilized egg to leave the ovary once every 28 days; the egg is then picked up by the fingerlike edges of the fallopian tube, where it may be fertilized as it moves toward the uterus. To interrupt this cycle, "the pill" stops the hormones that release the unfertilized egg, as indicated by the black cross, and no egg is available for fertilization.

Running the gauntlet

The journey of a chemical compound from witch doctor's caldron or chemist's flask to the shelves of the neighborhood pharmacy is a laborious and costly one. The great majority of chemicals fall by the wayside. The first step is to determine, by administering the substance to animals, what organ or organs it affects, and how it affects them. In one case in thousands, the results will be of sufficient medical interest to make further research worthwhile. The drug will then undergo very extensive batteries of animal tests to compile data on its physiological effects, good, bad or indifferent. Only if its useful actions far outweigh its harmful ones will it be tried even tentatively on human beings. And if it reaches this point it still has only a slim chance of achieving the final goal of general medical acceptance.

Because so many substances are rejected by this screening, a mountain of new compounds may have to be mined to find one valuable drug. The record for this downward progression was probably set by the National Cancer Institute, which between 1955 and 1967 studied the effects on cancer of no less than 272,700 chemicals, old and new. The net result was some 25 drugs with some value in controlling the disease; none proved to be a cure for it.

The pharmacologist who turns up a medically useful drug simply by his own screening considers himself remarkably lucky. More often, his tests will at best do no more than identify a compound that has some useful properties, but that is too toxic, or too slowly absorbed, or too rapidly eliminated from the body, to be of any medical use in its existing form. At this point he calls in the pharmaceutical chemist, who begins a complex game sometimes called "molecular roulette." This involves the reshaping of the original molecule—adding an atom here, knocking off a group of atoms there—so as to retain the substance's useful properties while eliminating its disadvantages.

The tailoring of "the pill"

The "tailoring" of a molecule in this manner is exemplified in the story of norethynodrel, the compound that was the basis of the first contraceptive pill. The story is significant not only as an example of pharmacological methods but for its impact on society. "The pill" has had an influence on mankind as great as that of any other drug in history. It has opened up new prospects for solving the population explosion, changed patterns of sexual behavior and raised delicate religious and political questions.

The tale begins far back in prehistory when it was first noticed that a woman cannot conceive a child while she is pregnant. It took a long time before anyone bothered to wonder why this should be true, and even longer before scientists discovered the reason: during pregnancy a woman ceases to produce the ova that, if fertilized, develop into babies. Only 30 years ago was it learned that this halt in ovulation is caused primarily by the hormone progesterone, whose manufacture in the mother's body is greatly stepped up during pregnancy. In 1937 experiments at the University of Pennsylvania showed that injections of progesterone into female rabbits could keep the animals from ovulating, an obvious method of birth control that was not fully appreciated until more than a decade later.

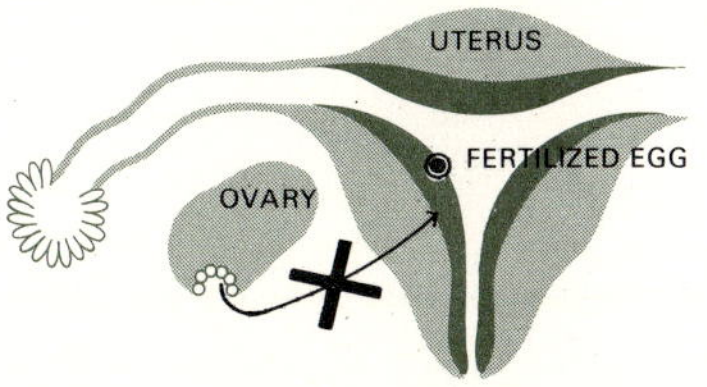

A PROPOSED NEW PILL, which interrupts the reproductive process at a late stage, forestalls pregnancy after an egg has been fertilized. Normally a fertilized egg implants itself in the wall of the uterus, where it will develop. But it can do this only if the uterus wall has been made ready for the egg by a hormone *(dashed arrow)* sent from the ovary. The blocking of this hormone by the contraceptive *(indicated by the black cross)* prevents implantation of the fertilized egg and forestalls pregnancy.

At about the same time, progesterone began to be used in medicine for other purposes. However, the drug had two major disadvantages: it was exceedingly costly, since it had to be extracted gram by gram from the ovarian tissue of animals; and, more serious, injection of the drug frequently produced painful reactions. Yet when given by mouth, the drug was ineffective except in enormous doses.

The cost problem was solved in the early 1940s by Russell Marker, then at Pennsylvania State University. Marker discovered that the *Dioscorea,* a large Mexican yam, contains a substance, diosgenin, whose structure is akin to that of progesterone, cortisone, cholesterol and the whole large class of chemical compounds known as steroids. What was more important, Marker developed a method of using the yam's plentiful diosgenin as a raw material for synthesizing almost any steroid.

Marker's discovery greatly stimulated medical interest in all steroids. In 1949, for example, the first reports on the use of cortisone in rheumatoid arthritis were published. Two years later, Gregory Pincus of the Worcester Foundation for Experimental Biology launched the first major research program on the use of steroids to prevent conception by blocking human ovulation.

"Too hot to handle"

From the beginning, Pincus and his associates were faced with two unusual problems, one pharmacological, one sociological. First, the anti-ovulation compound they were looking for had to be effective when given by mouth instead of by injection, because it would probably have to be taken often, and for months or years at a time—and nobody was likely to accept injections on that scale simply for contraception. Second, in seeking new steroids to test, Pincus found most drug companies reluctant to cooperate. "They felt that chemical birth control was too hot to handle," he recalls.

An exception was G. D. Searle & Co., of Skokie, Illinois. The president of Searle, as it happened, was personally concerned about what was beginning to be called the population explosion and saw the need for new methods of checking it. Moreover, the company had on hand a large and able group of steroid specialists—35 Ph.D.s in all—recruited for a research project that had not panned out.

The Searle team had already compiled a great mass of information on the properties of steroids. They knew which of the compounds possessed progesteronelike properties, and which ones were highly active when given by mouth. What was more important, they could spot specific resemblances between the molecules of steroids that both resembled progesterone and were active when given orally. On the basis of this data, they were able to set forth on paper the chemical composition of a number of substances that ought to possess all the properties they were looking for. Some 15 of these were synthesized; three turned out to have the predicted combination of properties: oral activity, suppression of ovulation and so on. It was also found that the addition of much smaller quantities of another steroid, mestranol, markedly increased the potency of the progesteronelike substances.

In 1953, the three new compounds were shipped off to Pincus for testing. The best of the experimental drugs, norethynodrel, proved to be both more reliable and far more potent than progesterone. When given by mouth, a 300 milligram dose of progesterone would prevent ovulation about 85 per cent of the time. Norethynodrel in 10 milligram doses (plus a fraction of a milligram of mestranol) was close to 100 per cent effective. (Subsequently, it was found that even this small dose could be safely reduced by half and in some cases by three quarters.) With this masterpiece of pharmacological ingenuity, ovulation can be controlled throughout a woman's childbearing years, and controlled with such precision that other bodily functions are hardly affected.

In 1960, after further extensive testing required by the U.S. Food and Drug Administration, the norethynodrel-mestranol pill went on sale as a contraceptive. "The pill," as it quickly came to be called, was soon joined by other oral contraceptives of the same general type. By 1965, they were being systematically used for family planning by an estimated five million American women, or about one of every eight women of childbearing age.

The norethynodrel story is a success story. Not all ventures into molecular roulette are so fortunate. The relationship between molecular structure and physiological activity is still imperfectly understood, and even when—as in the case of norethynodrel—the pharmacologist knows what type of molecule he is trying to construct, he is not always able to construct it. For nearly half a century chemists have been tinkering with the intricate morphine molecule, hoping to obtain a substance that relieves pain as effectively as morphine but that does not create physical dependency and depress respiration, as morphine does. There have been indications that radical reshaping of the molecule may have solved the physical dependency problem, and the answer to the respiratory problem may lie in the same reshaped molecule. Indeed, chemists are still not certain what structural characteristics of the morphine molecule produce its pain-killing action.

Playing computer games

New light on such problems may come from a project launched in 1965 in Columbus, Ohio. There, the Chemical Abstracts Service, working with federal funds, began feeding massive amounts of pharmacological information into a computer. Ultimately, the Service hoped to include data on several million compounds, including their structure, their chemical and physical properties and their biological effects on both humans and animals.

When information of this kind is stored in a computer, "we can start playing games," explains George J. Cosmides, a pharmacologist associated with the project. The computer can be programed, for example, to list the common characteristics of all known heart stimulants or all known anesthetics. If such a comparison showed that the greater an anesthetic's solubility in fats, the more effective it is, this fact would certainly be of inestimable value in creating new anesthetics.

Computerized information of this sort should also bring nearer the pharmacologist's ultimate goal: the ability to develop a drug from scratch by designing a molecule on paper that will have precisely the combination of qualities desired. The achievement of the goal would bring modern science full circle back to the Reverend Edward Stone's "rational" approach to pharmacology: learn what has gone wrong in an ailing human body, decide what must be done to the body to cure it, and find—or better still, create—the drug that will do the job.

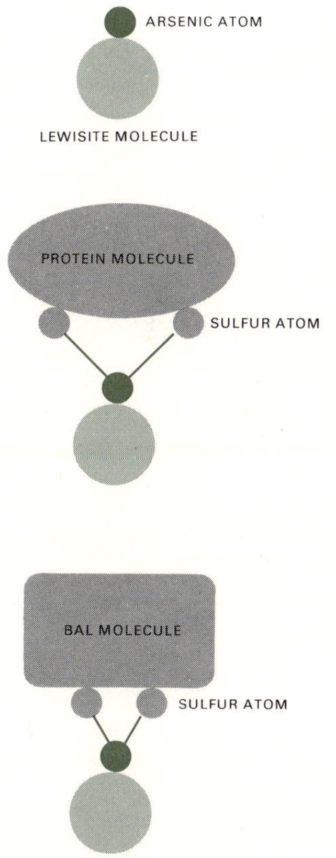

A MADE-TO-ORDER DRUG, BAL, is an antidote for lewisite, a poison gas developed during World War I. Scientists knew that lewisite is poisonous because its molecule *(top, light green)* includes an arsenic atom *(dark green)*. In the body or on the skin, the arsenic atom joins with loosely spaced sulfur atoms of a protein molecule *(gray, center)*, preventing the protein from performing vital body functions. To offset this effect, the BAL molecule *(gray, bottom)* was designed with two tightly spaced sulfur atoms that give BAL a stronger attraction for arsenic than protein has. When the antidote is injected into the body, these sulfur atoms lure arsenic away from protein and render the lewisite harmless.

Remedies from Roots and Molds

Constantly emerging from the laboratory stage are new drugs that result from the pharmacologists' unending search in strange places for improved remedies; some of these substances may have as much impact in the coming decades as yam-extract contraceptives *(opposite)* and snakeroot tranquilizers have had in the recent past. Candidates for future prominence include two synthetics that are among the first ever to show results against virus infections and a pain-killer, potent but nonaddictive, that may replace dangerous morphine. And the skin of a certain tiny frog has yielded a paralyzing venom of potential help for muscle ailments.

Discoveries like these are the rewards of an intensive effort to follow every clue that may lead to a useful drug. Scientists study ancient folklore remedies, extract chemicals from sea creatures and comb the jungles for valuable raw materials. Often the quest runs into a costly dead end. One company displays, as evidence of what it calls its "$160 million failure," samples of 40,000 compounds tested since 1937; only 55 of them proved useful. Yet the search goes on, sustained by the incalculable boon to mankind that would be provided by cures for cancer or even the common cold.

CONTRACEPTIVES FROM ROOTS

In the jungle in the state of Veracruz, Mexico, a laborer cuts *Dioscorea,* or Mexican yams, which yield diosgenin, the raw material for oral contraceptives. Using diosgenin, Carl Djerassi of Syntex Corporation pioneered in the synthesis of hormones that are active ingredients in the various forms of "the pill," one of the revolutionary new drugs of this century.

New Weapons against Infections

Although the great lifesaving discoveries of recent decades have been vaccines, sulfa drugs and antibiotics that prevent or cure infection, pharmacologists are still searching for other drugs to cope with the germs that cause infectious diseases. This continued search is necessary because many bacteria, including those responsible for staph infections, gonorrhea and tuberculosis, develop resistance to drugs; remedies become powerless and must be replaced.

A more difficult problem is presented by viruses that cause diseases like hepatitis, influenza and colds. Until recently, there were no drugs that cured virus diseases; vaccines, which do not kill viruses but stimulate the body to do so, have not always proved satisfactory.

Today better vaccines are being sought, and the first drugs effective against viruses have been found. One is a preparation, IDU, which blocks reproduction of the virus of an external infection. Another, amantadine, a synthetic chemical developed by Du Pont, acts like vaccines, preventing rather than curing an infection.

SAVING EYESIGHT WITH IDU

The rabbit at left was blinded by a viral infection, herpes keratitis. The bright-eyed one at right recovered from infection within 72 hours after receiving IDU (for iododeoxyuridine), a chemical drug that stops viruses without seriously harming body cells invaded by the viruses. IDU, first used to treat infection in 1961 by Herbert Kaufman of the University of Florida, seems to act by imitating thymidine, a body-cell component that the virus needs for growth. Fooled by the resemblance, the virus accepts the unusable IDU, passes up essential thymidine—and cannot multiply.

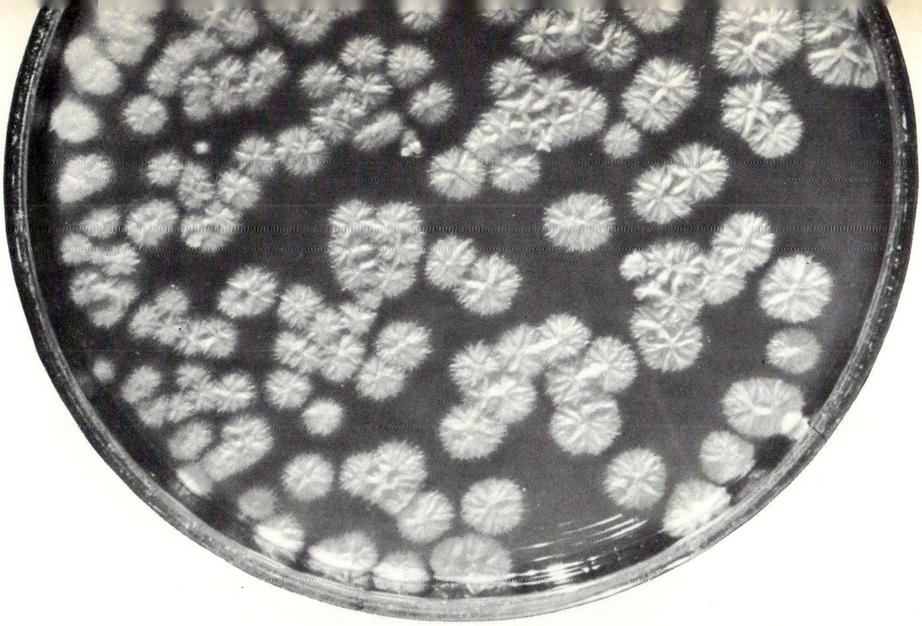

GROWING A NEW ANTIBIOTIC
The clumps on the culture dish at left are *Cephalosporium*, a bacteria-killing fungus discovered in 1945 in sewage. From this fungus chemists at Eli Lilly and Company, in Indianapolis, developed an antibiotic that kills many bacteria, including previously resistant staphylococci.

GIVING A FERRET A COLD
A ferret—one of the few animals that catch human colds—is given drops containing viruses as part of a search for cold vaccine at the Smith Kline & French Laboratories in Philadelphia. Making such a vaccine has proved difficult because at least 100 kinds of infectious agents can cause colds.

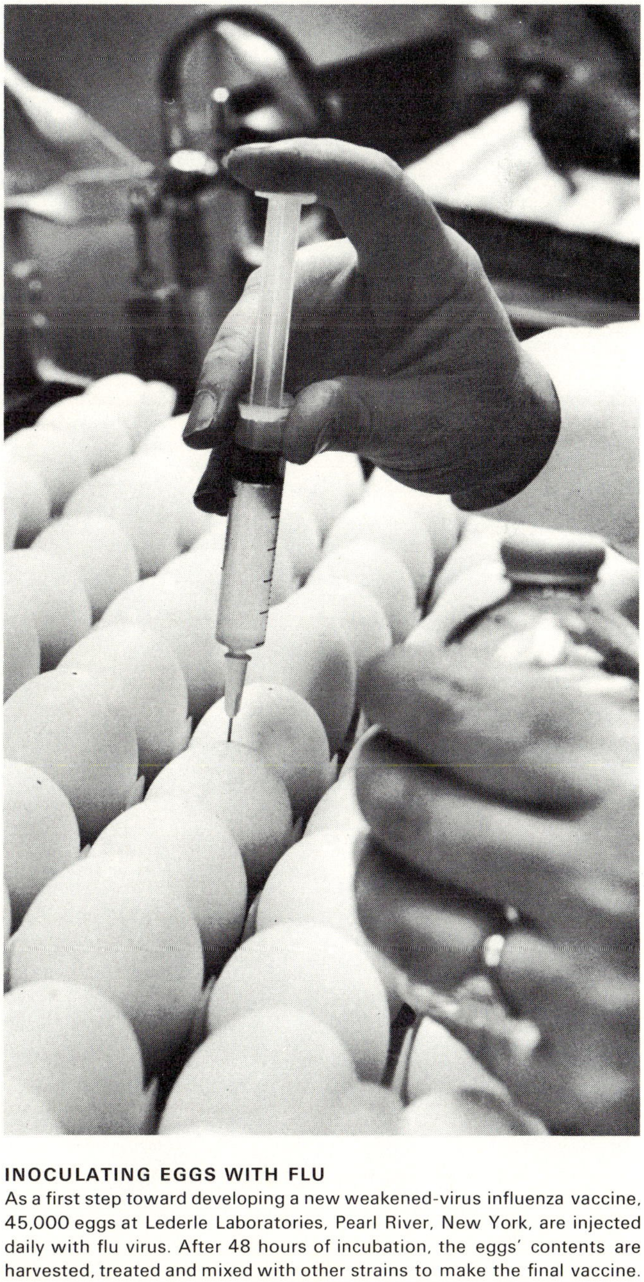

INOCULATING EGGS WITH FLU
As a first step toward developing a new weakened-virus influenza vaccine, 45,000 eggs at Lederle Laboratories, Pearl River, New York, are injected daily with flu virus. After 48 hours of incubation, the eggs' contents are harvested, treated and mixed with other strains to make the final vaccine.

Relief for Troubled Minds

Among the first drugs that man used were those, such as alcohol, that eased his pains and worries by their effects on his central nervous system, and the search for similar compounds continues. In this age of anxiety, the need for new and improved kinds of tension-relievers calls for elaborate research efforts *(below)*.

Old medications, too, must be improved or superseded. The opium poppy—and its derivative, morphine—has long been the basis of the most effective pain-killers, but opium is addictive and it so depresses the brain's respiration control center that it can easily stifle breathing. Only now are these drawbacks being overcome by new analgesics, synthesized in the laboratory; these drugs approach morphine in pain-relief potency but lack some of its faults.

PAIN-KILLER PILOT PLANT
Noel Albertson, developer of a new analgesic pain-killer called pentazocine, stands before a maze of pipes and tanks used to make the drug at Winthrop Laboratories in Rensselaer, New York. Pentazocine seems free of the addictive properties that make morphine troublesome.

TESTING AN ANTIDEPRESSANT
In a test of an antidepressant, a monkey *(below)* at Merck Sharp & Dohme Research Laboratories in West Point, Pennsylvania, presses a lever to avoid electric shock. Its reactions to stress, computed by the machines at rear, indicate whether the drug interferes with alertness.

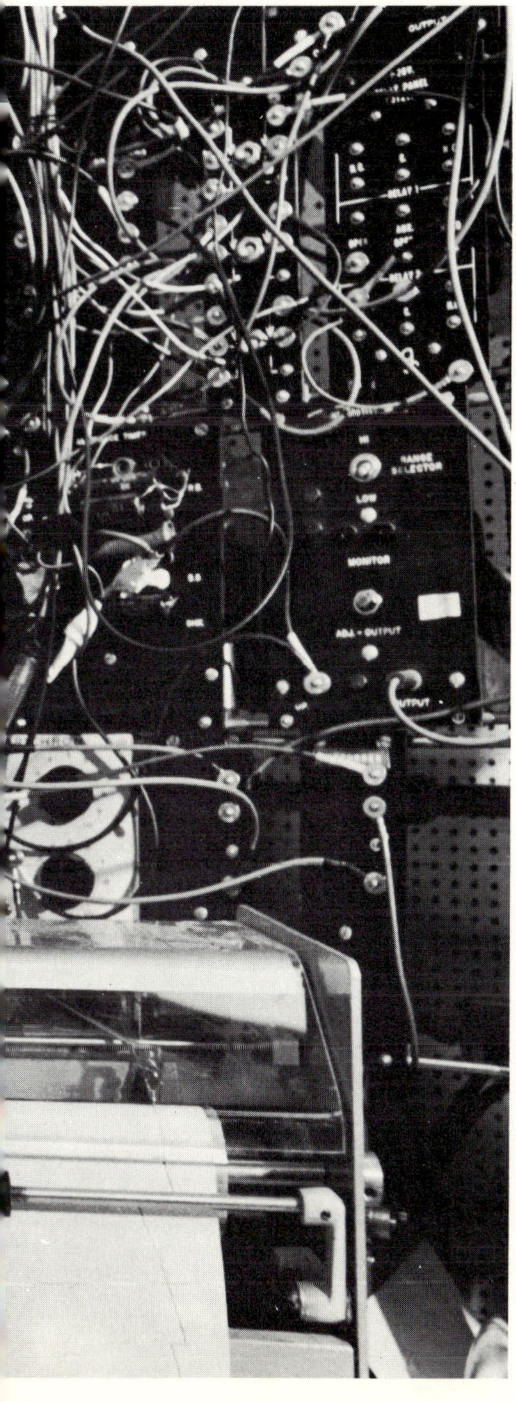

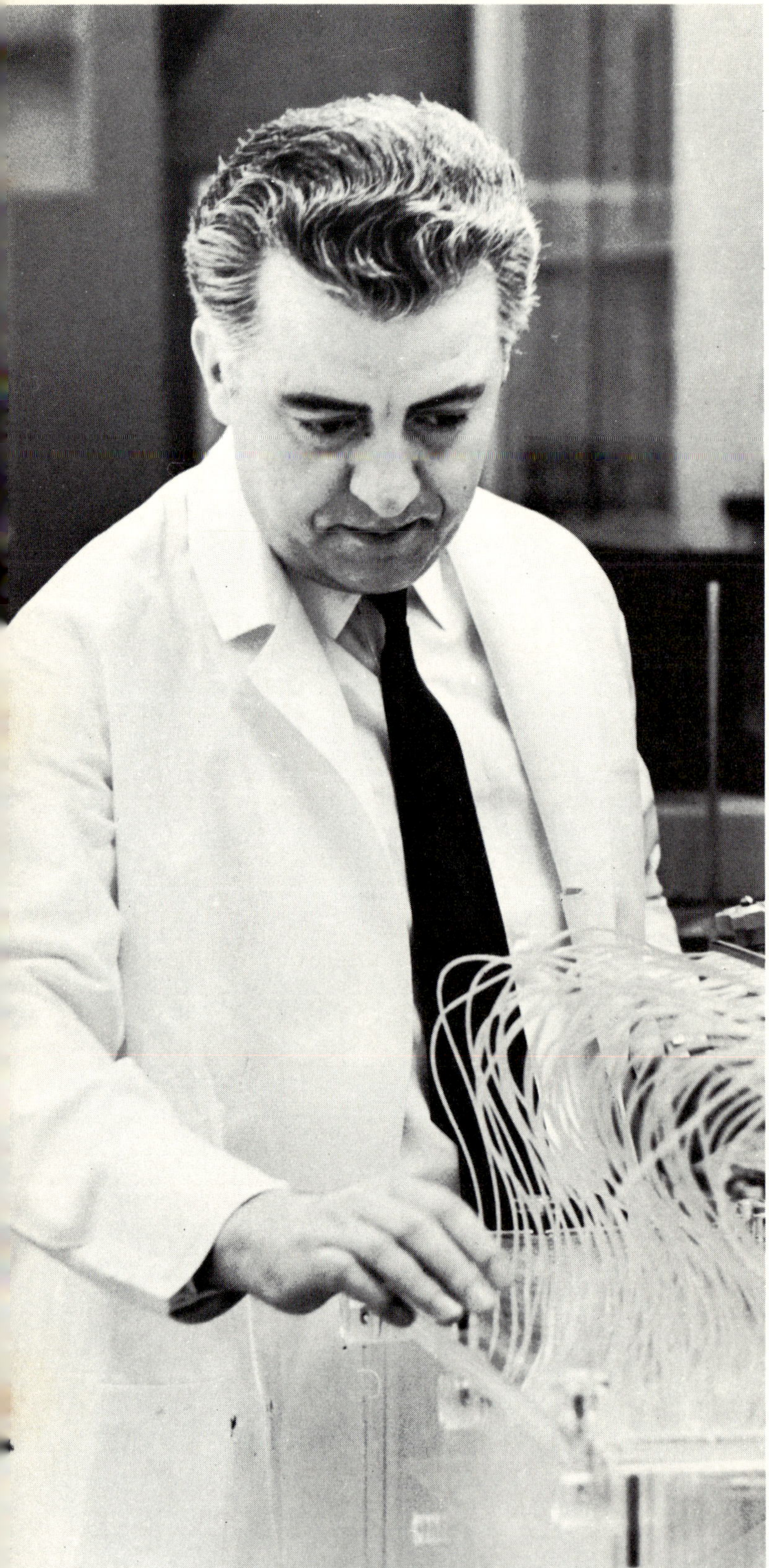

ANALYZING INSULIN'S STRUCTURE
Seeking an improved form of the insulin he has synthesized for diabetes, Panayotis Katsoyannis of Brookhaven National Laboratory, Upton, New York, uses a machine that separates components of natural insulin and collects them in tubes. He then compares them with synthetic components.

TESTING AN ARTHRITIS DRUG
Immersing the paw of a rat in a container of mercury, G. W. Nuss of the Merck laboratories gauges the swelling by the amount of mercury displaced. After the use of indomethocin, an experimental arthritis drug, has reduced the swelling, he will measure a comparative displacement.

SEPARATING A CLOT-DISSOLVER
Alex Lesuk uses test tubes to collect some urokinase, an experimental drug against dangerous blood clotting. The drug is the end product of the separation of urine components that is taking place in the columns in the foreground at Sterling-Winthrop Research Institute, Rensselaer, New York.

Combating the Chronic Diseases

The most elusive prizes pharmacologists seek are remedies for chronic diseases: heart and blood vessel ailments, which are the main causes of death in the United States today; cancer, the second biggest killer; debilitating diseases, such as arthritis; and metabolic ills, like diabetes, that develop when organs fail to function normally. No cures have yet been found for any of these ills, but their victims can often be helped by drugs.

One new medication may prevent deaths from circulatory disease by eliminating blood vessel clots, which can bring on strokes or may damage the heart muscle. When a clot forms in the bloodstream, blood flow in the area may cease; this will kill the surrounding tissue. But the damage may be avoided if the clot is dissolved before it can cut off blood flow. Among the promising clot-dissolvers is urokinase, an enzyme found in human urine. Purified and crystallized only recently, urokinase was found to break up clots by activating another enzyme, plasmin, which destroys the protein that is involved in the formation of the blood clots.

For arthritis, there are new drugs to reduce the disease's painful joint inflammation. For the 25 per cent of diabetics who are allergic to the natural insulin hormone, the mass production of a synthetic, nonallergenic insulin has come closer with the laboratory synthesis in the 1960s of the insulin molecule. And for cancer, perhaps the most frustrating disease of all, a massive hunt for causes and cures has already turned up some significant clues to new treatment.

For Cancer: 270,000 Trials

Probably the most exhaustive search for new drugs is the hunt for cancer remedies. Over 270,000 compounds have been screened in laboratories all over the world. About two dozen have been found that, alone or as adjuncts to surgery, help to check spreading tumors. These drugs stop the wild multiplication of cancer cells by interfering at one point or another with their reproductive processes. Some of them, such as the powerful nitrogen mustards, partially prevent the cells from reproducing their genetic material, the essential first step before cell division can begin. Other drugs, like the newly discovered vincristine, disrupt cell division itself. But no drug has been wholly effective, and the pursuit of a cancer cure goes on with undiminished vigor.

NARROWING A STOREHOUSE
At the Sloan-Kettering Institute in Rye, New York, cabinets containing about 30,000 possible anticancer drugs flank a table displaying eight drugs frequently used against one type of cancer, leukemia. Among these useful compounds, one of the newest and most effective is vincristine sulfate *(far right, foreground)*, extracted from the wild periwinkle, *Vinca rosea (above)*, a tropical herb. Fifteen tons of periwinkle leaves and 16 weeks of processing yield only one ounce of vincristine.

For Leukemia, Hope in Vaccines

The greatest discovery of the many-sided quest for cancer treatment will be an explanation of the disease's cause. For if a microbe is guilty, a vaccine might be developed that would confer immunity.

In at least one form of cancer, a microbial agent has already been implicated: there is some evidence that viruses cause leukemia. No one has proved that they do, but scientists have shown that mouse and fowl leukemia is virus caused, and particles resembling the viruses of mouse leukemia have occasionally been found in the blood and tissues of human leukemia victims.

To follow up this virus lead, the U.S. government allotted over $16.5 million for fiscal 1967 to support 74 research projects in laboratories here and abroad. At one of them, the Bionetics Research Laboratories in Kensington, Maryland *(right)*, doctors are attempting to transfer human leukemia to one of man's nearest relatives, the monkey, through injections of blood and tissue extracts from a human patient. If these experimental animals can be given leukemia, and if viruslike particles are then found in their blood, the scientists will attempt to grow the virus in quantity as the next step toward the development of a leukemia vaccine.

INJECTIONS FOR INFECTION
Using rubber gloves attached to a nearly germ-free plastic "isolator," a doctor and technician inject blood from a human leukemia victim into the arm of a monkey. In the background are other monkeys, in isolators bearing their names, which have already received similar injections.

956
DISMAL

PRETTY BUT POISONOUS
Staring into a laboratory aquarium *(above)*, Robert Endean of the University of Queensland studies poisonous creatures whose toxins may furnish clues to useful drugs: a beautifully striped butterfly cod, a repulsive bearded ghoul fish *(left)* and a collection of cone shells *(right)*.

A DEADLY BENEFACTOR
Robert Endean and David McColm *(at left)* extract venom from a stonefish, the world's deadliest fish. In modified form the venom is used experimentally to lower blood pressure. Other drugs have been extracted from the blue-ringed octopus and the sea wasp *(in jars at left)*.

New Drugs from Odd Fish

To drug hunters, the depths of the oceans are among the most promising frontiers waiting to be explored. The waters along Australia's 1,250-mile Great Barrier Reef, for example, house exotic, poisonous creatures whose toxins have already shown great promise. Toxin from the toadfish has been used to assist brain surgery, some sponges manufacture a substance that destroys bacteria, and the toxin of the Crown-of-Thorns starfish may inhibit growth of tumors.

Reef dwellers like these are the specialty of Australian zoologist Robert Endean, who tries to develop useful drugs from their deadly venoms. Endean has studied sea wasp poison (which normally will kill a man in seconds) as a possible muscle drug. Other Reef dwellers, the cone-shell mollusks, have yielded two promising toxins: a muscle relaxant resembling curare; and a muscle contractor that may some day help victims of such diseases as muscular dystrophy.

Sifting Truth from Legend

Folk medicine, despite its large humbug content, has proved so prolific a source of valuable drugs—quinine, opium, digitalis, reserpine—that modern scientists turn to it again and again for clues to the medications they seek. Renewed surveys of these traditional "kitchen remedies" are now underway in many parts of the world, but particularly in the Orient.

In India 80 per cent of the people are treated by practitioners of two ancient forms of folk medicine. One of these forms is Unani medicine, based on herbal remedies. An outgrowth of early Greek pharmacology, Unani was brought to India by 8th Century A.D. Arab invaders. The other is Ayurvedic medicine. It uses a variety of substances (some 7,000 prescriptions, 600 for purgatives alone) and may be as old as Indian civilization; its medicines are said to have been developed by physicians of the Hindu gods. Though Ayurvedic physicians often recommend such exotic but useless remedies as gold, diamond and ruby dust and rhinoceros horn, they were among the first to use rauwolfia, from which came the first modern tranquilizers. Today, Indian and Western researchers are using modern techniques to study Unani and Ayurvedic drugs, hoping to find substances that can benefit mankind in the 20th Century.

REEXAMINING OLD POTIONS
At the Unani Institute of the History of Medicine and Medical Research in New Delhi, India, Major J. S. Chowhan, head of the research department, extracts the juice of an herb for tests of its effect on blood pressure and respiration.

TRADITIONAL DRUG MAKING
Workers *(above)* grind ingredients of Ayurvedic drugs. In tins and bags are, counterclockwise from upper left: rust scrapings from a foundry, given for liver trouble; gray iron shavings from machine shops, for adult liver and brain ills; Asoka tree bark for uterine disorders; kantkari fruit for fevers, asthma, dropsy; harhar fruit for piles, hiccoughs, worms; spreading hogweed, for practically all ailments. In the courtyard *(opposite)*, women sort Unani herbs.

Hamdard

7

The Test: Does It Work? Is It Safe?

Rat fetuses, stored in glycerin, will be examined for malformations caused by experimental drugs fed their mothers. New drugs must pass this test, one in a series of four basic types, to be considered safe for trials on humans.

FINDING OUT IF A NEW DRUG WORKS would seem to be easy enough. The doctor gives it to a sick patient. If the patient gets better, the drug works; if he fails to improve, the drug does not work.

Unfortunately, such a straightforward procedure yields nothing but confusion. Proving a drug is one of the most difficult tasks of modern science, calling for broad knowledge, inventiveness, meticulousness—and a sharp eye for the pitfalls that lie on every side.

The causes of the difficulties are several. First of all, most patients recover from their ailments whether they get drugs or not. Many others recover as a result of the psychological effects of receiving treatment (particularly if it seems new), even when the "drugs" they receive are placebos, totally innocuous substances that do not affect physiological processes. And often it is even impossible to predict that a drug will not harm the patient, let alone cure him, for preliminary trials on animals can be misleading (animals react differently from humans), and tests on a few volunteers are inconclusive (people vary widely in their reactions).

Yet these uncertainties have been overcome to provide mankind with thousands of new remedies that save lives that once would have been lost and banish suffering that once had to be endured. Thanks to delicate and ingenious testing methods, it is possible to determine that these new drugs are safe and effective—if not for 100 per cent of the people 100 per cent of the time, at least for most people most of the time. The fact that no more can be said testifies to the difficulties that still plague even the most scientifically sophisticated tests. The fact that this much can be said is a tribute to the genius of pharmacologists who have discovered how to tell whether a new drug is worthy of use.

The modern drug tester draws on the accumulated knowledge of half a dozen scientific disciplines: not merely chemistry and pharmacology but also physiology (of man and many other animals), psychology (because drugs can affect the body through the mind as well as directly in the body), and even mathematics (for an indication of the role that chance plays in test results). A pharmacologist may spend seven years evaluating one new drug—trying it on several different species of animal, administering it to successively larger groups of people, analyzing his findings—before he finally convinces governmental authorities that the drug should be admitted to medical respectability. And after a drug has won acceptance, its evaluation still cannot stop, for prolonged and widespread use may turn up effects that no testing program, even if it includes thousands of subjects and lasts several years, could predict.

The first question in assaying a drug is: how safe is it? And the first step toward answering that question is a series of trials on animals.

Under current U.S. regulations, every new drug, before being given to human beings, must be tested on at least two species of mammal. The animals are tested in groups, to secure various kinds of information. One group will receive large quantities of the drug, in order to ascertain how much of a dose will prove fatal. Another will be given smaller doses—proportional to the dose that is expected to be medically useful in man—

then will be studied over a period of months for long-term damage. In this process, the testers will ask such questions as: do the animals gain or lose weight; are they unusually active or inactive; do they show any rashes or lesions of the skin? Whatever the answers, the animals will ultimately be killed and their vital organs examined for subtler signs of damage. The drug will also be given to young animals, to ascertain whether it affects their growth.

Tests against tragedies

In recent years, still another type of animal testing has become obligatory: administration of the drug to pregnant females, to discover whether it produces any ill effects on their offspring. Such tests became routine as a result of the thalidomide tragedy of 1962, in which thousands of European women who had used the sedative drug thalidomide during early pregnancy gave birth to deformed babies. Since then, testing procedures have been stiffened in both the United States and Europe—and physicians have become considerably more cautious about prescribing any drug for a pregnant woman.

Though animal tests are a necessary first step, their relevance to human beings is often uncertain. The reason lies in the truism that animal species are not alike. The obvious differences between, say, a man and a mouse—size, shape, furriness, diet, habits and so on—are themselves the results of less obvious but equally extensive chemical differences. And since the chemistry of an organism influences the effects a drug has on it, these effects may well differ between man and mouse.

In innumerable cases, one species' drug may be another's poison. Penicillin, for example, is one of the least toxic of substances—to a man. To a guinea pig, it is fatal in small doses.

Even when species are alike in their basic response to a drug, their tolerance for it may vary wildly. A dose of morphine that would kill a man will merely anesthetize a dog. Fluoroacetic acid, found in a poisonous South African plant, will kill a dog in one-milligram doses, but a rat can take about 100 times this quantity and a toad 10,000 times as much.

The reasons for various species differences in responses to drugs are sometimes bizarre. Penicillin is lethal to a guinea pig, for example, not because it poisons the animal, but because it destroys certain vital intestinal bacteria. Squill, an ancient heart drug, is useful rat poison partly because rats (which like its taste and eat it voraciously) are unable to vomit. A man would throw up an overdose of squill, probably before it could do him serious damage; the rat cannot do so, and dies.

More frequently, however, species differences involve subtle differences in internal chemistry—notably in the enzymes that regulate bodily processes. It is an enzyme, for example, that causes one of the most remarkable of these less obvious species differences. The painful disease called gout, characterized by excess uric acid in the blood, strikes only human beings and the great apes. These species lack an enzyme called uricase that, in other mammals, renders uric acid innocuous.

For years, drug testers sought a way to study compounds that would prevent gout through their ability to cut uric acid production or hasten its excretion. But research was hampered by the difficulty of finding an experimental animal that could accumulate uric acid in its blood. Apes were expensive and difficult to work with; the conventional laboratory animals—guinea pigs, cats, rats, mice and dogs—were useless because the uric acid in their blood is quickly eliminated by uricase. Then a surprising fact emerged: not all dogs have uricase in their blood. The Dalmatian coach dog, it was found, resembles man in lacking the enzyme, and is therefore a suitable subject for testing gout drugs—but only, it appears, if it is a pure-bred Dalmatian.

The difficulty faced by the gout-drug testers exemplifies another perennial problem associated with animal testing: the scarcity of animal "models" for human diseases. The tester would like to try his experimental drug not only on healthy animals but also on animals suffering from the disease that the drug is aimed at. Such a test is usually impossible. Though animals become diseased quite as often as humans, their diseases are seldom similar enough to human complaints to be of much scientific use. For example, no animal develops leprosy spontaneously. And while atherosclerosis (the most common form of human heart trouble) occurs spontaneously in some animals and can be induced artificially in others, in neither case do its mechanisms bear much resemblance to those of the human disease. A condition superficially resembling human congestive heart failure can be caused in experimental animals—but it does not respond to the drugs such as digitalis that effectively relieve the disease in human beings.

The step from animal to man

The only important category of animal disease that closely parallels human disease is infection. Microbes that attack human beings will usually attack other species, and a drug that cures the infection in the animal will usually cure it in man. This fact helps to explain why anti-infection drugs are the only important group of curative substances yet devised. For these drugs, the step from animal to human subjects has been relatively easy.

For every drug, however, that step must be taken. When a drug tester has completed his animal studies, he must go on to ascertain how far his animal findings apply to human beings. He begins his tests on humans with a very small group of healthy volunteers—often convicts who are

THE AGONY OF GOUT, which causes excruciating pain in the big toe, is lampooned in an 18th Century cartoon showing the devil applying a hot coal to an English gentleman's toe. Gout was long a subject of ridicule because it was blamed on overindulgent living. While too much wine or rich food can bring on an attack, the disease itself is caused by an inherited tendency of the body to accumulate uric acid, which may crystallize and form painful deposits in the joints. Although drugs can alleviate or prevent attacks of gout, they cannot cure the disease.

attracted by the break in routine and the modest payments they receive. This small, "preclinical" group receives very limited doses of the drug at first. If nothing happens, the dose is gradually increased until something does happen; when the subjects begin to show toxic effects, the dose is cut back to a lower level. Meanwhile, the physical condition of the volunteers is studied exhaustively.

If these early trials indicate that useful amounts of the drug can be administered without harm, the volunteer group is expanded. The tester's concern is still with the drug's safety rather than its effectiveness; his aim is to determine the "dose response curve," which shows how the effect of the drug changes with changes in the amount that is administered. Human beings vary in their responses to drugs, as they do in height, intelligence and every other characteristic, and it is important to know how far this variability affects responses to the drug being tested. (In some extreme cases, an identical dose of a drug can cure one man, poison another and leave a third unaffected.)

Only after the drug has been proved safe for human use does it come to the crucial part of testing: the study of effectiveness. Will the new compound help the disease for which it is intended? The question can be answered only by giving the drug to diseased people; and getting an unequivocal answer often makes the tester's earlier difficulties—species differences, dose curves and all—seem like child's play.

The problems stem from two ancient difficulties of the pharmacologist: placebo effect and spontaneous recovery. For a clinical trial to have any meaning, the investigator must be able to report, not merely that the patients improved, but that the improvement was due to the drug's pharmacological action rather than to its psychological effects as a placebo or to the body's own disease-combating mechanisms.

A place for placebos

Paradoxically, the standard method for dealing with both these problems involves the use of placebos. The technique, developed only about a generation ago, requires two groups of patients as similar as possible —in general physique as well as severity of illness. The first, or "treatment" group, is given the experimental drug, while the second, or "control" group, is given innocuous placebos disguised as active remedies; in all other respects the two groups receive identical treatment.

The response of patients in the control group provides a standard for judging the worth of the drug to the treatment group. In both groups, there should be an equal number of patients who get better because of spontaneous recovery or the placebo effect. Those two sources of error are thus canceled out. And if there is then a preponderance of recoveries in the treatment group, the drug has obviously helped some patients.

TESTING A NEW DRUG involves many steps that may take many years. The procedure followed with an antibiotic, sodium cephalothin, illustrates the careful preliminaries that precede approval of a drug for public use. As shown at the right, the drug was first injected into dogs, rabbits and pregnant rats. Judged safe for human testing, it was given to adults, children, pregnant women, newborn babies and premature infants. It was then compared for effectiveness with other antibiotics and finally the results of all the tests were forwarded to the Food and Drug Administration for approval.

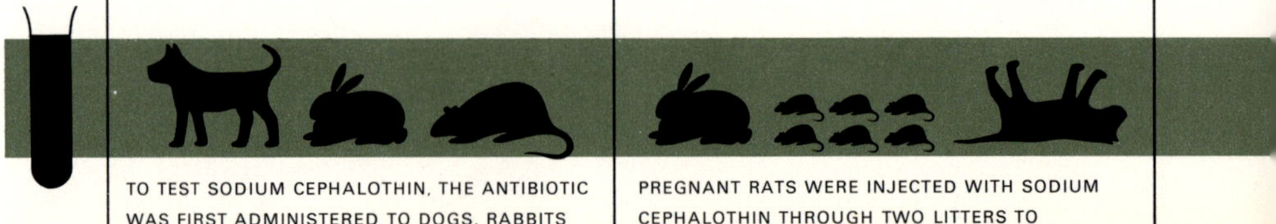

TO TEST SODIUM CEPHALOTHIN, THE ANTIBIOTIC WAS FIRST ADMINISTERED TO DOGS, RABBITS AND RATS. THIS STAGE OF THE TESTING SHOWED THAT THE DRUG WAS READILY ABSORBED, RAPIDLY EXCRETED AND WELL TOLERATED BY ANIMALS.

PREGNANT RATS WERE INJECTED WITH SODIUM CEPHALOTHIN THROUGH TWO LITTERS TO DETERMINE ITS EFFECT ON SUCCEEDING GENERATIONS. THE TESTS SHOWED NO ILL EFFECTS IN THE YOUNG. LETHAL DOSAGES OF THE DRUG WERE ALSO ESTABLISHED.

If there were no more than that to drug testing, the pharmacopoeia would be a far more certain guide to medical treatment than it is. But pharmacologists have learned that spontaneous recovery and psychological influences affect trials in subtle and intricate ways. Many a drug—like the bee venom once touted as a remedy for arthritis—has been successful in one series of tests, only to fail miserably in later ones. In some cases a drug works wonders when administered by a beautiful nurse; when dispensed by a male orderly, it does nothing at all.

Fooling the patient—and the doctor

Such vagaries have forced the drug testers to adopt elaborate precautions. No longer is the placebo a simple sugar pill; now it is compounded as carefully as the drug itself, duplicating it in shape, color and taste. Nor is much reliance placed on concealing the nature of the placebo from the patients alone; this "single blind" method is not enough to outwit the placebo-susceptible person. So long as doctor or nurse knows which pill is placebo and which is not, the patient may respond to the gleam (or lack of it) in his attendant's eye.

Today drug testers use a "double blind" technique, in which neither patient nor doctor knows which preparation is being administered. Both drug and placebo are identified only by code numbers, known to those who make up the preparations, but not to those who administer them. Not until the test is ended is the code revealed, so that the two groups of patients can be identified and their responses compared.

Further precautions are taken to assure uniformity between the treatment (drug) and control (placebo) groups. The progress of a disease, like the response to a particular drug, can be affected by a host of seemingly extraneous influences: age, heredity, sex, weight, and a score of other factors that can be summed up as "general physical condition." In theory, if the test group includes a woman of 29, with three children, somewhat overweight and with low blood pressure, the control group should include an identical twin with the same weight, blood pressure and family size. In practice, this kind of match is almost impossible, but the investigator tries for a close equivalence of factors that are believed to affect the disease and drug responses. One serious limitation on this attempt is the fact that people of a particular age group, for instance, do not get sick to order.

The laborious problem of matching can sometimes be avoided by what is called the crossover technique, in which each subject under treatment also serves as his own control, so that the two "groups" are truly identical. For perhaps two weeks, a patient gets the drug; during the next two weeks he gets a placebo. The technique serves very well in dealing with conditions, such as diabetes and high blood pressure,

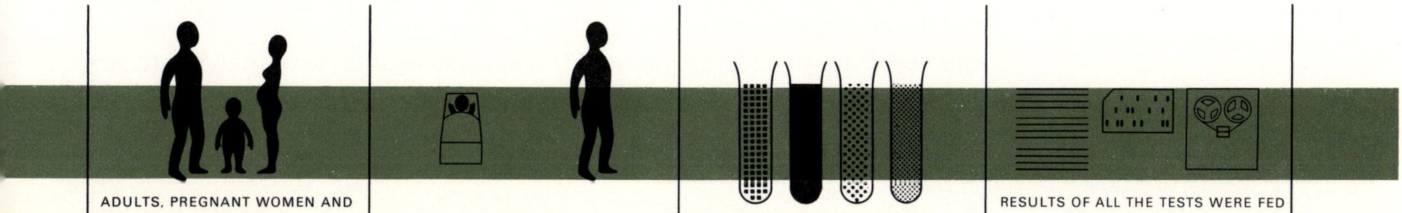

ADULTS, PREGNANT WOMEN AND CHILDREN WERE GIVEN THE DRUG. IT WAS EASILY ABSORBED, RAPIDLY EXCRETED AND WELL TOLERATED, CONFIRMING EARLIER ANIMAL TESTS.

CHILDREN AND ADULTS WERE INJECTED WITH VARYING AMOUNTS OF THE DRUG AND APPROPRIATE DOSAGES WERE ESTABLISHED.

THE DRUG WAS COMPARED WITH OTHER ANTIBIOTICS FOR EFFECTIVENESS SO THAT IT COULD BE ASSIGNED ITS PROPER PLACE IN COMBATING INFECTION.

RESULTS OF ALL THE TESTS WERE FED INTO A COMPUTER. THIS INFORMATION WAS THEN SENT TO THE FOOD AND DRUG ADMINISTRATION, AND APPROVAL OF THE DRUG FOLLOWED ANALYSIS OF THE DATA.

in which the character and severity of the disease changes very slowly. But in rapidly developing ailments, such as most infections, crossovers are useless. A person suffering from typhoid fever—or for that matter, a common cold—is not the "same" patient on Tuesday that he was on Monday. In such cases, the investigator is forced back to matching and to hoping that he has not overlooked any relevant factors.

Having solved as best he can the problems of eliminating the placebo effect and other forms of bias, the investigator is not yet out of the woods. He must still collect his results and decide what they mean.

To the extent that he can measure the results by objective methods—blood tests, X-rays, and so on—he is in luck. Too often, however, he is forced to rely at least in part on the patients' own reports of their progress—and these reports are frequently inaccurate. Patients are prone to talk about how they feel at the moment, forgetting that a few hours earlier they may have felt much better, or much worse. The way the doctor phrases his questions to the patient may help determine the answer. "Did you feel nauseated after taking the pill?" is quite likely to elicit a "Yes"—regardless of how the patient actually felt. "How did you feel after taking the pills?" will stand a better chance of getting an accurate report. Such subjective factors help to make the gathering of clinical data inaccurate and often exasperating. As one of the authors of this book has written elsewhere, "There are few investigations in any other scientific discipline in which so critical a part in the collection, storage and interpretation of observations is left in the hands of an interested, biased and untrained assistant—the subject himself."

Eventually, the investigator will come up with a set of figures that should tell him whether the drug is in fact doing what it is supposed to do. But do they?

Sometimes the decision is easy. The condition known as subacute bacterial endocarditis—an infection of the lining of the heart—had a death rate, before antibiotics, of 99 per cent. When antibiotics were tried, they cut the rate to about 15 per cent—and it was then no great feat of judgment to conclude that the drugs were in fact responsible.

Why did they get well?

But tests with such definitive results are rare. In most tests, the majority of patients recover or show improvement, whether they receive drugs or not. The tester may face a situation in which half the patients receiving a drug showed improvement, but a third of those receiving a placebo also showed improvement. He must decide whether it was the drug that caused improvement in the treatment group, or simply chance—the possibility that this group happened to have an unusually large percentage of spontaneous improvements.

At this point the tester usually calls on mathematics for help. By mathematical formulas, he can figure what the odds are that a particular result may occur by chance. If the odds against a chance result are no better than 20 to 1, he will usually consider his test meaningless and undertake further tests before making a decision. Fortunately, the odds against chance results increase rapidly as the number of patients treated increases (all other factors remaining equal). Thus, a large number of subjects helps to ensure that the tests will be meaningful.

For this reason a drug must usually be tested successfully on at least 5,000 to 15,000 people before the U.S. Food and Drug Administration will approve it. After so many trials, obviously, the drug must clearly be safe at least in comparison with the risks of giving no drug. Obviously, but not necessarily, for even 15,000 patients cannot exhaust the quirks of human physiology and all the combinations of circumstance.

Problems in blood and in cheese

Consider, for example, the strange cases of the antibiotic drug chloramphenicol and the antidepressant drug tranylcypromine. Chloramphenicol is used, among other things, for treating typhoid fever and typhus. Occasionally, however, it destroys not only the microbes of these diseases but also blood-forming cells of the patient's bone marrow. This potentially dangerous—even fatal—outcome was not discovered during the clinical tests of the drug because it occurs only in about one case out of 150,000. Furthermore, out of 150,000 people, one or two may well develop a similar blood disorder spontaneously, drug or no drug. It took experience with more than five million cases before physicians realized that something unusual was occurring and that chloramphenicol rather than chance was responsible. Once they knew this, of course, they could take precautions, testing individuals receiving the drug and stopping its use if signs of bone-marrow destruction appeared.

Tranylcypromine, during its clinical trials as an antidepressant, seemed to be safe. Later, however, a few patients treated with it showed a dangerous jump in blood pressure. Only after lengthy study did it become clear that this result occurred only if the patient had eaten certain cheeses. Tranylcypromine, it turned out, prevents the body from destroying tyramine, a substance contained in cheese—and when tyramine accumulates in the body, the blood pressure goes up.

Under federal law, drug advertisements in medical journals must include long lists of "indications" (when to use the drug) "contraindications" (when not to use it), "warnings," "precautions" and "side effects." This information represents the distilled clinical experience with the drug, including the findings of physicians who have used it. The expansion of these lists as experience accumulates shows that no testing program can gather all the facts about a drug or substitute for the careful observation and judgment of the conscientious physician. Testing can evaluate a drug; it is the doctor who must evaluate the patient.

In itself, drug testing is an inherently inexact science. Because it is inexact, several hundred Americans may die every year who would have lived had they not been given some drug. But because testing is a science, hundreds of thousands of people now lead productive lives, who would be incapacitated or dead were it not for modern drugs.

"Good for What Ails You"

The second half of the 19th Century was the gaudy, golden era of patent medicine in the United States. In the cities, drugstore racks groaned beneath hundreds of nostrums, each advertised as a cure for anything from coughs to consumption—and, with rare exceptions such as Castoria and Lydia Pinkham's, almost all of them worthless. Medicine shows traveled the countryside, making one-night stands in "one-horse towns," extolling remedies like Kickapoo Indian Sagwa and Hamlin's Wizard Oil. Before the federal government began cracking down in 1907, cure-alls like Kennedy's Medical Discovery *(opposite)* had boosted patent-medicine sales to over $80 million a year.

The faith of the buyers was exceeded only by their gullibility. In an enthusiastic endorsement, Jane Demee of Utica, New York, wrote that, after five years of using Phoenix Bitters, Life Pills, Brandreth's Pills, Phelps Arcanum, Smith's Anti-Mercurial Syrup, Swaim's Panacea, Conway's Boston Medicine and Fowler's Solution of Arsenic, without observing any improvement, "I am satisfied that my life has been preserved and my health entirely restored by the blessing of God and the use of Bristol's Fluid Extract of Sarsaparilla."

AN ANGELIC CURE-ALL

A poster for Kennedy's Medical Discovery typifies flamboyant patent-medicine advertising, which stressed trademarks and ignored ingredients. Kennedy's advertised: "It seldom takes hold of two people alike. . . . Beginning at the stomach, it goes searching . . . for any hidden humor. . . . Soon you thank me for making something that has reached your weak spot."

KENNEDY'S MEDICAL DISCOVERY
AN ANGEL OF MERCY IN EVERY HOUSEHOLD
CURES SCROFULA, ERYSIPELAS, SCALD HEAD, SALT RHEUM, LEPRA, SCURVY,
PIMPLES, ULCERS, CANKER & EVERY DISEASE OF THE SKIN OF WHATEVER NAME OR NATURE.

PLEASE HANG UP.
Pratts HEALING OINTMENT
FOR MAN AND BEAST
PRATT FOOD CO.
WE BOTH USE IT!
CURES
HARNESS AND SADDLE GALLS,
OPEN WOUNDS, CUTS, SORES, SCRATCHES, BURNS,
EVERY BOX GUARANTEED.
GET IT HERE TO DAY!

A Beginning from Bilious Pills

American patent medicines and their extravagant advertising are both the brainchildren of a shrewd Connecticut Yankee named Samuel Lee. In 1796 he mixed a cathartic resin called gamboge with aloes, soap and potassium nitrate and patented the bitter concoction under the name of Bilious Pills. These he marketed as a sure cure for yellow fever, jaundice, dysentery, dropsy, worms and "female complaints." There is no evidence that the pills ever cured anything, but Lee soon had a host of imitators.

Relatively few of the 19th Century patent medicines were actually patented, since this required disclosure of their ingredients. Rare was the medicine-maker who cared to admit that his ballyhooed panacea was little more than a hand-me-down folk remedy or simply a horse salve that also offered relief to humans *(left)*.

Here and there among the medicines were a few honest remedies. One of these was Castoria *(below)*, a patented formula of a syrup containing senna mixed with sugar, Rochelle salt and a number of aromatic spirits including pleasant-tasting wintergreen. A popular and effective remedy for children's digestive disorders, Castoria is still sold.

Another surviving formula is that of Dr. Miles's Compound Extract of Tomato, a popular patent medicine of the 1830s. Although it vanished long ago from drug counters, Compound Extract of Tomato can be purchased today—as ordinary catsup.

". . . TWO FOR A HORSE"
A poster for Pratt's Healing Ointment, a 19th Century farm remedy, stresses its value for both man and beast. Patent-medicine manufacturers mixed horse-liniment ingredients like camphor, ammonia, chloroform, alcohol and turpentine into combinations that were also useful to humans. A familiar dosage instruction for internal use was "One for a man, two for a horse."

PLUGGING FOR A USEFUL REMEDY
A vivid advertising card of 1885 shows the famous circus elephant Jumbo feeding Castoria—one of the few old remedies that has proved useful—to Tom Thumb, his pygmy companion.

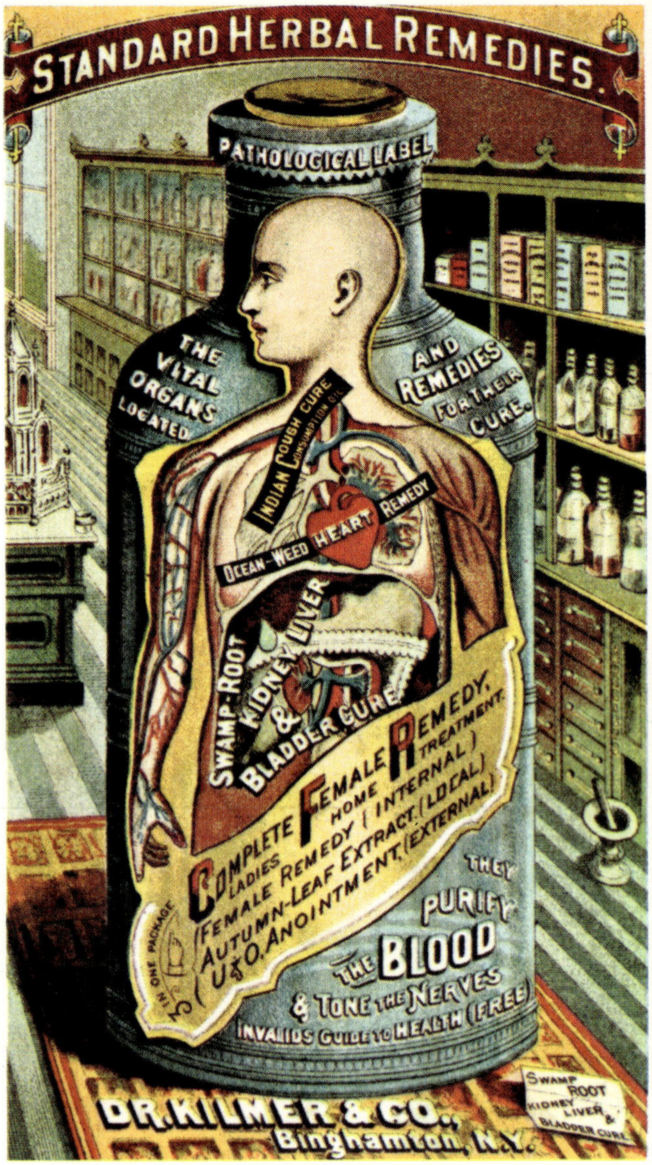

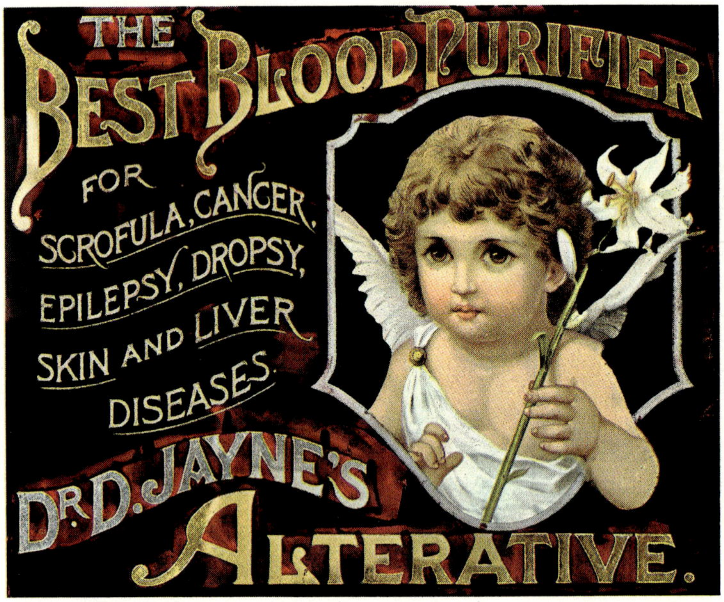

The Battle of the Billboards

In the heyday of patent medicines the names and claims of thousands of remedies assailed the public at every vantage point, from the risers of elevated railway station steps in New York City to the paint-splashed walls of Niagara Falls and the Grand Canyon. Manufacturers, locked in a fierce competitive struggle, overlooked no gimmick in their massive advertising campaigns. Newspapers were loaded with patent-medicine advertising—often paid endorsements disguised as news items—and the almanac put out by Ayer's Sarsaparilla was a familiar item in many American households. Owners of strategically located barns allowed the names of patent medicines to be proclaimed in huge letters—in exchange for a free coat of paint. No settlement was too small or remote for the far-ranging medicine shows and pitchmen, whose entertainment and elixirs were equally well received.

There seemed to be no limit to the public's acceptance of patent remedies, and a bemused English visitor wrote: "We breakfast on aloes, dine on cassia, sup on logwood and myrrh, and sleep on morphine and prussic acid." He neglected to mention the most prevalent ingredient of all: alcohol. Many a teetotaling temperance advocate saw no cause for suspicion in the pleasant glow produced by the popular "blood tonics" like those advertised on these pages, most of them containing over 25 per cent alcohol.

AYER'S SARSAPARILLA
CURES
SCROFULA,
DYSPEPSIA,
SORES,
CATARRH,
BOILS,
Rheumatism,
DEBILITY,
HUMOURS,
All Disorders
TETTER,
OF THE
ECZEMA.
BLOOD.
AYER'S
AYER'S SARSAPARILLA
The DEACON. "Land sake 'Liza, the very sight of that bottle makes me feel like another man."
MPOUND CONCENTRATED EXTRACT-THE STRONGEST-BEST-CHEAPEST BLOOD MEDICINE

BURDOCK BLOOD BITTERS

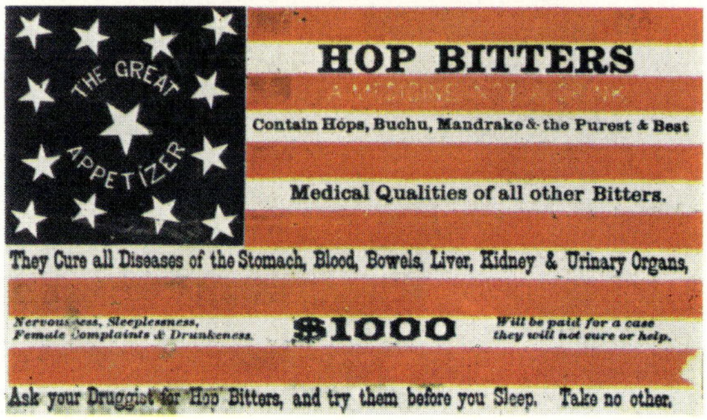
THE GREAT APPETIZER
HOP BITTERS
Contain Hops, Buchu, Mandrake & the Purest & Best
Medical Qualities of all other Bitters.
They Cure all Diseases of the Stomach, Blood, Bowels, Liver, Kidney & Urinary Organs,
$1000
Will be paid for a case they will not cure or help.
Ask your Druggist for Hop Bitters, and try them before you Sleep. Take no other.

"Cures" for the Incurable

"But drink the draught, 'twil save you
That bids consumption fly,
Take Dr. Swayne's Wild Cherry,
And do not, do not die!"

The best customers for 19th Century patent medicines were those suffering from the slow, wasting respiratory diseases—influenza, pneumonia and "consumption" (tuberculosis)—that accounted for approximately 25 per cent of all adult deaths in the United States in 1900.

Although these three diseases were then considered incurable, hundreds of patent medicines were advertised

as sure cures. The most popular were the sweet-tasting cherry pectorals, like Wistar's Balsam of Wild Cherry *(opposite)* and Dr. Swayne's brand that inspired the verse opposite. In most cases the chief ingredient, disguised by a pleasant cherry flavor, was opium. The narcotic drug provided temporary relief from chest pains but had absolutely no effect on the germs that cause respiratory ills. Dr. King's New Discovery for Consumption contained both chloroform, to ease the wracking coughs of tuberculosis, and opium, to give the patient a false—and often fatal—sense of well-being.

A more subtle approach was employed by Dr. Samuel Hartman, the millionaire manufacturer of Peruna. In his widely distributed booklet, "The Ills of Life" *(above, right)*, Hartman insisted that his medicine cured only one thing: catarrh. But then Hartman went on to define consumption and pneumonia as "catarrh of the lungs," enteritis as catarrh of the intestines, heart disease as catarrh of the heart, measles as catarrh of the skin and dozens of other ailments as other forms of catarrh.

The cure for all these could be accomplished, according to Hartman, by using his compound of seven vegetable drugs in "cologne spirits," his flowery name for alcohol. Chemical analysis showed the seven drugs to constitute less than half of one per cent of the Peruna formula. Of the other 99½ per cent, more than 70 per cent was water—and 28 per cent was alcohol, making a drink as strong as a stiff highball. The only "ill of life" that Peruna could really cure was the endemic thirst for liquor in legally dry towns. In this it succeeded so well that by 1905 the Peruna habit had helped make the "catarrh remedy" the nation's best-selling medicine.

RESIDENCE & LABORATORY OF G. G. GREEN

Palaces from Patent Medicines

The patent medicines made millionaires of many 19th Century nostrum hucksters, who often vied with one another in ostentatious displays of wealth. G. G. Green built a showplace mansion and "laboratory" *(left)* with earnings from his remedies, German Syrup, August Flower and Ague Conqueror. Dr. Joseph Schenck, of Pulmonic Syrup and Sea Weed Tonic fame, boasted both a Philadelphia mansion known as Schenck's Palace and a 300-acre estate in the country. Swamproot millionaire Willis Kilmer owned five estates plus a stud farm.

For years, the citizens of Rochester, New York, were treated to the spectacle of feuding patent-medicine tycoons spending their fortunes to upstage each other. After Asa Soule had brought a major-league baseball team to Rochester and named it for his product, Hop Bitters, his rival H. H. Warner went him one better by building an astronomical observatory and offering Warner's Safe Cure prizes to anyone discovering a new heavenly body. Then Soule, desperate to regain stature, offered $100,000 to the University of Rochester if it changed its name to Hop Bitters University. Rebuffed, Soule threw in the towel and headed west for Kansas and a new career as a land speculator.

A MANSION BUILT ON SYRUP
The impressive home of German Syrup millionaire G. G. Green, located across a handsomely landscaped lawn from his plant in Woodbury, New Jersey, is shown in this front-cover illustration from Green's Diary Almanac. Proud of his affluence, Green, pictured on the urn at lower right, often added an illustration of his ocean-going steam yacht to the almanac's back cover.

Collier's
THE NATIONAL WEEKLY
SWAMP-ROOT
PRICE $1.00
DOPE
PRICE
$
DOPE
AGAIN!!!
VOL. XLIX NO 8
NEWS-STAND EDITION
MAY 11 1912

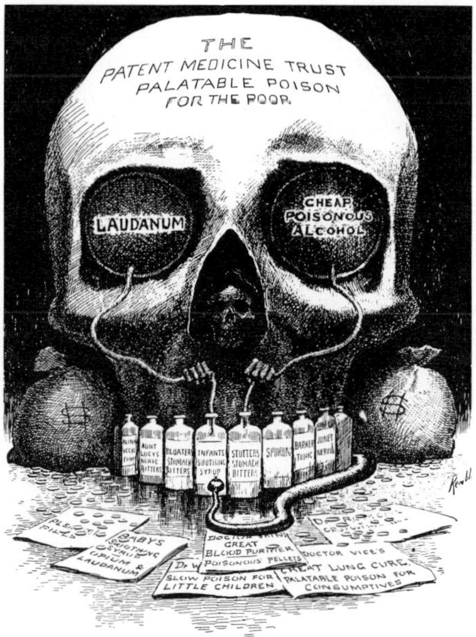

"A Goblin-Realm of Fakery"

The growing ground swell of criticism directed against patent medicines in the 19th Century by physicians, druggists and a handful of newspapers reached flood-tide proportions in the first decade of the 20th Century, as influential national magazines began attacking patent remedies.

In 1905, a remarkable series of articles began to appear in *Collier's*. The series was widely ballyhooed in advertisements that used fanciful, snakelike designs *(border)* to point to the grim cartoon above—a skull representing "the patent medicine trust" filling toothlike bottles from sockets labeled "laudanum" (opium) and "cheap poisonous alcohol."

In the very first paragraph of the lead article, reporter Samuel Hopkins Adams stated a theme he would document with devastating accuracy in each of the installments that followed: that the purchasers of patent medicines "swallow huge quantities of alcohol, an appalling amount of opiates and narcotics, a wide assortment of varied drugs ranging from powerful and dangerous heart depressants to insidious liver stimulants; and, far in excess of all ingredients, undiluted fraud."

Describing patent-medicine advertising as "a veritable goblin-realm of fakery," Adams proceeded to attack 264 nostrums and their manufacturers by name. Peruna was "the maker of drunkards"; Liquozone, the leading "germ-killer" of the day, was a product of "pseudo-scientific charlatanry"; Orangeine, a popular headache powder, was a "subtle poison" because it contained acetanilid, a heart depressant that could be fatal to people with cardiac conditions.

Even before the series was completed in 1906, an aroused Congress passed the first Pure Food and Drug Act, requiring names and amounts of such drugs as alcohol, opium and cocaine to appear on patent-medicine labels. By 1912, when *Collier's* undertook a new campaign *(left)*, the freewheeling golden era of patent medicine was virtually over; a new era of scientific medicine had begun.

Lydia Pinkham's: A Hardy Survivor

The transformation of patent medicines from fraudulent cure-alls to the often helpful remedies sold in drugstores today can be traced in the changing content and claims of one of the old era's survivors: Lydia Pinkham's Vegetable Compound.

A home remedy sold by the original Lydia Pinkham in 1875 as a common cure for all female disorders, the vegetable compound was first prepared in the kitchen of Lydia's home in Lynn, Massachusetts. It was a blend of quaint ingredients: true unicorn root, false unicorn root, life root, pleurisy root, fenugreek seed, black cohosh—and 20 per cent alcohol.

An intensive advertising campaign centered around a shrewd theme—"A woman best understands a woman's ills"—made Pinkham's one of the best-selling patent medicines at the turn of the century. Lydia's benign features appeared on every box and her grandchildren were pictured on giveaway advertising cards *(below)*.

Beginning with the passing of the Pure Food and Drug Act in 1906, however, both the alcoholic content and advertised claims of Pinkham's have been steadily reduced. Today the compound contains a number of new ingredients, including vitamin B_1, and while the liquid version contains 13½ per cent alcohol—about the strength of a glass of wine—most of the million-dollar annual sales comes from the nonalcoholic tablets.

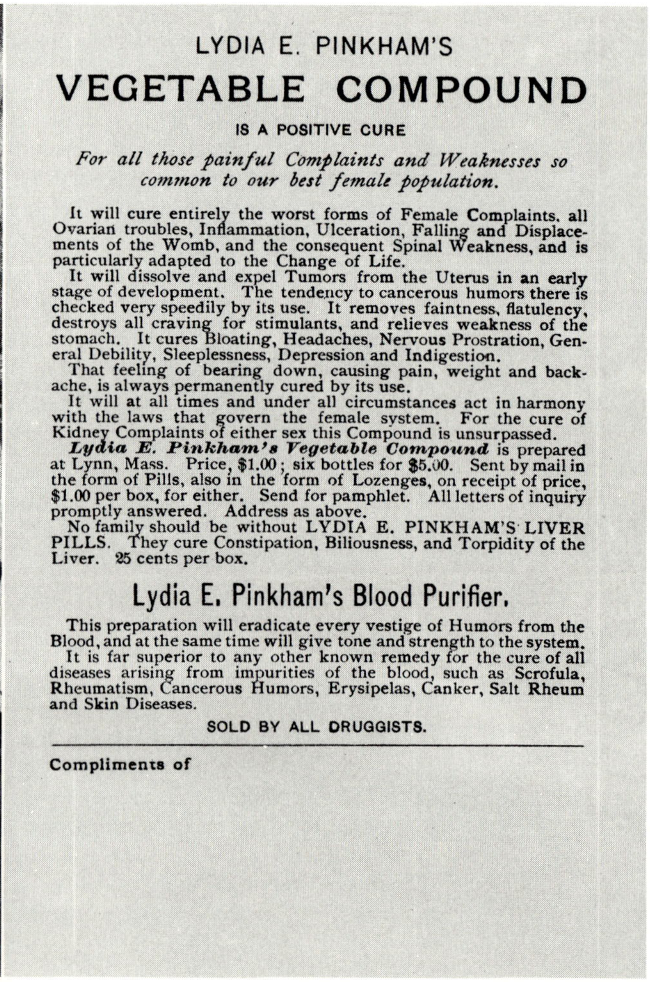

BEFORE AND AFTER

An 1889 advertising card for Lydia Pinkham's Compound *(above)* displays granddaughters Lucy and Marion Pinkham on the front and a long list of "cures" on the back, including "kidney complaints of either sex." By contrast, the 1915 advertisement *(right)*, conforming to new laws restricting label claims, offered nothing more than a cautiously worded recommendation for use in unspecified "weaknesses and disorders."

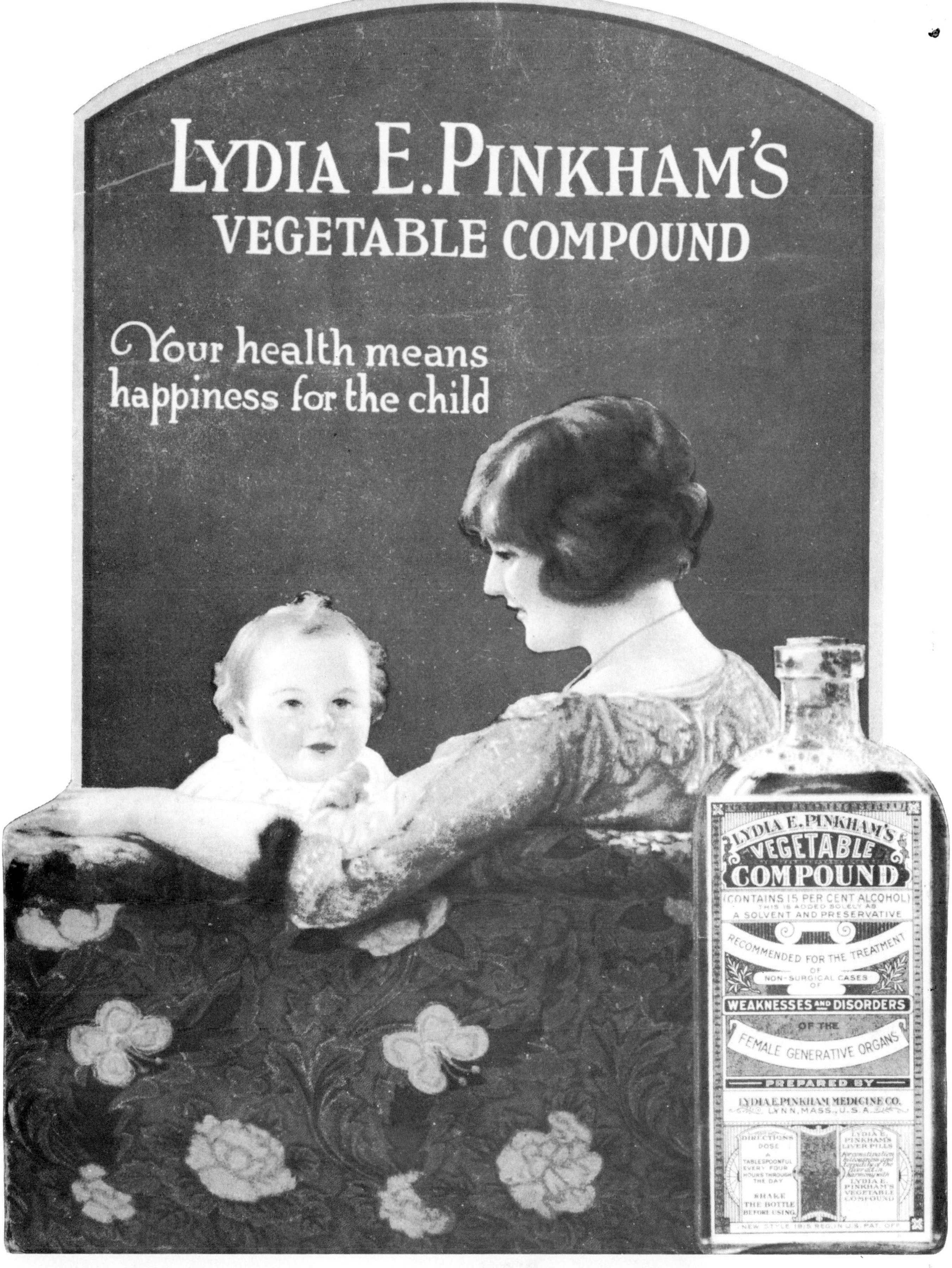
LYDIA E. PINKHAM'S
VEGETABLE COMPOUND
Your health means happiness for the child
LYDIA E. PINKHAM'S
VEGETABLE
COMPOUND
(CONTAINS 15 PER CENT ALCOHOL)
THIS IS ADDED SOLELY AS
A SOLVENT AND PRESERVATIVE
RECOMMENDED FOR THE TREATMENT
OF
NON-SURGICAL CASES
OF
WEAKNESSES AND DISORDERS
OF THE
FEMALE GENERATIVE ORGANS
PREPARED BY
LYDIA E. PINKHAM MEDICINE CO.
LYNN, MASS., U.S.A.
DIRECTIONS
DOSE
A
TABLESPOONFUL
EVERY FOUR
HOURS THROUGH
THE DAY
SHAKE
THE BOTTLE
BEFORE USING
LYDIA E.
PINKHAM'S
LIVER PILLS
LYDIA E.
PINKHAM'S
VEGETABLE
COMPOUND
NEW STYLE 1915 REG. IN U.S. PAT. OFF.

8
The Challenge

Clutching his brush in a hand crippled by arthritis, the impressionist artist Pierre Auguste Renoir struggled to continue painting despite his painful ailment—one of the serious degenerative diseases that continue to challenge pharmacologists.

THE 1937 EDITION of the *United States Dispensatory,* the standard American reference book on drugs, contained some 3,090 entries. Thirty years later, 2,470 of these preparations were no longer listed because they had been proved worthless—but new drugs had brought the total to 1,508. These figures symbolize the pharmacological revolution, which promoted the science of drugs from a rather humble collaborator with medicine to its most intimate associate.

Of the revolution's significance in human terms there is hardly need to speak in detail. In the United States, as in all other countries where modern drugs and medical services are widely available, people live longer—and more productively—than ever before. Of the serious infectious diseases, many can be cured with drugs; many of those impervious to drugs can be prevented by vaccination. Progress in treating mental disease has been almost as remarkable, largely due to the use of new drugs. Even the degenerative diseases—notably those prime killers that cause heart and blood vessel disorders—can often be alleviated by drugs that permit a victim to lead a tolerable if circumscribed existence.

For all its achievements, however, this revolution has shown the same limitations as have history's social and political revolutions: modern pharmacology has not solved all the problems of disease, and even while solving certain problems has created new ones. For some diseases there are literally too many drugs, so that physicians have difficulty deciding on a rational basis which to use. Other diseases, for which there are too few useful drugs, have suddenly grown into serious threats to human welfare and probably will not be overcome without major new discoveries. But making such discoveries is increasingly difficult. In part this is because fresh basic knowledge must be accumulated to inspire new discoveries; in part because drug research involves human experimentation that poses difficult ethical questions.

If these problems can somehow be solved, they might open the way to still another pharmacological revolution and supply remedies for cancer and arthritis, a preventive for old age, even stimulants to intelligence and drugs to improve the very nature of the human race. However, such a new victory would, in turn, bring problems of its own. For already it is clear that whatever direction drug progress may take in the future, it will not merely affect the individual for whom a drug is prescribed, but will exert potent effects on society at large.

Today, the most obvious "drug problem" stems from the sheer multiplicity of drugs. There are, for example, some 44 different antibiotics now being sold in the United States, including 15 varieties of penicillin alone. Part of this array is accounted for by the existence of several major categories—the penicillins, the tetracyclines and so on—each of which has its own peculiar characteristics that adapt it for use against particular kinds of diseases and in particular kinds of circumstances. But *within* each category there are many compounds whose effects differ from one another marginally; even experts cannot always agree on which is most effective. The list of things that drugs can do has expanded rapidly over the past 30 years; but the list of drugs has expanded faster.

The explanation for this duplication and reduplication of drugs lies in the economics of the pharmaceutical business. Drug research is always costly. But it is far less costly to develop a slightly different—and, hopefully, a better—variation of an existing drug than to undertake the lengthy and too often unsuccessful search for an altogether new type of drug. Breakthroughs in drug research (or any other kind) do not happen to order; often, indeed, they depend on the infrequent lucky accident. Any drug company that devoted its research efforts to the pursuit of breakthroughs, though it might just possibly usher in a new medical era, would be far more likely to land abruptly in bankruptcy court.

But the proliferation of new and not always easily distinguishable drugs poses troublesome problems for the practicing physician. Keeping track of the scientific literature on the properties, uses and side effects of all new drugs is far beyond the capacity of any doctor primarily concerned with looking after patients. Some harassed physicians have stopped trying to make their own appraisals of new drugs solely from the professional literature and rely on information supplied by the advertisements and sales representatives of the drug companies. This situation, observes pharmacologist Louis Lasagna, is disturbing to many who would prefer to see doctors guided by "groups less likely to have a bias arising out of the need to earn money for the stockholders."

These problems are quite likely to get worse before they get better. Breakthroughs in pharmacology, rare enough in the past, may be even rarer in the immediate future. Ernst Boris Chain, one of the "Oxford group" that developed penicillin, has declared: "The dazzling success and rate of development . . . in the last few decades cannot be maintained in the future at the same level . . . unless there is a flow of new ideas based on the discovery of new biologic phenomena. We are, at present, living on inherited capital, a very large capital to be sure, but not inexhaustible." Chain, like many scientists, is concerned over a growing tendency, in and out of government, to pursue immediate practical goals at the expense of the theoretical advances that often seem useless—but on which tomorrow's successful applications depend.

A DEATH-DEALING EXPERIMENTER of the First Century B.C., King Mithridates VI, ruler of the ancient kingdom of Pontus in Asia Minor, investigated the action of poison drugs by trying them on condemned convicts. Through these cruel tests—which grew out of his desperate fear that he would be poisoned by plotters—Mithridates discovered what he believed was a universal antidote, a useless concoction made mainly from walnuts, salt and dried figs. His work gained him great fame and little censure—for the use of human guinea pigs was an accepted practice in his time.

Answering the basic questions

Lasagna, at a symposium titled "The Medicated Society," spelled out a few of the specific questions to which basic research must address itself: "How do our drugs work? How do they interact with other drugs . . . ? How much do people differ in their handling of drugs . . . how do children differ from adults. . . ? What genetic factors are important in determining drug effects? Why do some drugs lose their effect on continued use?" Without answers to these and other perhaps even more fundamental questions, the pharmacological revolution may soon be largely a memory.

The business of getting such answers has been further complicated by the question of how research should be carried out on human subjects. No one doubts that some research of this sort must be conducted if progress in drugs, and in medicine generally, is to continue. But when, and under what circumstances?

Doctors have been especially sensitive to this problem since World War II. At the war crimes trials that followed the hostilities, it was revealed that certain Nazi physicians had forced concentration camp inmates to serve as experimental subjects. Many of the experiments were extremely cruel; some, indeed, seemed designed rather to gratify the experimenters' sadism than to advance medical knowledge.

Shocked by these revelations, physicians throughout the world felt compelled to reexamine their own beliefs governing human experimentation. Their conclusions were formalized in such ethical codes as the Declaration of Helsinki, adopted in 1964 at a meeting of the World Medical Association. The Declaration lays down stringent guidelines for clinical research, in particular making clear that it should be carried out only with the patient's consent. This Declaration has been endorsed by medical groups in many countries, including all the major U.S. organizations of medical researchers.

Problems of "the patient's consent"

But just what is involved in "the patient's consent"? The difficulty of answering this question has been highlighted by several incidents in which researchers have carried out experimental work on individuals who, as it turned out, were not informed of the precise nature of the experiment. They had "consented"—but their consent was based on faith in the doctors, not on knowledge. As a result, both the Declaration of Helsinki and regulations of U.S. government bodies concerned with research now require that individuals taking part in almost any kind of drug experiment must first register their informed consent.

On the face of it, this provision seems no more than reasonable. If human beings should not be forced to undergo experimental treatment—and everyone agrees that they should not—surely they should not be permitted to volunteer to do so unless they understand what they are volunteering for. But like many ethical questions, this one is not quite so simple as it looks.

To ascertain the worth of a new drug, results with the drug are often compared with the results obtained when a placebo is used. A patient in the study group must, if he is to give his informed consent, be told that he may receive a placebo if the luck of the draw runs that way. Quite likely he will object; why, after all, should he take the chance of receiving no medication? In such situations clinical researchers are finding patients reluctant to sign the required consent forms.

How the "informed consent" requirement might hamper vital medical research is best shown by describing the valuable information obtained from an experiment that could not have observed this rule. In India, not long ago, a group of doctors undertook an investigation of treatments for tetanus. Tetanus is a serious public health problem there, ranking

A RESPECTER OF LIFE. Roger Bacon, the pioneering English scientist of the 13th Century, opposed the use of human beings as guinea pigs in drug tests. Bacon, a leader in the rebellion against medieval reliance on written authority, was one of the first scholars to recognize the need for experimentation. True knowledge, he believed, could only be gathered through the observation of nature and the testing of theories. But he condemned experiments that used people because he felt that "the nobility of the material" made the possibility of mistakes unacceptable.

among the four leading causes of death. Obviously a better understanding of the disease is an important and worthwhile goal for Indian medical researchers, and for the population generally.

Tetanus is treated with antitoxin, which neutralizes the poisons liberated by the tetanus bacillus. Or so, at least, it was thought. Antitoxin does not always work—and the Indian physicians were brash enough to wonder whether it *ever* worked.

They thereupon set up four groups of tetanus patients. Three received antitoxin, though in different doses, the fourth received no antitoxin at all. The result, in terms of current medical practice, was startling: the groups showed no differences. Regardless of whether they had received antitoxin, or how much they had received, about half of each group recovered and the rest died.

If these results are confirmed by other research teams they will constitute an important contribution to medical knowledge. If a drug is worthless, the sooner doctors know it the better, especially since a worthless drug may make some patients even sicker (tetanus antitoxin in particular produces a good deal of "serum sickness"). Moreover, misplaced faith in a drug can lead to poorer general treatment.

In the United States, under current regulations, such an experiment would almost certainly be impossible. Few tetanus patients if any would consent to receiving no antitoxin; indeed, few physicians would be courageous (or foolhardy) enough to suggest it. Yet it is hard to avoid the feeling that some experiments of this sort must be carried out if worthless old drugs are to be weeded out of the pharmacopoeia and new and better ones included.

This ethical dilemma has been summarized clearly by Samuel Bukantz of New York University, a physician well acquainted with the problems of drug research. "No declaration of principles, however widely endorsed, no system of regulations, however rigorously enforced, can evade the need for making ethical choices and ethical compromises," he declares. "Sick people want—and are entitled to—the best care obtainable. Well people want—and are entitled to—a rapid advance in medical knowledge against the time when they too may fall sick. And sometimes the interests of the sick individual and those of the society of which he is a part are going to conflict. Putting it at its bluntest, there will be times when the researcher must decide whether he is prepared to risk one life in the hope that he can later save thousands."

Frontiers of pharmacology

Despite the scientific and ethical problems that stand in the way of drug progress, pharmacologists can see exciting prospects ahead. They cannot predict what wonder drugs are about to be found, let alone when. But it is possible to single out the challenging areas of pharmacology, the scientific frontiers that promise discoveries revolutionary in their impact on mankind.

By all odds the most immediately challenging area is that of the degenerative diseases, whose dangers have been made even more apparent by the success of drugs against infection. Drugs, if they have not conquered infectious diseases, have at any rate shown how to contain many of them; in those parts of the world where infection is still a serious menace, the problem is less that of finding suitable drugs than of making existing drugs, together with medical and sanitary services, available to the population.

But when it comes to cancer, rheumatoid arthritis, or disorders of the heart and blood vessels, we find that their toll has gone up, not down, during the pharmacological revolution—and in precisely those prosperous countries where drugs are most readily available. In a sense this is a tribute to medical progress, since the increased incidence results in part from the fact that more people are living long enough to develop these diseases. But it is hardly cause for rejoicing.

Although degenerative diseases can almost never be cured, their progress can sometimes be checked. The derangements they produced in the body can often be ameliorated by drugs that derange the body in the opposite direction, as some drugs do in the case of high blood pressure. But deranging the body, even for the patient's benefit, is not the physician's true aim; his goal is the restoration of normal functioning.

Pinpointing a process

To cure degenerative diseases will require pharmacological sharpshooting—in the technical phrase, the use of drugs with a very high specificity of action. Drugs have been successful in knocking out microbes because high specificity is not essential to that task. The targets are organisms whose physiology differs radically from that of man; there is, therefore, a reasonable probability that a drug damaging to microbes will not seriously damage the human body. But in degenerative disease the target is some abnormal process of the patient's own body. Generally physicians do not know precisely what process is at fault; even if they did, they would still face the delicate task of correcting the deranged process without disrupting other, normal processes on which life depends. There are, for example, hundreds of drugs that will destroy cancer cells. But their effects on normal cells are so similar, and thus so serious, that they can seldom be used in adequate doses or for periods of time sufficient to eradicate the cancer. In tackling degenerative disease, the pharmacologist resembles a policeman who, armed only with a shotgun, is trying to disable a killer in a crowd of innocent bystanders. To do the job safely, he needs a rifle.

The search for more specific drugs is already leading pharmacology into an even broader area than the control of degenerative disease: the control of growth. In a sense, many degenerative diseases involve disorders of growth. In cancer, the growth of certain cells is out of control; in rheumatoid arthritis, growth is inadequate—that is, the body lacks sufficient capacity to repair itself. But control of growth raises possibilities far more radical than a cure for cancer or arthritis; it could, for

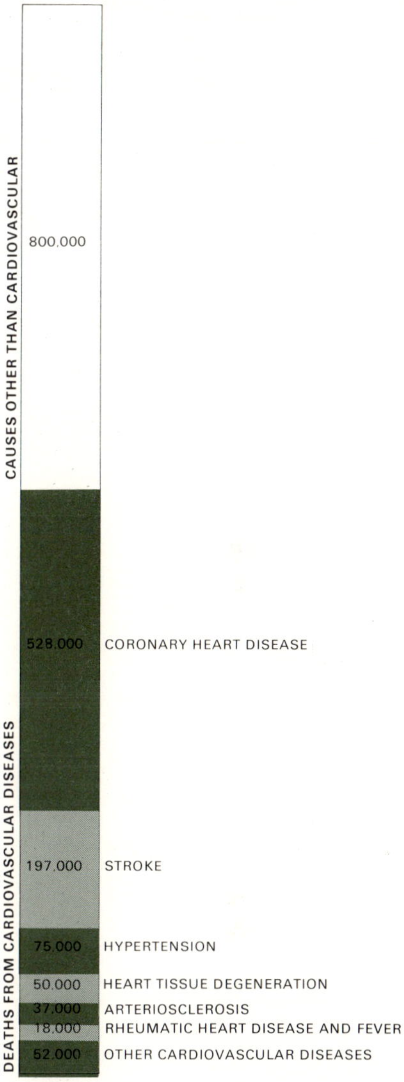

CHIEF CAUSE OF DEATH in the United States is the group of cardiovascular diseases—the heart and blood-vessel ailments—for which few effective drugs have been found. The chart shows that in 1962 deaths from various cardiovascular diseases outnumbered fatalities from all other causes of death in the United States. The sizes of the green bands indicate the relative importance of each disease. By far the biggest killer, causing half a million fatalities, was coronary heart disease—the heart attack.

example, show how to regenerate an amputated limb. A worm can grow a new head, and a salamander can regenerate a leg. But this capacity to repair bodily damage decreases markedly among the higher and more complex animals; a man can regenerate only a fraction of an inch of most organs (the only important exceptions are the skin, and the liver, which for some unexplained reason will grow back to near-normal size even after much of it has been surgically removed).

An answer to old age

Nobody knows how a salamander manages to grow its new limbs. The process almost certainly involves chemical changes in certain cells that enable them to multiply far more profusely than they did before, yet with sufficient organization to form a limb, not a tumor. If the nature of these changes can be pinpointed, drugs could presumably be devised to bring about similar changes in human tissues. Amputees could be supplied with natural, not artificial limbs; weakened heart muscles could grow new fibers, restoring themselves to youthful vigor; rheumatic joints could replace their rough, inflamed linings with smooth, healthy new ones.

If drugs can ever manipulate growth to this extent, mankind will be in sight of victory over the ultimate disease: old age. For old age, too, results from a breakdown in the body's self-repair mechanisms. In nearly all organs, cells are constantly being used up and replaced; eventually, for reasons still unkown, the body becomes unable to replace the cells as fast as they die off. Muscles grow lean and stringy; heart, stomach and kidneys lose cells and perform less efficiently; brain cells vanish, taking memories with them. Although most old people die of some disease other than senility, it is nonetheless age that kills them: their waning organs lack the capacity to withstand the disease. Drugs that could restore the body's capacity to repair itself would bring the human race close to immortality.

As drugs help man toward a healthier and longer—perhaps much longer—life, they may also help him toward a better life, by expanding both his intellectual and his physical capacities. One drug whose effects on animals are already being studied seems to speed up learning and improve memory; a few clinical studies with elderly people suggest that it may have similar effects on man. It is not inconceivable that in another 10 to 20 years men will be able to take pills to step up their intelligence.

Drugs may also be able to improve man in another way: by manipulating his heredity. The Rockefeller University's distinguished geneticist Edward L. Tatum is even willing to speculate about the possibility of "genetic engineering," which could suppress harmful traits, emphasize desirable ones and eventually, perhaps, even synthesize genes to order. Parents might be able to "design" their children according to their own plans—and even redesign themselves. Man's hereditary defenses against disease might be strengthened to the point where most drugs would become unnecessary, thus achieving the ultimate goal of pharmacology, a healthy society rather than a medicated society.

No one can predict when, or if, any of these miraculous drugs will be discovered. What can be predicted with certainty is that their discovery will pose social problems and new medical problems beside which current preoccupations with pharmacological side effects and medical ethics will seem trivial.

The impact of drugs on society is already obvious. The population explosion—which threatens a serious gap between the number of people and the world's supply of foodstuffs, not to mention its effect on urban sprawl, traffic jams and smog—has resulted from a sharp fall in the death rate caused in part at least by drugs. It does not take much imagination to foresee the increase in population that would accompany cures for degenerative diseases or the discovery of some form of longevity pill. To be sure, contraceptives (pills or other types) can lower the birthrate, but only if people can afford them—and take them. Manipulating man's procreative behavior is—perhaps fortunately—a good deal more difficult than manipulating his reproductive machinery.

Again, genetic engineering of unborn children would doubtless permit, among other things, a choice between a boy or a girl baby. In countries in which male children are considered a blessing and females a curse, the result might be a generation with nine men to every woman.

Terror of drugs misused

Thus drugs that are innocuous or even constructive when employed on a small scale suddenly assume frightening aspects when employed on a mass scale. We have already had a taste of this in the case of the drugs with which our air, water and soil are being permeated. One farmer applying insecticide to his fields increases his crop; a thousand farmers doing the same thing destroy songbirds and fish. The exhaust from one car is, at worst, an unpleasant odor—but vapors from 10,000 cars destroy vegetation, inflame our eyes and damage our lungs. In assaying the social impact of drugs, the whole is often a great deal more than the sum of its individual parts. And when we consider what might happen if drugs were deliberately misused, the possibilities are truly terrifying. If drugs can increase intelligence, they can decrease it, producing a dim-witted population controlled by a self-perpetuating elite. If genetic engineering can produce a superrace, it can produce a subrace.

These possibilities may sound like the fantasies of horror-science fiction. They are not. Many sober scientists believe that advances in biology and pharmacology will raise social issues as vital as those created by atomic weapons. Failure to consider these issues in advance and deal with them wisely could lead to a biological Hiroshima.

To achieve new pharmacological breakthroughs will require immense amounts of knowledge. But to determine how new substances are to be used—to hold death at bay or to bring it closer, to move man toward a golden age of health, longevity and intelligence or thrust him back toward savagery, oppression and famine—will require something much rarer than knowledge: wisdom.

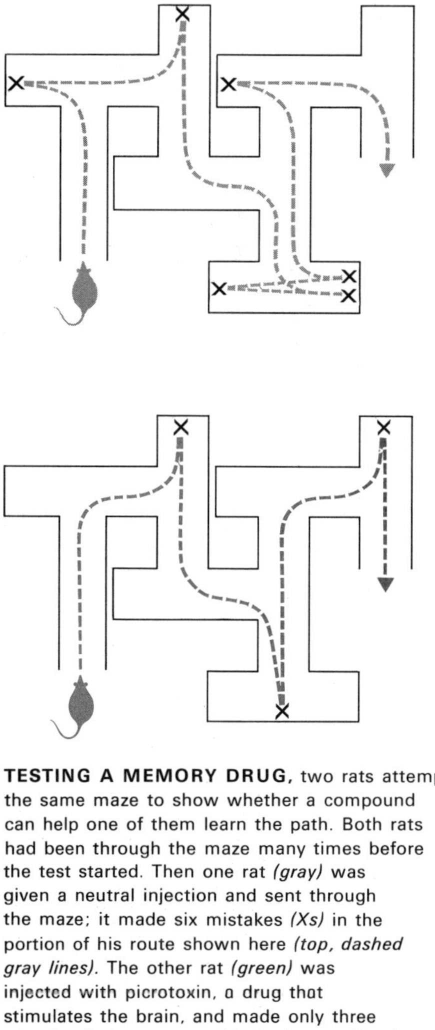

TESTING A MEMORY DRUG, two rats attempt the same maze to show whether a compound can help one of them learn the path. Both rats had been through the maze many times before the test started. Then one rat *(gray)* was given a neutral injection and sent through the maze; it made six mistakes *(Xs)* in the portion of his route shown here *(top, dashed gray lines)*. The other rat *(green)* was injected with picrotoxin, a drug that stimulates the brain, and made only three mistakes in its passage *(dashed green lines)*, an indication that the drug had helped the rat to learn from his previous experiences.

An Outpouring of Pills and Potions

In 1946, America's pharmaceutical manufacturers had sales of about $520 million. Two decades later their sales totaled over $5 billion—a phenomenal tenfold increase—and theirs had become one of the most important and most profitable industries in the country. By then the drug companies were employing 121,000 people in 1,700 plants located in every state, and were satisfying a national demand for 12 billion prescription tablets and capsules each year.

To achieve this growth, the industry had developed drug production methods radically different from those of the old-time pharmacist who pounded herbs with mortar and pestle and rolled pills by hand in the back of his shop. Today gleaming machines in tiled, aseptic rooms prepare and mix materials that come both from natural substances imported from all parts of the world and, more and more often, from synthetics concocted in the chemist's vats. But the most remarkable change in the drug industry is the increased importance of research and testing—a development strikingly illustrated by pharmaceutical companies' annual requirements for laboratory animals: 7.6 million mice, 2.2 million rats, 620,000 chickens, 190,000 guinea pigs and 2,590,000 other creatures.

SHAPING THE CAPSULES

Red-tinted molten gelatin drips over stainless steel pins, forming capsules that will hold one of the 7,000 medications the U.S. pharmaceutical industry now produces. Capsule making, like the other steps of drug manufacturing, has become a highly developed art, for the sanitary containers must be mass-produced to exacting standards of size, color and content.

Strange Sources for Drugs

Bats' wings and ground pearls, two favorite ingredients of the medieval alchemist-pharmacists, are no longer raw materials for drug makers, but modern pharmaceuticals are derived from sources hardly less exotic.

Microbes originally found in soil produce the antibiotic chlortetracycline. Horse blood yields tetanus serum. Human placentas—obtained by collecting the afterbirth that follows a baby from its mother's womb—are the main source of the infection-fighting substance gamma globulin. The common autumn crocus provides colchicine for gout; ouabain, a heart stimulant, comes from an exotic African dogbane shrub.

Although animals and plants furnish many drug components, modern manufacturers tend more and more to create their own materials, which are purer and more uniform than nature's. Today about three fourths of all prescription products available are concocted in the chemists' vats.

A NATURAL SUPPLY OF BLOOD
Frozen human placentas, thawing in plastic bags at Lederle Laboratories, Pearl River, New York, provide blood for the production of gamma globulin, used to treat or prevent infectious hepatitis. In a five-week process, gamma globulin is separated from the blood and then purified.

A SPAGHETTI-LIKE DRUG
Strands of a synthetic drug that stimulates kidney action are squeezed through small holes to complete the mixing of its ingredients, chlorothiazide and an inert paste. After drying, the material will be formed into tablets at Merck Sharp & Dohme in West Point, Pennsylvania.

Close Attention to a Container

All the ingredients of a medicine—even the inert filling substances that produce no pharmacological effect—must be prepared to the same high standards of purity and precision. Among the substances this applies to are the hundreds of millions of gelatin capsules made each year to hold together the powders that cannot be compressed into tablets. So important are these simple little containers that their production has become an industry in itself.

The pure gelatin used for capsules is extracted from animal bones and hides. Gelatin is an ideal container because it melts readily at body temperature, is tasteless and does not react with the drugs. Normally colorless, the gelatin may be tinted to one of 80,000 possible color combinations to guard drugs from deterioration by light; in some cases, colors identify the drug content.

When the gelatin has been molded into capsule shape the formed containers are dried *(below)* at constant temperature and humidity, assembled and sent to the first inspection station *(right)*, where they are examined for physical defects. Only after the capsules have passed several additional inspections can they go on to another part of the plant—or sometimes to another company—where they will finally be filled with drugs.

FINISHING THE CAPSULES

Endless rows of stainless steel pins support films of blue gelatin drying into hard capsules at the plant of Eli Lilly and Company in Indianapolis. Each pin must be precisely shaped and the coating process must be closely monitored so the capsule walls will vary by an amount less than one third the thickness of this page; otherwise the body and the cap will not fit snugly.

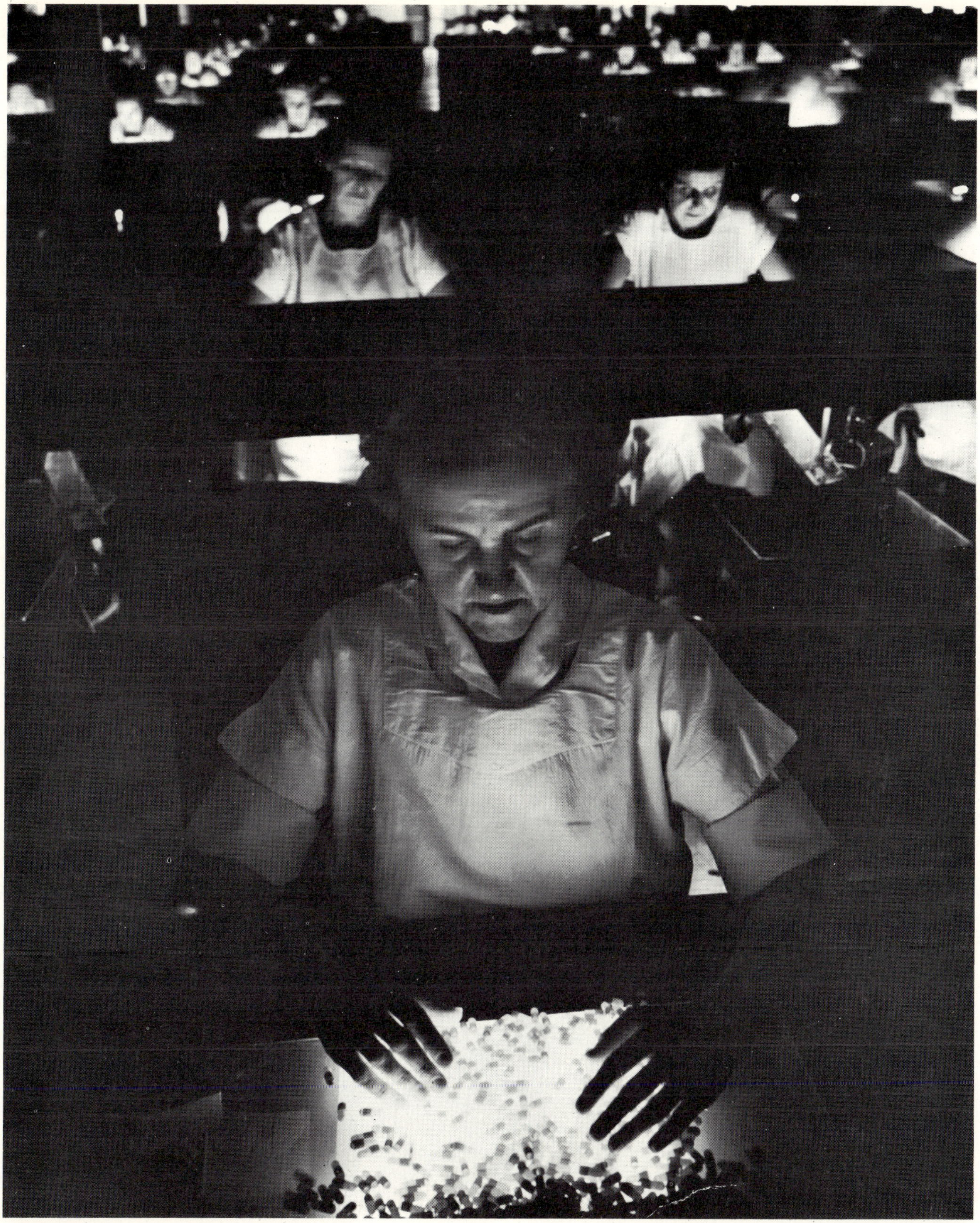

AN ENDLESS INSPECTION JOB

Spreading capsules across lighted tables, workers at Parke, Davis & Co. in Detroit look for defects; dents, discoloration or rough edges mean rejection. After this inspection, the capsules are loaded into drums, but they are not yet ready for use. Before they are filled with drugs, samples are taken and checked again. If defective capsules are found, the entire lot is rechecked.

A SPLASHING SEPARATION

By rocking a hundred glass tubes at once, the purifier above analyzes a crude drug mixture. The machine splashes the mixture through tubes of solvents so each solvent can dissolve a different amount of each component. Finally nothing but pure materials will remain in the tubes.

SPOTTING A NEW DRUG

To identify drug materials, a chemist uses a process called chromatography. In each jar a paper spotted with a drug is suspended in solvent. The solvent dissolves the ingredients and carries them down the paper, each at a different rate so that it appears as an identifiable smear.

Drugs' Secret Ingredients

Two unseen ingredients go into the making of every drug. One of them is research; the other is testing. Within the past four decades, pharmaceutical manufacturers' research has mushroomed into a $470-million-a-year effort to discover and develop new medications. Of the drugs most often prescribed today, 75 per cent were not in existence a decade ago.

The starting point of drug research is isolating and identifying likely materials *(opposite and above)*. Few chemicals remain untried. The antimalarial compound, atabrine, was originally prepared as a yellow dye, and the antidepressant, iproniazid, was derived from hydrazine, a component of rocket fuel.

Even the old drugs, long extracted from plant or animal products, are the subject of intensive research. For if their active ingredients can be isolated and reproduced in the laboratory, the drugs may be improved. With synthetic drugs, manufacturers are no longer tied to undependable or seasonal natural supplies. Most important, the drug can then be manufactured with consistent quality, simplifying the production tests that serve to guarantee uniform products.

Rabbits in a row—some of the 120,000 employed every year in drug testing—await temperature checks that help to determine the purity of

A Ceaseless Policing Program

Long after a drug has been discovered, developed and accepted for medical use, its testing continues. At every stage of manufacture, repeated inspections check whether the compound is, in fact, what its specifications call for. This continuing quality control is more expensive than the combined cost of raw materials and manufacturing; it accounts for nearly one fifth of all production employees and requires more animals for the laboratory than inhabit all the zoos in the world.

Quality control may involve more than 100 different kinds of tests, some as simple as measurement of a tablet's thickness and weight, others as complex as delicate analysis of chemical ingredients, and still others

water used in the manufacture of a compound. The water, injected into the rabbits, causes fevers if impurities have made it unsafe to use.

as elaborate as the precautions taken to ensure the purity of the water used in manufacturing processes.

The most stringent tests are made on the so-called biologicals, such as vaccines and most antibiotics, which cannot be synthesized but must be obtained from living microorganisms. Since living things vary in unpredictable ways, their products are seldom uniform. Each batch of certain biological drugs is tried on animals to see that it conforms to standards of safety and potency—a lengthy procedure not often necessary for synthetic drugs. Quality control does not end when a drug leaves the plant, for manufacturers periodically collect samples from druggists' shelves to test for deterioration.

Sugarcoating the Medicine

Most drug compounds, so arduously assembled, elaborately tested and painstakingly processed, end up in prosaic tablet form. But the humble tablet is not as simple as it looks. It contains many other elements in addition to the drug. A binding material, often a sticky form of sugar, holds the tablet together. And to make certain it breaks up after it is swallowed, the tablet also includes a "disintegrator" like cornstarch; when moistened by stomach liquids, the starch swells, breaking the tablet and releasing its ingredients.

Covering these substances is the coating, often the most complex part of the pill. A tablet may be coated with as many as 100 layers, requiring 20 days to apply. Each layer serves a special purpose, such as protecting against chipping or adding an agreeable flavor. Some tablets get an outer coating of highly refined shellac to protect them from being broken up by stomach acids and to make sure they arrive in the intestines before dissolving. Other coatings divide a single tablet into separate compartments, each containing its own specific drug. These coatings permit combining into one dose drugs that might ordinarily react if mixed.

A PAN FOR PILL POLISHING
Inside canvas-lined pans, antibiotic tablets are tossed and tumbled, half an hour at a time, for polishing and buffing. Each pan holds about 80,000 tablets, which are buffed with talc and given a shine by beeswax-carnauba polish.

START
STOP

A perforated disk, its holes filled with finished drugs, counts up to 12,000 tablets an hour and carries them to waiting bottles.

Marching Off the Assembly Line

When tablets have been coated and polished, and capsules loaded with drugs, they roll off conveyor belts by the hour and drop into automatic labelers. There a mechanical printer *(below, right)* tirelessly stamps newly made drugs with identifying names and numbers at a dizzying speed.

As the conveyor belt dumps its nonstop procession of tablets into shipping drums *(below, left)*, vigilant inspectors pull out an occasional chipped or unlabeled pill. The drugs flow by chute to automatic counters and loaders like the one on the opposite page, and are double-checked.

As the loader's filled slots spill their tablets into sterile bottles, one team of inspectors pulls bottles at random to count the contents. At the same time the quality control department takes its own samples for analysis. Labels for the bottles are guarded in locked cases and checked against the drug's contents before loading into the labeling machine. Each step assures that wherever the prescription is filled, at any of the nation's 55,000 pharmacies or 7,000 hospitals, it will be exactly what the doctor ordered.

A LAST-MINUTE LOOK
Spilling into a drum at the end of a conveyor belt, tranquilizer pills are culled by hand at the Smith Kline & French plant in Philadelphia before they reach the packaging machines at left.

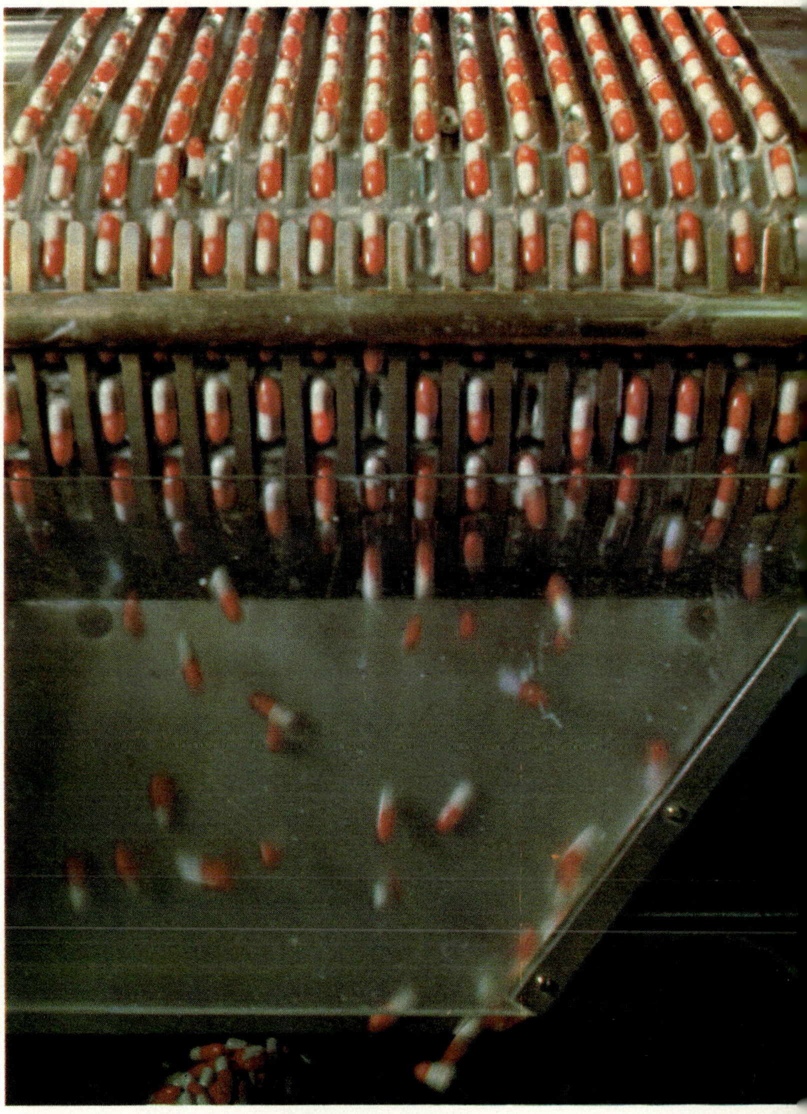

STAMPING FOR SAFETY
Capsules speeding through a printer at Eli Lilly and Company in Indianapolis receive code numbers so if they are separated from their labeled bottles, they can still be identified by the code.

In the great outpouring of drugs, a sampling of which is displayed at McKesson & Robbins, Inc., Hicksville, New York, the antibiotics make

up the largest single category of prescription medications: 44 basic drugs formulated into 144 kinds of pills, ointments, syrups and serums.

Great Men of Drugs

IN AN AGE of sulfa drugs, antibiotics, hormones and vitamins, it is hard to realize that many of our most valuable drugs did not exist less than a century ago, when medicine still relied on remedies hardly changed from Nero's time. Only since pharmacology emerged as a science in the late 19th Century have dedicated men, like the ones cited on these pages, made our most important drug discoveries. Paul Ehrlich found Salvarsan 606 in a chemical dye in 1910; Alexander Fleming discovered penicillin in a speck of bread mold in 1928. And, as this book indicates, the search is really just beginning.

PEDANIUS DIOSCORIDES *(First Century A.D.)*, a Greek physician who served with Rome's armies, produced the most complete catalogue of ancient drugs. His five-volume *De Materia Medica*, describing some 900 medications, was a standard reference work for over 15 centuries.

THEOPHRASTUS VON HOHENHEIM *(1493-1541)*, known as Paracelsus, was a Swiss physician who advocated chemical cures for all diseases. He is credited with introducing such valuable remedies as mercury, sulfur, iron and distilled extracts into Renaissance Europe.

HUMPHRY DAVY *(1778-1829)* was a brilliant English chemist whose distinguished career began with his discovery of nitrous oxide at the age of 20. After experimenting with this compound, which came to be called "laughing gas," Davy correctly predicted its role as an anesthetic.

François Magendie

FRANÇOIS MAGENDIE *(1783-1835)*, a pioneer in experimental pharmacology, undertook systematic tests of the effects of drugs on animals and humans. He was responsible for securing medical acceptance of such drugs as strychnine and morphine.

FRIEDRICH SERTÜRNER *(1783-1841)*, a German chemist, produced the alkaloid morphine from opium in 1806, the first isolation of the active component of a natural drug. He also showed how other medications could be derived from opium.

JAMES SIMPSON *(1811-1870)*, a Scottish obstetrician, was the first to use an anesthetic drug —chloroform—to ease the pain of childbirth. His technique was widely opposed at first, but won acceptance after it was used to help Queen Victoria deliver her eighth child in 1853.

CLAUDE BERNARD *(1813-1878)*, a French physiologist, provided the first scientific explanation of how a drug works when he described the poisonous action of carbon monoxide. Bernard also explained the muscle-relaxing ability of curare, a deadly poison used by jungle warriors.

HORACE WELLS *(1815-1848)*, a Connecticut dentist, successfully experimented with the anesthetic nitrous oxide in 1845. Ridiculed when a publicized demonstration to a group of surgeons in Boston ended in a fiasco, he brooded over the failure and committed suicide at the age of 33.

William Morton

JAMES BLAKE *(1815-1893)*, an English physician who emigrated to America in 1847, established the principles that the chemical structure of drugs determines their effect on the body, and that drugs become active only upon reaching responsive tissues

WILLIAM MORTON *(1819-1868)* was a Boston dentist who proved the utility of ether as a surgical anesthetic. A month after he first used ether in 1846, Morton anesthetized a hospital patient, permitting painless removal of a tumor on the jaw.

RUDOLF BUCHHEIM *(1820-1879)* helped make pharmacology—the science of drugs—a separate and important branch of medicine. His model pharmacology laboratory at Dorpat, Estonia, the first of its kind in the world, was widely imitated by 19th Century European scientists.

CARL BINZ *(1832-1913)*, a noted German pharmacologist, demonstrated that low concentrations of quinine could kill fever-causing microorganisms without dangerous side effects. Binz also compiled much of the 19th Century knowledge of drugs into a highly regarded textbook.

OSWALD SCHMIEDEBERG *(1838-1921)* was the Russian educator whose textbook and techniques set the pattern for modern instruction in pharmacology. Schmiedeberg also did important research into the effects of the heart stimulant digitalis and the nerve drug muscarine.

THOMAS BRUNTON *(1844-1916)*, an English pharmacologist, studied the effects of drugs on the circulatory system. His findings produced greatly improved heart stimulants, among them amyl nitrite, which Brunton introduced to medicine as the first remedy for angina pectoris.

JOSEPH VON MERING *(1849-1908)*, a German biochemist, teamed with chemist Emil Fischer to produce the first commercial barbiturate, Veronal, in 1903. Von Mering also showed that a secretion of the pancreas—later identified as insulin—could regulate the symptoms of diabetes.

WILLIAM HALSTEAD *(1852-1922)*, first professor of surgery at Johns Hopkins Medical School, injected cocaine into a patient's lower jaw before an operation in 1884 and proved the drug's remarkable effectiveness when used as a local anesthetic.

JOHN LANGLEY *(1852-1925)* was an English physiologist best known for his studies of the body's autonomic nervous system and its responses to drugs. He was the first to explain how nicotine offsets the paralyzing effect of curare on muscle nerves.

John Langley

Paul Ehrlich

PAUL EHRLICH *(1854-1915)* proved it was possible to create chemical drugs that would cure infections by killing particular organisms. His trypan red for sleeping sickness and Salvarsan 606 for syphilis initiated medicine's new era of chemotherapy.

JOHN ABEL *(1857-1938)*, the "father of American pharmacology," trained two generations of pharmacologists at Johns Hopkins University. His great achievement was the isolation of the valuable hormone epinephrine from the adrenal glands in 1898.

HENRY DALE *(1875-   )*, an English biologist, did research on rye mold that led to the isolation of acetylcholine, which reduces high blood pressure, for which he shared the 1936 Nobel Prize with Otto Loewi. Dale also led a world movement to standardize drugs and dosages.

ALEXANDER FLEMING *(1881-1955)*, a Scottish bacteriologist, discovered in 1928 that bread mold contains a substance that kills bacteria without damaging human cells. The substance, called penicillin, was later to become one of the first and finest of the modern antibiotic drugs.

ALFRED CLARK *(1885-1941)*, a British pharmacologist, discovered that some drug combinations are antagonistic, causing the drugs to counteract each other, while others are synergistic, producing jointly a greater effect than if used separately.

JOHN TREVAN *(1887-1956)* was a British pharmacologist who took guesswork out of drug dosages by establishing standards based on tests with large numbers of animals. His technique was first used to find safety margins for digitalis and insulin.

Alfred Clark

SELMAN WAKSMAN *(1888-   )*, a Russian- American microbiologist, coined the term antibiotics for the family of bacteria-killing drugs obtained from microorganisms. He earned the 1952 Nobel Prize for discovering streptomycin, the first drug effective against tuberculosis.

FREDERICK BANTING *(1891-1941)* was the Canadian physician who found a way to extract the hormone insulin and proved that it could control the abnormal amounts of blood sugar that made diabetes mellitus a slow killer. For this achievement, he shared a 1923 Nobel Prize.

TRACY PUTNAM *(1894-)*, a Los Angeles neuropathologist, enabled epilepsy victims to lead near-normal lives with his introduction in 1937 of diphenylhydantoin, better known by its trade name of Dilantin. It was the first drug to control seizures without producing drowsiness.

Carl Dam

CARL DAM *(1895-)*, a Danish biochemist, discovered vitamin K, the body's blood-clotting substance, while studying the effects of cholesterol on hens. He shared the 1943 Nobel Prize with Edward Doisy, who synthesized vitamin K from plants.

GERHARD DOMAGK *(1895-1964)*, a German biochemist, began the golden era of the wonder drugs in 1935 when he used Prontosil, the first sulfa drug, to produce an amazing recovery in his daughter who was dying from a streptococcus infection.

TADEUSZ REICHSTEIN *(1897-)*, a Polish-Swiss chemist, played a key role in isolating the hormones produced by the adrenal cortex. From these hormones came such wonder drugs as cortisone, the first effective remedy for rheumatoid arthritis.

HOWARD FLOREY *(1898-)*, an Australian-English pathologist, led the wartime crash program that isolated penicillin from its mold in 1940. First used to treat war casualties in Tunisia and Sicily, the drug is the workhorse of modern medicine.

Gerhard Domagk

K. K. Chen

K. K. CHEN *(1898-)*, a Chinese-American pharmacologist, isolated many useful drugs from ancient Chinese medicines. The best known is ephedrine, from the shrub *Ephedra sinica*, a remedy for such allergic conditions as asthma and hay fever.

JOHN GADDUM *(1900-)*, a British physiologist, has done important research in autopharmacology, the body's ability to produce drugs like vitamins and hormones. Gaddum also helped perfect testing techniques to determine safe and lethal doses.

RENÉ DUBOS *(1901-)*, a French-American microbiologist, in 1939 introduced tyrothricin, the first antibiotic used in medical practice. Two years later, Dubos isolated the active component gramicidin D, a drug that still enjoys wide use for ear, nose and throat infections.

Gregory Pincus

GREGORY PINCUS *(1903-)*, an American physiologist, has earned fame as a developer of the first successful female oral contraceptive, from progestin and estrogen hormones. Pincus then turned to research on a similar male contraceptive pill.

ULF VON EULER *(1905-)*, a Swedish physiologist, was studying the effects of hormones on respiration and circulation when he discovered noradrenaline in 1946. The hormone increases blood pressure by constricting passages in the blood vessels.

KARL FOLKERS *(1906-)*, an American chemist, was among the first to establish the chemical structures of B-vitamins and streptomycin. His most important achievement was the isolation of vitamin B_{12}, a drug which has eliminated the deadly threat of pernicious anemia.

ALFRED GILMAN *(1908-)*, an American pharmacologist, introduced the first effective cancer drug in 1942. He proved that nitrogen mustards, from the same compound that produces deadly mustard gas, cause some cancerous tumors to regress without affecting healthy cells.

CHOH HAO LI *(1913-)*, a Chinese-American biochemist specializing in hormones of the pituitary gland, was responsible for the isolation of cortisonelike ACTH and the growth hormone STH, medicine's first effective weapon against pituitary deficiencies that stunt human growth.

FURTHER READING

History of Pharmacy

Castiglioni, Arturo, *A History of Medicine*. Alfred A. Knopf, 1947.

Holmstedt, B., and G. Liljestrand, *Readings in Pharmacology*. Pergamon Press, 1963.

Kremers, Edward, and George Urdang, *History of Pharmacy*. J. B. Lippincott Company, 1963.

Rapport, Samuel, and Helen Wright, eds., *Great Adventures in Medicine*. Dial Press, 1961.

Sigerist, Henry E., *A History of Medicine*, 2 vols. Oxford University Press, 1961.

Thomson, Charles John Samuel, *The Mystery and Art of the Apothecary*. John Lane The Bodley Head Limited, 1929.

Drugs and Infectious Diseases

Burnet, F. M., *The Integrity of the Body*. Harvard University Press, 1962.

Carter, Charles F., *Principles of Microbiology*. C.V. Mosby, 1961.

Cook, J. Gordon, *Virus in the Cell*. Dial Press, 1957.

Dubos, René, *The Unseen World*. Rockefeller Inst. Press, 1962.

Fiennes, Richard, *Man, Nature and Disease*. Weidenfeld and Nicolson, 1964.

Simon, H. J., *Microbes and Men*. McGraw-Hill, 1963.

Central Nervous System Drugs

DeRopp, Robert S., *Drugs and the Mind*.* St. Martin's Press, 1957.

Keys, Thomas E., *The History of Surgical Anesthesia*.* Schuman's, 1945.

Prescott, Frederick, *The Control of Pain*. Thomas Y. Crowell, 1965.

Roueché, Berton, *Alcohol*.† Grove Press, 1962.

Taylor, Norman, *Narcotics: Nature's Dangerous Gifts*. Dell, 1963.

Patent Medicines

Carson, Gerald, *One for a Man, Two for a Horse*. Doubleday, 1961.

Holbrook, Stewart H., *The Golden Age of Quackery*. Macmillan, 1959.

Young, James Harvey, *The Toadstool Millionaires*. Princeton University Press, 1961.

Other Topics

Kreig, Margaret, *Green Medicine*. Rand McNally, 1964.

Maisel, Albert Q., *The Hormone Quest*. Random House, 1965.

Modell, Walter, and Doris Place, *The Use of Drugs*. Springer Press, 1957.

Rogers, Terence, *Elementary Human Physiology*. Wiley, 1961.

Talalay, Paul, ed., *Drugs in Our Society*. The Johns Hopkins Press, 1964.

Taylor, Norman, *Plant Drugs That Changed the World*.* Dodd, Mead, 1965.

*Available also in paperback.
†Available only in paperback.

ACKNOWLEDGMENTS

The editors of this book are indebted to the following persons and institutions: Charles E. Alford, Sterling-Winthrop Research Inst., Rensselaer, N.Y.; Dr. William Apple, Executive Director, American Pharmaceutical Assoc., Washington, D.C.; Dr. Otto Bettmann, Bettmann Archive, Inc., NYC; Dr. Junius Bird, American Museum of Natural History, NYC; Dr. John Blake, Curator, National Library of Medicine, Bethesda, Md.; Carmen Buonfiglio, Merck Sharp & Dohme, West Point, Pa.; Dr. Richard Costello, The Rockefeller Univ., NYC; Dr. William D'Aguanno, Food and Drug Administration, Washington, D.C.; Mrs. Helen Davidson, Eli Lilly and Co., Indianapolis; Dr. C. R. Garcia, Univ. of Pennsylvania School of Medicine, Philadelphia; Dr. McKeen Cattell, Professor Emeritus, Cornell Univ. Medical College, NYC; Dr. George Cosmides, National Institutes of Health, Bethesda, Md.; Dr. Gordon Ekholm, American Museum of Natural History, NYC; Alma Eshenfelder, Marine Historical Assoc., Mystic, Conn.; Dr. Ed Feldman, American Pharmaceutical Assoc., Washington, D.C.; Dr. Stanley Freed, American Museum of Natural History, NYC; A. Robert Garofalo, Lederle Laboratories, Pearl River, N.Y.; Dr. Leon A. Greenberg, Director of Research, Center of Alcohol Studies, Rutgers Univ., New Brunswick, N.J.; George B. Griffenhagen, Director of Communications, American Pharmaceutical Association, Washington, D.C.; Vera Grove, Merck Sharp & Dohme, West Point, Pa.; Mr. and Mrs. Lurelle Guild, Noroton, Conn.; Dr. Bruce Halstead, Director, World Life Research Institute, Colton, Calif.; Dr. Sami Hamarneh, Curator, Div. of Medical History, Smithsonian Institution, Washington, D.C.; William Helfand, Merck Sharp & Dohme, West Point, Pa.; Carl Henn, Eli Lilly and Co., Indianapolis; Richard Hughes, Arthur D. Little, Inc., Cambridge, Mass.; Dr. Lawrence E. Hinkle, Jr., New York-Cornell Medical Center, NYC; Robert Hurt, Smith Kline & French Laboratories, Philadelphia; Everett Jackson, Smithsonian Institution, Washington, D.C.; Dr. Norman Kahn, College of Physicians and Surgeons, Columbia Univ., NYC; Dr. Stanley Kern, Exec. Director, Control Division, Eli Lilly and Co., Indianapolis; James Kieley, Chief, Public Info., National Cancer Institute, Bethesda, Md.; Dr. Nathan S. Kline, Director, Research Center, Rockland State Hospital, Orangeburg, N.Y.; Dr. Irving Ladimer, National Better Business Bureau, NYC; Alan Lapiner, NYC; William Learnard, Smith Kline & French Laboratories, Philadelphia; Robert Liebsen, Drug Trade News, NYC; John A. MacCartney, Parke, Davis & Co., Detroit; Dr. Robert McCleery, Food and Drug Administration, Washington, D.C.; Dr. Lloyd C. Miller, U.S. Pharmacopoeia, NYC; Dr. Roderick Murray, National Institutes of Health, Washington, D.C.; Robert Newell, Eli Lilly and Co., Indianapolis; Mrs. M. W. Nilsson, Merck Sharp & Dohme Research Laboratories, Rahway, N.J.; Michael Noar, Merck Sharp & Dohme, West Point, Pa.; Dr. Charles R. Noback, College of Physicians and Surgeons, Columbia Univ., NYC; Herman Oppe, Winthrop Laboratories, Rensselaer, N.Y.; Edwin Pickard, McKesson & Robbins, Inc., NYC; Dr. Arthur Pollotta, Bionetics Research Laboratories, Inc., Kensington, Md.; Dr. William H. Prusoff, Yale Univ. School of Medicine, New Haven; Dr. Irving Putter, Merck Sharp & Dohme Research Laboratories, Rahway, N.J.; Dr. Martin Rizack, The Rockefeller Univ., NYC; James B. Russo, Pharmaceutical Manufacturers Association, Washington, D.C.; Paul Schuette, Food and Drug Administration, Washington, D.C.; John Shepherd, Smith Kline & French Laboratories, Philadelphia; Stafford Smith, Communicable Disease Center, Atlanta; Charles D. Solomonsen, G. D. Searle & Co., Chicago; Dr. Max Tishler, President, Merck Sharp & Dohme Research Laboratories, Rahway, N.J.; Dr. A. Trakatellis, Brookhaven National Laboratory, Upton, N.Y.; Dr. S. C. Wang, College of Physicians and Surgeons, Columbia Univ., NYC; Ellen Wells, National Library of Medicine, Bethesda, Md.: Dr. George D. Wessinger, Assoc. Director, Sterling-Winthrop Research Inst., Rensselaer, N.Y.; Paul Westphal, E. R. Squibb & Sons, NYC; Dr. Steven Wyte, Columbia Presbyterian Hospital, NYC; Ray Zettel, McKesson & Robbins, Inc., NYC; these persons of Cook County Hospital, Chicago: William McCoy, Director; Dr. Vincent Collins, Chief of Anesthesiology; Dr. Alon Winnie; the staffs of the anesthesiology dept. and pain and emphysema clinics.

INDEX

Numerals in italics indicate a photograph or painting of the subject mentioned.

E

F

G

H

I

J

K

L

M

PICTURE CREDITS

The sources for the illustrations that appear in this book are shown below. Credits for the pictures from left to right are separated by commas, from top to bottom by dashes.

Cover—Bruce Roberts from Rapho Guillumette courtesy Eli Lilly and Company.

CHAPTER 1: 8—Arthur Seller. 10—The University Museum, University of Pennsylvania. 11—Derek Bayes courtesy Wellcome Historical Museum. 12—The Biblioteca Laurenziana, Florence. 14—Viking Press. 15—Courtesy Columbia University Libraries. 17—Courtesy George Griffenhagen *Les Oeuvres Pharmaceutiques,* Jean de Renou. 18, 19—Eddy van der Veen courtesy Bibliothèque Nationale, Paris—Eddy van der Veen, Nicholas Muray courtesy the Dumbarton Oaks Collection, of the Smithsonian Institution, Freer Gallery of Art. 20—Skira courtesy The Topkapi Saroyi Museum. 21—Courtesy George Griffenhagen and The Topkapi Saroyi Museum. 22, 23—Frank Lerner courtesy The Metropolitan Museum of Art. 24, 25—Courtesy George Griffenhagen and the Biblioteca Casanatense, Rome—Henry B. Beville courtesy National Library of Medicine, Bethesda, Md., Bibliothèque Nationale, Paris. 26, 27—Robert Lackenbach from Black Star courtesy The German National Museum, Nürnberg, courtesy George Griffenhagen. 28, 29—Derek Bayes courtesy The Worshipful Society of Apothecaries, London, David Lees courtesy The Stockholm Apothecary Society, Robert Lackenbach from Black Star courtesy The German National Museum. 30, 31—Henry B. Beville courtesy National Library of Medicine, Bethesda, Md., except extreme top right Derek Bayes courtesy Wellcome Historical Museum.

CHAPTER 2: 32—Mark Kauffman. 34—Courtesy The Vatican Library. 39—Drawings by Donald and Ann Crews. 41—Drawing by Otto van Eersel—Adger Cowans. 42, 43—Drawings by Otto van Eersel, Lawrence Schiller from Pix, Inc. 44, 45—William Holland from Smith Kline & French Domestic Design Department—drawings by Otto van Eersel. 46, 47—Herbert Migdoll—drawings by Otto van Eersel. 48, 49—Drawing by Otto van Eersel, United Press International; U.S. Army Photo.

CHAPTER 3: 50—Bruce Roberts from Rapho Guillumette. 52—Drawing by Donald and Ann Crews. 54—The Bettmann Archive. 58—The New York Public Library, Astor, Lenox and Tilden Foundations. 59—Henry B. Beville courtesy The National Library of Medicine, Bethesda, Md. 61 through 75—Cornell Capa from Magnum.

CHAPTER 4: 76—Gjon Mili. 78, 79—The Bettmann Archive. 82—Drawing by Donald and Ann Crews. 85 through 93—Drawings by Leslie Martin except pages 90 and 91—Leslie Martin adapted from Paul Peck courtesy Merck Sharp & Dohme.

CHAPTER 5: 94—Yale Joel. 96, 97—Drawings by Donald and Ann Crews. 98—Drawing by Gloria Cernosia. 99—Drawing by Donald and Ann Crews. 101—Courtesy Communicable Disease Center, Atlanta, Ga. 103 through 119—Collages by David Gordon except pages 116, 117—right Nancy Genet. 103—Background Donald Miller and Yale Joel, portrait Charles Moore from Black Star. 104—Background Donald Miller, portrait Jon Brenneis. 105—Top background Donald Miller, portrait Dr. H. Zinram—Donald Miller (2). 106—Donald Miller. 107—Background Yale Joel and Donald Miller, portrait Dr. H. Zinram. 108, 109—Left background Yale Joel, portrait Dr. H. Zinram, right Donald Miller. 110—Donald Miller. 111—Donald Miller except portrait top left Donald Getsug from Rapho Guillumette. 112, 113, 114—Yale Joel. 115—Left Donald Miller, right portrait Dr. H. Zinram, background Yale Joel. 116, 117—Donald Miller, Yale Joel. 118, 119—Donald Miller, Yale Joel.

CHAPTER 6: 120—Cornell Capa from Magnum. 124 through 127 and 129—Drawings by Donald and Ann Crews. 131—Ezra Stoller for FORTUNE. 132—Don Uhrbrock. 133—Courtesy Eli Lilly and Company—Bruce Roberts from Rapho Guillumette. 134 through 137—Bruce Roberts from Rapho Guillumette. 138, 139—Courtesy Eli Lilly and Company, Fritz Goro. 140, 141—Yale Joel. 142, 143—David Moore from Black Star. 144, 145—Baldev-Pix.

CHAPTER 7: 146—Joe Baker. 149—Culver Pictures, Inc. 150, 151—Drawings by Donald and Ann Crews. 155, 156, 157—The Warshaw Collection of Business Americana. 158—The Warshaw Collection of Business Americana except bottom left Robert S. Crandall courtesy of P. F. Colliers. 159, 160, 161—The Warshaw Collection of Business Americana. 162, 163—Albert Fenn courtesy The New-York Historical Society, The Bella C. Landauer Collection. 164—Pat Towle from Robert S. Crandall Associates. 165—The New York Public Library Picture Collection. 166, 167—The Warshaw Collection of Business Americana.

CHAPTER 8: 168—Culver Pictures, Inc. 170—Culver Pictures, Inc. 171—The Bettmann Archive. 173—Courtesy American Heart Association, Inc. 175—Drawing by Donald and Ann Crews. 177—Bruce Roberts from Rapho Guillumette courtesy Eli Lilly and Company. 178, 179—Bruce Roberts from Rapho Guillumette courtesy Merck Sharp & Dohme, Bruce Roberts from Rapho Guillumette courtesy Lederle Laboratories. 180—Bruce Roberts from Rapho Guillumette courtesy Eli Lilly and Company. 181—Joe Clark courtesy Parke, Davis & Co. 182, 183—Michael Rougier courtesy Eli Lilly and Company, Bruce Roberts from Rapho Guillumette courtesy Merck Sharp & Dohme. 184—Michael Rougier courtesy Eli Lilly and Company. 186, 187—Bruce Roberts from Rapho Guillumette courtesy Eli Lilly and Company. 188—Bruce Roberts from Rapho Guillumette courtesy Smith Kline & French except extreme right courtesy Eli Lilly and Company. 190, 191—Robert Phillips courtesy McKesson & Robbins, Inc. 193, 194, 195—Drawings by James Barkley. Back Cover—Donald and Ann Crews.

A STONEHENGE BOOK

PRODUCTION STAFF FOR TIME INCORPORATED

John L. Hallenbeck (Vice President and Director of Production), Robert E. Foy, Caroline Ferri and Don Sheldon
Text photocomposed under the direction of Albert J. Dunn and Arthur J. Dunn